3,500 Good Jokes
for Speakers

3,500 Good Jokes
FOR SPEAKERS

By Jerry Lieberman

MAIN
STREET
BOOKS

DOUBLEDAY
NEW YORK LONDON TORONTO SYDNEY AUCKLAND

A MAIN STREET BOOK
PUBLISHED BY DOUBLEDAY
a division of Bantam Doubleday Dell Publishing Group, Inc.
1540 Broadway, New York, New York 10036

MAIN STREET BOOKS, DOUBLEDAY, and the portrayal of a
building with a tree are trademarks of Doubleday, a division of
Bantam Doubleday Dell Publishing Group, Inc.

Portions of this book have previously appeared in the following
publications written by Jerry Lieberman and published by Pocket
Books in New York:

Off the Cuff, Copyright © 1956 by Jerry Lieberman
The Laff Parade, Copyright © 1957 by Jerry Lieberman

Library of Congress Cataloging in Publication Data
Lieberman, Jerry
   3500 good jokes for speakers
    1. American wit and humor.   I. Title
PN4193I5L5   817'.5'408   74-29354

ISBN 0-385-00545-8
Copyright © 1975 by Jerry Lieberman
All Rights Reserved
Printed in the United States of America

27 29 31 33 35 36 34 32 30 28

To Joe Laurie, Jr.

Contents

viii

(They couldn't afford a rising orchestra pit, so they made the musicians stand up slowly.)

(Everything is so overcrowded today that the cemeteries are only selling standing room.)

FAMILY...FRIENDS...

tender reflections of things past

(We were so poor we couldn't afford a watchdog. When we heard a noise at night we'd bark ourselves.)

The panhandler approached Uncle Stanley. "Kin ya spare five bucks for a cuppa joe?" he said.

"Five dollars!" Stanley was taken aback. "Isn't that a lot of money for coffee, my good man?"

"Well, I'll tell ya," said the bum. "It's me wife's boithday and I wanna knock off early."

"Who was that man I saw you kissing last night, daughter?"

"What time was it?"

Everyone in my family was called Irving except my mother. Couldn't call her Irving . . . her sister's name was Irving.

There were three kids in the family . . . one of each sex.

The Wall Street man was standing at the curb when a friend from his old home town, whom he hadn't seen in years, approached. They embraced but the friend seemed mighty serious. "I'm awful sorry to tell you this," said the visitor, "but your old and dear Aunt Cecily is in jail."

"Glad you told me," said the broker. "It's good to hear she's provided for."

Every father was a kid once . . . and every mother is trying to make the neighbors believe she is still one.

The lifeguard approached the distinguished gentleman. "Sir," he said, "I've just resuscitated your daughter."

"What?" shrieked the gent. "Then, by God, you'll marry her."

Father got so angry he hit the ceiling, knocking large chunks right out. It was the first time he got plastered without going out.

Mamma's yearning capacity is greater than papa's earning capacity.

"I'm against liquor. That was the cause of my father's death."

"Drank too much?"

"No. A case fell on his head."

Two friends of long standing met at their club. "Johnathan, old chap," said one, looking morosely into his drink. "As your best friend I hate to tell you this— but your wife is fickle."

"Ah," sighed Johnathan. "So she's thrown you over too."

There's no place like home . . . after the other places close.

Father's learning a trade . . . so he'll know what kind of work he's out of.

It was one of those family fights that took place every Saturday night right after the card game, which took place right after services. This time the feudin', fightin' and fussin' was more than he thought his mother ought to hear. "Mom," he said. "Leave the room."

"All right," agreed the gentle, sensitive soul. "But please, boys, talk loud."

Brother got the electric chair. Every year we put a wreath on the fuse box.

"How could you have a son that age?"
"I didn't. When I had him he was just a baby."

"I'll never forget grandfather. He used to drink gallons of water. Then he'd sit back in his rocking chair, just sit there and slosh around all day.

"My ancestors all followed the medical profession."
"Doctors?"
"No. Undertakers."

"Father," said the rich man's son, "I'm marrying an older woman. I just can't stand those giddy young girls. There's something more to an older woman."

"Well, all right, son," his father replied. "But I'm warning you. Don't ever come to me for money to have her face lifted."

Every spring we'd start spring cleaning by throwing out the Christmas tree.

It wasn't ma's fault that we kids were raised in dirt and filth. Why our place was so dirty the neighbor's dog used to cross over the yard to bury his bone in the living-room rug.

Father was always bothered by flat feet. They kept giving him tickets for speeding.

"My name is Montgomery S. Epstein."

"What's the S stand for?"

"Nothing. My father dropped a noodle on my birth certificate."

Next door to uncle's was a widow tendin' her own farm. They grew potatoes, corn and friendly.

"What's a pauper?"

"The guy who married mamma."

Uncle's with the FBI now . . . they caught him in Chicago.

Auntie had a lovely complexion. It brought out her ugliness.

Sister had a problem. "Father," she said. "Who should I marry? Handsome Percy or Steady Sam?"

"Sam."

"Why?"

"I been borrowing money from him for the last six months and he still comes to see you twice a week."

We gave mother a beautiful set of L-shaped dishes. In case she misses father . . . they come back to her.

We had fourteen girls and eleven boys . . . I was scorekeeper.

If he drinks your brand, smokes your cigars, lets you pay the dinner check and flirts with your wife . . . he's your pal. But—if he also wears your clothes, borrows your car and sleeps in your bed . . . then he's a relative.

"Did we throw a big party in our basement last night."

"Was your Uncle Tim there?"

"Was he? He was the big party we threw in the basement."

They were all tap dancers in my wife's family. Then she married me . . . and not one of them has done a tap since.

Two Britishers greeting each other on the street.

"How's your business, yourself, your folks and all that sort of rot?"

"Fine. How's your father, sisters, brothers, wife and all that sort of rot?"

"Rotten."

The charity ran a raffle. First prize was $10. Second prize was uncle's check for $500.

As a kid father was a man of few words. He said choo . . . instead of choo choo.

"Have your bees done well this year?" asked the honey buyer.

"Well, they haven't given much honey," said the breeder, "but they stung my mother-in-law."

"That dog is a pet. Just like one of the family."

"Yeah? Which one?"

Uncle is very popular in prison. He's the lifer of the party.

The rich, old, dying man called his lawyer to him for the purpose of disposing of his worldly goods. "How many children have you?" the lawyer asked.

"That, sir," said the old-timer, "will be decided by the courts when my will is contested."

"Tell your mother to come to school next month," the teacher told the Hollywood actor's son.

"I can't tell mother," he replied.

"Don't you know where she's going to be next month?"

"I don't even know who she's going to be next month."

She was named after General Sherman . . . not long after him either.

Brother started off working for peanuts until he proved his salt. Now he gets salted peanuts.

"He changed the faucets in the bathtub when he was a kid."

"Was his father mad?"

"He will be when he finds out."

I have a lot of distant relatives . . . including one brother and two sisters.

"My uncle made a speech from a platform. The platform gave way."

"Did he get hurt?"

"No. Luckily the rope around his neck broke the fall."

The child was bad in school so he was told to bring a parent with him the next day. But they were both busy, so he brought his elderly grandparent.

"Who is that man?" the teacher asked.

"That's my grandfather."

"Is he on your mother's side or your father's side?"

"Oh, he sticks up for both of them."

She comes from such an old family . . . it's been condemned.

"Was daddy a bashful man, Mommie?"

"Well, if he wasn't you'd be six years older."

Brother has all the girls eating out of his hand. He's a waiter.

Grandmother was a famous writer. She wrote *Drugging Horses for Fun and Profit.*

Friendship is a deeper emotion than love . . . but not as entertaining.

Song title: "Don't Put on Your Swim Suit, Mother, It's Not that Kind of a Dive."

The piano tied our family together . . . or maybe it was the payments.

"Uncle's horse took sick so uncle put a powder in a pipe and put one end in his mouth and the other end in the horse's mouth. But the horse blew first."

"Was the powder strong?"

"Strong? Why uncle sneezed twice after he died."

My uncle would never steal. He worked in a bathhouse for five years and never took a bath.

Father took Sonny to see a show which featured fifty of the most naked performers in the country. "Phooey, phooey, phooey," father kept muttering all during the performance.

"Whatsa matter, Pop? Don't you like the show?" Sonny asked.

"Sure I do," he replied. "I was just thinking of your mother."

"My aunt collects fleas for a living."
"What does your uncle do?"
"Scratches himself."

The woman was shopping in the super market and as she went from counter to counter she kept humming and singing to herself.

"You seem to be very happy," the clerk remarked, smiling in the face of all this good cheer.

"I have every reason to be," replied the woman. "I have a beautiful home, two lovely children, a snug sum in the bank, my husband's life is insured for $100,000 . . . and his health is far from robust."

The boss was anxious to have the staff salesman marry one of his daughters so that he wouldn't go to work for a competitor. The salesman was anxious to marry one of the boss's daughters so that she wouldn't marry a competitor.

"You can marry any one of my three daughters," the boss said, pointing to two young ladies seated in the office. "Here are two of them and the other will be along in a minute."

The salesman stared. "If you don't mind sir," he replied, "I'll take the one that's coming."

9

For weeks the son had been praising his new fiancée, until his parents felt they should invite the girl to the house for dinner. The next day the boy's father asked him to reiterate his feelings about the girl. "She is all the world to me, Father," replied the boy.

"Then, son," father said, "you'd better see more of the world."

Kravetz was worried about his daughter not being married. Now she was invited to a party that would be fertile with eligible bachelors. "You know, darling," Kravetz said, "I shoulda bought you a new dress."

"I'll go without one."

"No," said Kravetz. "Without a dress the boys wouldn't even look at you."

Grandma had her hair bobbed. Now she doesn't look like an old lady any more . . . she looks like an old man.

"Pardon me, sir. Do you have the time?" Montgomery Epstein asked.

The elderly gentleman removed the watch from his vest pocket, studied it and then put it back without telling the young man the time.

"I say, old chap, do you have the time you know?" Montgomery repeated, in his best British accent.

Once more the elderly gentleman repeated the process of looking at his watch and putting it back into his pocket without telling him the time.

"Why do you do that?"

"It's like this," the elderly gent explained. "If I told you the time you'd start asking me where I come from. Then you'd visit me. Meet my beautiful daughter. Fall in love with her and she'd fall in love with you. Then you'd ask for her hand in marriage and I couldn't refuse. AND I'LL BE DAMNED IF I WANT A SON-IN-LAW WHO CAN'T AFFORD A WATCH."

"My sister goes in the bathroom and takes off her rouge, lipstick, false eyelashes, switch of hair and takes off her leg makeup."

"That ain't a bathroom. That's a separation center."

It was a sad day in the O'Leary house, for old O'Leary was breathing his last. His lawyer sat by his bedside writing the last will of the sick man as he dictated it. "The old lady can have the house," O'Leary said faintly. "My son should get $5,000, my brother Mike $3,000, my good friend Pat $2,500 and my Uncle Rednose O'Bulb $2,000."

The lawyer's eyes brightened. "Where is all this money coming from?" he asked.

"Let 'em work for it like I did!" roared O'Leary.

"Was your friend shocked over the death of his mother-in-law?"

"Shocked? He was electrocuted."

They were arguing violently over her selection of a fiancé.

"But, Mother," she cried, "he said he'd put the earth at my feet."

"My darling," mother said, calming down, "you already have the earth at your feet. What you'll be needing is a roof over your head."

This watch has been in the family for years. Been handed down from pawnbroker to pawnbroker.

Thirty days has September, April, June and Uncle Jake, who'll be out Saturday.

"I know you need a lawyer and I'd like to recommend my boy Sol."

"But your son has never won a case."

"I know. But in your case he can lose for you cheaper than any other lawyer in New York."

"My uncle's in Who's Who."

"Who ya kiddin'? Which Who's Who?"

"Who's Who in the Hoosegow."

"Did you hear the news? My rich uncle fell off a cliff."

"Were you very close to him?"

"Just close enough to push."

The stuttering son told his short-legged father how his impediment would not be noticed. "Walk with one leg in the g-g-g-gutter and one l-l-l-leg on the s-s-s-sidewalk," advised the son.

So the father took his son's advice and was hit by a car. When his son came to visit him in the hospital he said, "Son, I've a way to cure your stuttering."

"H-h-h-how?"

"KEEP YOUR DAMNED MOUTH SHUT."

"You're an old gossip. You can't call Jimmy a pickpocket. Not our Jimmy, even if he is a pickpocket."

"But you admit he's a pickpocket?"

"Of course he is. And he killed a coupla guys too."

"But you're talkin' about him yourself."

"Why not? Who's got a better right? After all I'm a relative."

The father was angry because of the usual morning procedure.

"Who gets into the bathroom at seven and stays a solid hour?" he demanded angrily.

"Your brother, Daddy."

"I have no brother. What makes you say such a thing?"

"Well, every morning you bang on the bathroom door and yell 'Oh brother, are you still in there?'"

I used to lick all the kids on the block, except the O'Briens. Had trouble with them. They were boys.

"Why are you leaving us?" the master asked the hired girl. "Haven't we always treated you like one of the family?"

"Yes," she said. "And I'm tired of it."

"Stork brought your baby brother. Wanna see your baby brother?"

"No, I wanna see the stork."

Uncle Harry was the real lazy one. He used to put coffee grounds in his mustache and drink hot water.

I was so surprised at my birth, I couldn't speak for a year and a half.

Mother drinks to forget that she drinks.

Father was very mechanically inclined. He invented a double-decker bathtub for people who sing duets.

Uncle Herman was a scientist. He disproved the theory of heredity. He had one glass eye and his son didn't.

There were eighteen kids in the family. And no toys. We used to play with the stork.

Father never raised his hand to me. He was afraid of breaking a cobweb under his arm.

Cousin Sam was a singer. He played a hot towel in the *Barber of Seville*.

"You say your cousin swallowed two dozen firecrackers? How's he getting along?"
"We're getting favorable reports."

The kid interrupted his mother for the tenth time that day and she was getting pretty much annoyed with it. "Children," she said, gritting her teeth, "should be seen and not heard."
"Leave him alone," father roared angrily. "I sold three of his bright sayings last week."

Father wasn't a heavy drinker. He weighed only 110 pounds.

They just listed father in Booze Who.

The family is all Norse . . . he's souse.

"Father is suing the city of New York. A patrol wagon went around the corner at sixty miles an hour—"
"And hit him?"
"No. The back door opened and he fell out."

Mother loves to sit by the spinning wheel. Last night she won $50 on the red.

Grandma lay back on her pillow, a comfortable look on her face. "I feel much better today," she said. "I don't think my appendix will have to be removed." She beamed happily. "But it was nice of the minister to call and see me."

"Grandma," said Lulubelle, "that wasn't the minister. That was a specialist from the city who examined you."

"Oh," granny replied. "I thought he was a little familiar for a minister."

He used to sit around Saturday nights thinking about taking a bath. We were poor . . . but clean-minded.

Mother makes what is known as a sponge cake. She borrows the butter, she borrows the eggs . . .

The clock fell off the wall. If it was a minute sooner it would have hit my mother-in-law. That clock was always slow.

There used to be thirteen kids but one was killed. Father was superstitious.

Mother doing fine—father doing everybody—baby doing . . . well you know what babies do.

Uncle was a great hero. He had so many medals when he died that instead of burying him they junked him.

The young lady walked over to the room where she knew her friend was. "May I see Irving, please?" she said to the woman blocking the door.

"We don't allow anyone but relatives to see the patients," replied the woman. "Are you a member of the family?"

"Why-er-why, yes. I'm his sister."

"Oh, I'm so glad to meet you," said the woman. "I'm his mother."

Father was a man of broad vision. He could spot a broad a mile away.

"Money isn't everything," counseled the rich relative.

"Maybe not," said his impoverished kin. "But right now it's the only thing I can think of that I really need."

Uncle invented the slow-motion pictures . . . and is too lazy to take credit for it.

Uncle refuses to leave the jail. He might lose his seniority rights.

We're sending my mother a big surprise. Father.

Quadruplets: When you make four the hard way.

When we held him one way he looked like his mother and when we held him another way he looked like his father. Couldn't hold him that way too long. The blood would rush to his head.

A friend in need is a friend to feed.

I'm the father of twenty and never left New York. In fact I never left home.

The gallant gentleman held the lady's hand and said, "You're my oldest friend."

"B-b-but I just met you."

"I've known friends longer," said the cavalier. "But you're the oldest."

Song title: "Dear Old Dad Was a Junkie Who Left a Pile."

Sometimes—as a child—I'd wish mother didn't work in a poolroom.

We always left a light burning in the $2.00 window for father.

Cousin McSeymour was a Scotsman. He used to send grandpa pipe cleaners every Christmas. They were made up of dozens of dead caterpillars with rigor mortis.

He was a great hero. During the war he served in the Army and Navy stores.

"He's greater than the President, he's greater than the King."

"Is he greater than the Pope?"

"Well—he's young yet."

I'll never forget the excitement when grandpa shaved off his beard . . . and we found out it was grandma.

When the lad graduated from college he was taken into the corporation by his dad. He started as assistant treasurer, then gradually worked his way through the ranks to third vice president, second vice president, executive vice president, president and—finally—dislodged the old man as chairman of the board. The old guy took it kind of hard and Sonny tried to console him. "After all," he said, "there's no difference between your success and mine. We both worked our way up through the ranks."

"There's one difference," said the dethroned chairman. "I didn't have a rich father."

We didn't steal the family silverware. We bought it from a fence.

One night a burglar broke into our house . . . all he got was practice.

"Who's that man living at your house all these years?"
"Wife's second cousin . . . never removed."

"Get a job, my boy. Work. Save your money. Soon you'll have enough money to stop working."
"I ain't working now."

I hated to miss the sweet-sixteen party but father made me stay home and mark the cards.

The child rapped gently on the screen door. "Mrs. Scoogle," he said politely, "mamma wants to borrow some pots and pans."
"Having a party?"
"No ma'am," he said politely. "It's startin' to rain and the roof leaks."

We hide the presents from Irving but he always finds them. This year we're gonna hide Irving.

The skin you love to touch. Dad's old pigskin wallet.

Despite our congenital poverty we had cross ventilation. A hole in the floor and a hole in the ceiling.

Uncle was so short he used to wear out the seat of his pants just walking around.

I came from one of them royal families. Whenever I'd come home late there'd be a light burning . . . on ma's cigar.

My parents were radio performers. They appeared regular on "The Good Will Hour."

"Isn't it time he said 'daddy'?"
"We decided not to tell him who you are until he gets a bit stronger."

Father was vaccinated against work.

One day Cousin Zebulah came to see us from the west. He was so bandy-legged when he walked into the room he scratched the wallpaper.

We didn't expect anything from him . . . and he came through.

Father named me Weatherstrip . . . I kept him out of the draft.

Father was an old newspaperman. He read nothing but old newspapers.

Uncle Jim was extremely fat. One day they told him to stop pushing on the subway. "I'm not pushing," he said. "I'm just sighing."

When he got his shoes shined he had to take the man's word for it.

Uncle married a paleface. She had a face like a pail.

We put mother on a pedestal . . . to keep her away from father.

Grandpa Sidney was a politician. When his party won he was too dumb for the police department . . . so they put him on the school board.

The boy came running into the basement. "Father," he called, "you can take your finger off the leak in the pipe."

"Thank heavens," muttered father. "Is the plumber here at last?"

"No," said Junior. "The house is on fire."

Average person: What we all think we are not.

"He never smokes, drinks, goes to the movies or night clubs. He never swears or plays cards and he never married. He's going to celebrate his eighty-ninth birthday."

"How?"

Look at that doorman. Gold buttons on his right lapel, gold buttons on his left lapel, gold buttons on his right sleeve, gold buttons on his left sleeve, gold buttons on his collar and gold buttons down the front of his coat . . . but his pants he holds up with a safety pin.

The tombstone read: HERE LIES A LAWYER AND AN HONEST MAN.

"Times must be bad," said a visitor to the cemetery. "I see they're putting them two in a grave."

The girl was overcome by gas fumes while taking a bath. The next day she put this ad in the paper: "Miss Whosis owes her life to the watchfulness of the elevator boy and janitor of the Ritz Hotel, where she is staying."

"He said after the fight he's gonna run away with your wife."
"The fight's off. I ain't got the heart to hit a friend."

My girl got the most votes for being popular . . . that's why she's so disliked.

Goodman must believe in the hereafter. He just bought a suit to be buried in . . . with two pairs of pants.

Adam and Eve were the first bookkeepers. They invented the loose-leaf system.

Never cash a friend's check on Saturday. That leaves two days to worry about it.

"I had a policy on my first husband."
"What did you get out of it?"
"My second husband."

The man laughed and hung up the phone. "Boy that was great," he said.
"Who were you talking to?" his friend asked.
"Nobody," he said. "This is a party line."

21

"I just don't know what to give my son for his birthday. What do you think a twenty-year-old boy would want most?"

"A twenty-one-year-old girl."

In ye olden days folks used to wine and dine . . . now they dine and whine.

He's a toe head. His head is shaped like my toe.

The newly arrived convict was complaining to the warden.

"Warden, I don't like the food here. I don't like the quarters and I don't like your face."

"Anything else you don't like?"

"That's all for the time being. I don't want you to think I'm unreasonable."

Pat and Mike went into the fancy restaurant and ordered the de luxe dinner with all the trimmings. Then Mike haughtily called for the manager. "There's a fly in my soup," he said angrily to the distraught man. "This is terrible, horrible, awful. I never expected such a thing to happen in this place of all places."

"Ssh," pleaded the manager. "Not so loud. These things can happen. Won't you gentlemen have dinner on the house?"

After dinner the two men left and Mike pointed to a drugstore across the street. "Could you go for an ice-cream soda?" he asked Pat. "I've got one more fly left."

"I got a girl in a grass skirt tattooed on my arm. Do you know what happens when I make my muscle go up and down?"

"No."

"I get tired."

The human race has been able to improve everything but people.

An immigrant, Abe Cohen, went out and bought a book and studied it from cover to cover so that he would know the law of the United States. Finally, he went to get his papers.

"Who makes the laws of the United States?" asked the judge.

Without a moment's hesitation Cohen replied, "Friedman the printer, your honor."

My brother fooled everybody. For a long time after he was born we thought he was a baby.

Telegram: HAVING A WONDERFUL WISH, TIME YOU WERE HERE.

Two men were facing each other on the train. "I always knew my hearing wasn't good," said one, "but I never thought this would happen. I must have gone stone deaf. Here you've been speaking to me for an hour and I can't hear a word."

"I wasn't speaking," said his companion. "I was only chewing gum."

When you're a comic everybody thinks everything you say is intended to be or has to be on the humorous side. The other day I said I had a headache, my chest hurt, I had terrible pains in my back and my tongue was coated. One of the fellows at the club said he didn't think my remarks were especially funny.

Skeletons are nothing but a stack of bones with the people scraped off.

BUSINESS...
OCCUPATIONS...
PROFESSIONS

(The barber told me to use that hair tonic and my hair would come in heavy. Only one hair grew, but it weighed twelve pounds.)

American science is great. They just invented a new drug that cures penicillin.

The profession of meat-grinding is a dangerous one. See this little finger? It used to be my big finger.

"What's a Grecian urn?"
"About $25 a week . . . unless he owns a restaurant."

She was a stenographer. She married the boss. Now he takes dictation.

Promoter: A man that wants to sell you something you don't want that he ain't got.

The visitors to the farm were admiring the neatness and cleanliness of the place. "Your farmhouse is so nice and white," said one of the "girls." "Do you paint it every day?"
"Naww—ma'am," said the farmer. "It's hard to get them cows to lay on their backs."

A waiter is one that believes that money grows on trays.

Brother was a dismal failure as a surgeon. He was so chicken-hearted he couldn't even open up a conversation.

26

Talk's cheap . . . if lawyers don't do the talking.

"Answer the door."
"Hello, door."

The man applied for a job with the chain food store. "What's your experience with groceries?" the interviewer asked.

"Well," said the job seeker. "I'm eating them all the time."

You can always claim you're an artist . . . and nobody can prove you aren't.

Uncle's a swimming instructor. He gives drowning lessons.

I get paid for using my brains . . . it's like stealing money.

The first thing I did when I took over was to order a new switchboard. The old one was full of holes.

"When did your teeth start troubling you?"
"When I was teething."

He works all the time. He's a picket.

After the examination the doctor handed the patient a prescription and said, "Take this medicine after each meal."

"But, Doc," confessed the patient, "I haven't eaten in four days."

"Fine," said the doc. "The medicine will last longer."

Pawnbroker's holiday . . . Lent.

I was a garbage collector and happy at my work . . . then my cold cleared up.

"My husband wrecks houses."
"Make much?"
"He pulls down a few thousand a year."

A specialist is a man who knows more and more about less and less.

"Nurse, hold my hands so I can relax."
"I'll hold your hands so I can relax."

Any girl married to a plumber is sitting pretty.

"Open wider," said the dentist. "Wider—wider—wider."
"Look, Doc," said the patient. "If you're gonna get in I'll get out."

Buddenbender hired the lush-looking gal as his secretary. He immediately dictated a lengthy speech. "Got everything?" he asked after fifteen minutes.
"Yes," she said. "Except one thing. I haven't got a pencil."

"You know that old vase, Mum, you said was handed down from generation to generation?"
"Yes."
"Well, this generation has dropped it."

He's a good watchmaker. Nobody ever left a watch to be repaired that didn't come back a second time.

I'm going to maître d'school . . . learning how to de-burp radishes.

Father works for a law firm. He makes loopholes.

"How long did you work for your husband?"
"Until I got him."

I get shot from a cannon . . . I get three cents a mile and traveling expenses.

Mrs. Fiffkit was one of those women with a natural curiosity. She had to know everything about everything. "How is it," she asked the dentist one day, "that the little hole in my tooth feels so big to my tongue?"
"Well," said the dentist, "you know how a woman's tongue exaggerates."

"Now, son, you're coming into the family business. I'm going to give you $15 a week."
"Rather than take that I'll go to work."

Girls are like typewriters . . . press the wrong places and you get terrible words.

Calling Dr. Kinsey—Calling Dr. Kinsey—you should hear what they're calling Dr. Kinsey.

I'll call my lawyer . . . SHyster 4900.

My stocks fell so low I had to read the ticker tape in a decompression chamber.

Uncle had three heads—all bald. He got a job hanging upside down over a pawnshop.

Two specialists were called in for consultation. Both men put their hands under the covers and accidentally grasped each other's wrist. "Typhoid," said one. "No," said the other. "He's only drunk."

Barber: A clip-joint operator.

"Swell sermon, Parson."
"Today was nothing. You oughta hear me when I'm half drunk."

An urgent call was put in for a plumber at noon but he didn't arrive until eight hours later. "How is it?" he asked upon entering the house.
"Not so bad," replied the home owner. "While we were waiting for you to arrive I taught my wife how to swim."

"Hard at work, Mike?"
"I'm foolin' the boss. He thinks I'm workin' . . . but I'm carryin' the same lot of mortar up and down all day."

Mrs. Foofkit was instructing the new maid. "Sometimes, my dear," she said, "you'll have to help the butler upstairs. Understand?"
"Yes'm," said the maid. "I've worked with drunken butlers before."

I'm a mother-sitter. Same principle as a baby-sitter but more fun.

The stenographer was transferred to the New York office of the big advertising agency. "You'll find the work the same here as in our Chicago office," her supervisor instructed.
"Okay," she said. "Kiss me and let's get started."

"You need glasses," said the optometrist.

"I'm wearing glasses."

"Oh. Then I need glasses."

My brother's with the UN—He opens the door when the Russians walk out.

The old man arrived at the doctor's office at 2 P.M. for his appointment. Two—three—four hours later he was still in the waiting room. Finally, in disgust, he got up to go. As he passed the nurse he said, "Guess I'll go home and die a natural death."

"Where did you get that faraway look?"

"The fella on the next farm gets *Playboy*."

Gentleman farmer: A city guy who can raise only his hat.

The very high-society Vandervinnies were celebrating their fortieth anniversary. It was the gala event of the season. Among the guests called upon to speak were several ambassadors, three bankers, a prize-winning author and the president of the nation's leading industrial organization. "And now," said Mrs. Vandervinnie, "I would like to call on the surprise speaker of the evening. He doesn't know he's being called upon so it will be a surprise to him as well as everyone here. But he's a man who knows us better than anyone—for he's been in our employ from the day we were married. Would our beloved butler, Morgan, say a few words."

There was a smattering of stunned applause and the embarrassed Morgan cleared his throat. "Well," he said, raising a glass. "All I can say is you two have fought a good fight."

Early to bed and early to rise makes a man a rooster in disguise.

The boss told me to give customers three fingers of liquor. I quit. I got tired of those drunks licking my fingers.

"Have you weighed anchor?"
"Yeah. It hasn't gained an ounce since we left Shanghai."

Pneumonia isn't bad as long as you don't let it develop into a cold.

"Got anything to say before I fire you?"
"Yeah. How about a raise?"

What a catastrophe. They closed down the big plant . . . and threw four hundred pickets out of work.

I'm working for a good cause . . . 'cause I need money.

The agency sent the butler out to be interviewed and the dowager laid down the terms of employment. "Very well, madam," said the butler. "I accept your terms. "Twenty-five dollars a week, no washing done at home, my own room with radio, every fourth Sunday free, one outing a week. By the way ma'am," he added. "Are you jealous?"

I borrowed $2,000 from my father so I could study law. My first case was when my father sued me for $2,000.

Uncle worked for the post office. People handed him packages and he would say, "For me?"

"Where did you learn to weave?"

"I followed my old man home on Saturday nights."

He's got that soft touch on the piano. Learned it when he was on the night shift in a dairy . . . had to milk the cows without waking them up.

The lawyer was down and out. "How's business?" asked a contemporary.

"I just got eviction papers," he said sadly. "Wrote them up myself. Wouldn't of done it if I didn't need the money."

Bandleader: A man who can face the music.

The party who designed the Holland Tunnel got the idea from a public toilet.

The boss's wife tiptoed silently into his office, sneaked behind him while his head was down, clasped her hands over his eyes and said, "Guess who?"

"I told you there was no time for foolin' around," he shouted. "Now get those letters out."

"Are you a regular doctor?"

"I'll show you my revoked license."

I wanted to be a writer. But I quit when I found out writers don't use models.

Vet: A doctor who was in the war.

The dentist gave Foofkit the bad news. "I have to take out all your teeth," he said.

"Please leave one in front," Foofkit pleaded. "So when I smile it'll look good."

Side splitting: Usually referred to as an appendix operation.

Doctor: "Nobody lives forever."
Patient: "Mind if I try?"

Auntie works an escort service . . . she's a bouncer.

"Cheer up," said the physician. "I've had the same ailment myself."
"Yeah," said the patient. "But you didn't have the same doctor."

I come from a poor but honest family. Father didn't have enough education to be crooked.

I had to fire my steno for lack of experience. All she knew was shorthand and typing.

The handsome movie actor stopped the policeman and asked for instructions. Then he waited for some sign of recognition but none came. "Er—uh, don't you recognize me?" he asked the cop.
"Sure. You're the fellow's gonna buy that butcher shop on Seventh Avenue."
"No, no," said the actor. "Did you see me in pictures?"
"Yes. And take my advice. Buy that butcher shop."

Her husband is an accountant . . . but he can't figure her out.

Father was a novelty worker. It was a novelty when he worked.

He was admitted to the bar . . . then studied law.

"My uncle is a southern planter."
"You mean he owns a plantation."
"No. He's an undertaker in South Carolina."

Pop went broke. He had a hatcheck concession in an Orthodox synagogue.

He's a second-hand dealer. The first hand he lets you win—but the second hand . . .

"What's your father do?"
"He tests steamboat whistles."
"Where is he now?"
"He's out on a toot."

I worked in a saloon. I got $5.00 a week and all I could drink. Lost money. I spent $6.00 on pretzels.

The farmer sued the railroad for damages resulting from the death of one of his cows. The railway attorney was making every effort to rattle him. "Tell me," continued the lawyer, "was the cow on the line?"
"Well," said the farmer, "if you want me to tell the truth—the cow was bathing in the stream on the other side of the bank. The engine saw it, leaped the rails, dashed over the bank and, landing on the cow, strangled it to death without a word."

Artichoke: A man who designs buildings.

Father wasn't a very good watch repairer. He fixed the family cuckoo clock. Now it coos before it cucks.

The Sunday gospel shouter was in great form. "Everything God made is perfect," he preached.

A hunchback rose from the rear of the auditorium. "What about me?"

"Why," said the preacher, "you're the most perfect hunchback I ever saw."

"It will cost you $50 to repair this watch."

"Okay, if you'll take the watch as down payment."

I used to go to barber college. I was a shear leader . . . but they threw me out for cutting a class.

I gave uncle a walking stick—next year I'll give him the cup that goes with it.

The doctor met a former patient on the street. "Hello, Mr. Brown," he said. "Er—uh, that check you gave me came back."

"That's funny," said Brown. "So did my lumbago."

He's a writer. His wife helps him with his plays. She burns them.

Many a guy who isn't an engineer has started a girl off on the wrong track.

Mother had to let the maid go 'cause father wouldn't.

"Bring in a girl."

"Very good, sir."

"Not necessarily."

You don't know what you can't do till you try.

"Where are my spareribs?"
"Lady, I'm a butcher, not a doctor."

A lawyer is a guy who'll read a 10,000-word document and call it a brief.

After they become judges they stop practicing law.

The girl was hauled into court on suspicion of engaging in a shady profession. "Are you innocent?" asked the judge.
"Certainly not, Judge," she replied. "Are you?"

It was so hot the farmers had to feed the chickens cracked ice to keep them from laying hard-boiled eggs.

I always help with the diapers. It's a good way to make a little change.

The phone rang at the firehouse just five minutes after the men had all retired for their afternoon nap. "It's a terrible blaze at my house," the voice frantically cried. "The flames are licking through the basement and the first floor. Pretty soon they'll ravage the entire place."
"Did you try throwing water over it?" asked the fire chief.
"Yes!"
"Then there's no use our coming over. That's all we do."

I worked in a building that was so high the elevator boy wouldn't go up without a weather report.

No man who ever delivered groceries or ice is likely to be shocked at a burlesque show.

"Can you write shorthand?"
"Yes, but it takes me longer."

The dentist was afraid to give Father gas. How could he tell when he was unconscious?

The labor question: Is it six o'clock yet?

Just before leaving for the movie Mrs. Krupp decided to give the new maid instructions. "—and don't forget to clean out the refrigerator," she concluded.
"I did this afternoon," said the maid. "It tasted swell."

If two negatives make an affirmative, how many negatives make a photographer?

"What would you charge to alter my nose?"
"Five hundred dollars."
"Anything cheaper?"
"You can try walking into a lamppost."

The well-known shyster lawyer came down with pneumonia . . . from settling all his cases out of court.

It's natural for a stockbroker to take his vacation at a watering place.

"Will you give me something for my head."
"I wouldn't take it as a gift."

Operetta: A girl who works for the phone company.

She's a neat stenographer . . . before going home she puts the boss in his place.

As for his ability I can't say too much—I can't say too little . . . maybe I better keep my mouth shut.

Dr. Hirtz—swell name for a doctor.

"What tooth hurts you?"
"The cuspidor."
"You don't mean the cuspidor."
"Well, it's the one I spit through."

A chiropractor may not be able to see ahead any better than the rest of us . . . but he certainly sees more behind.

She's a lady carpenter. You ought to see her build.

The policeman uttered the following warning to the couple: "Hearken, no parkin', larkin' or sparkin'—and no foolin'."

"Dr. Shniblick, Dr. Shniblick, this is Dr. Martenson here," the excited voice shouted into the phone. "I've a patient with the most unusual disease. The nine-year itch. Do you know anything about it?"
"Yeah," said Shniblick. "It lasts two years longer than the seven-year itch."

"I'm a night watchman."
"What do you watch?"
"I don't know. It's so dark I can't see."

Father was a barrel kicker in a beer factory. He used to kick the barrels to see if they're full or empty.

Robin Hood: A fella who stole spark plugs.

The hired hand wasn't living up to his advance notices. "Say, look here," said farmer Gray. "You ain't gettin' as much milk from the cows as you used to."

"Nope," agreed the hired man. "Sorta lost my pull."

He's a gunner in a canning factory. He shells peas.

I send my shirts to an old-fashioned laundry. They still tear the buttons off by hand.

"I love you. I adore you. I truly love you. I love you as no man has ever dared to love any woman."

"What do you know about love?"

"I drove an ice wagon for eight years."

He's working himself to death. He's near-sighted and can't tell when the boss ain't looking.

"Did you water the plant, Sara?" called the mistress of the house.

"Of course, ma'am," Sara called back. "Don't you hear the water dripping on the carpet?"

I work in a pet shop. I get fifty cents a day—and all the flea powder I can use.

"What are your qualifications for the job of night watchman?"

"The slightest noise wakes me up."

In New York there is a lawyer for every criminal . . . and for other lawyers who go on trial occasionally.

"What's in the kitchen that looks good?"
"The maid."

"I worked for the great lawyers Hinkle & Finkle."
"What'd you do? Wash the windows?"
"Lucky guess."

I have vivid memories of my youth as an usher. Especially one story about a doctor. He was great. I saw the picture twice a day for three weeks—and he pulled her through every time.

The movie mogul called a meeting of the board. In his hand he held a newly arrived manuscript. "Gentlemen," he said, "it is the first time in my life I've seen a perfect scenario. There's absolutely nothing wrong with it. Make one hundred copies so I can distribute them to all the other writers so that everybody should see a really perfect script."
He paused, lit a cigar, sat back with a pleased smile. "And hurry," he added, "before I start rewriting it."

Chauncey is running for mayor. He's never been a grafter. All he wants is a chance.

I fought with the dentist not to pull my tooth. It ended in a draw.

I have an article here says a man laid 24,000 bricks. Gonna show it to my hens.

The doctor leaned over the man, tapped his chest and listened.
"Doctor," asked the patient, "why do you do that?"
"I don't know," said the doc. "I saw it in the movies."

The news broke that the ditchdigger had been willed one million dollars. The press services descended upon the excavation where he was working. "Will one million dollars make any drastic changes in your life?" asked one reporter.

"Certainly," said the laborer. "Now I can have a chauffeur drive me to work."

Uncle was a mounted policeman. He suffered from occupational calluses.

"What's your favorite sport, Doctor?"
"Sleighing."
"I mean apart from business."

I wouldn't mind work if it wasn't so confounded daily.

Auntie is a member of the horsey set. She's a bookie.

I have insomnia so bad . . . I can't even sleep when it's time to get up.

The bum appeared at the doctor's office doubled up with pain. After a careful examination the physician told the man he'd have to give up wine, women and song.

"But, Doctor," the man protested, not knowing what that had to do with his ailment. "I can't bend down."

"Oh yes," said the doc. "You'll have to give up smoking too."

"I object."
"Why?"
"I feel like a fool standing around doing nothing."

He's a landscape artist. He paints Burma Shave signs.

A dentist is a person who finds work for his own teeth by taking out those of others.

Doctors are round-shouldered from looking at people in bed.

The lawyer brought the results of the legal dispute to his client. "Great news," he said. "You don't have to pay alimony."

"No?" The client was gleeful.

"No. The judge gave you three years."

"Oh," and his face dropped.

"But don't worry," said the lawyer. "Your wife got six months."

"What? Oh no. What about my baby?"

"I got your baby off with a $2.00 fine."

The sign said Dr. Smith 2–4 . . . I didn't go in. On my life I want better odds.

"Has the depression affected your business as a door-to-door salesman?"

"I'll say it has. I now find twice as many husbands home as I used to."

Operator: A small opera.

She lives in a house with fourteen servants. Only thirteen there today. It's her day off.

The doctor saved my life . . . he didn't come.

"You sold me a button-down coat. It burst at the seams."

"Shows how well the buttons were sewn on."

"Hello, Doc. Make any grave mistakes today?"

The clerk recommended the latest book, titled *The Husband's Friend—or 500 Reasons for Staying Out Late.*

"Why will this interest *me?*" she asked, disturbed at his bad taste.

"Because on his way to work this morning," replied the clerk, "your husband picked up a copy."

She's of the opinion that she made a mistake when she took up stenography . . . and she's still making them.

The female author was being interviewed by *Time* magazine.

"What do you do between books?"

"I have three children."

"Every time?"

The time will come when a woman will get a man's wage . . . and it will probably be on Friday night.

The firm on the fourth floor is looking for someone. It's a great opportunity for a girl with a big corporation.

The gang was digging a deep hole when the foreman appeared.

"All right, me buckoes," he shouted. "All of yez out."

The men came trudging out of the deep hole and no sooner were they all out than the foreman ordered them all back in again. This went on for several hours. "Hey, whatza madda big Mike?" one of them finally asked.

"Me lads," said Mike. "Ye tack mur dirt out on yer boots then ye do on yer shovels."

She married her boss . . . now she works only afternoons.

"I can't sleep, Doctor," said the patient.

"Well, hire a beautiful nurse and kiss her every fifteen minutes," advised the doctor.

"Will that put me to sleep?"

"No. But it will be a pleasure to keep awake."

"Do you know the doctor well?"

"Not as well as he knows me. I never saw his x-rays."

The barber was shaving along at a merry pace when suddenly the man grimaced with pain. "Oh—I'm sorry," said the barber. "Did I cut you?"

"Can't *you* tell?"

"I could," said the barber. "If you'd bleed a little."

Brush fire: What happens when a Fuller man drops a match in his samples.

"Why didn't you walk the floor with the two-month-old kid when he cried?"

"I couldn't find his shoes."

He lives the life of Riley . . . while she spends all day at a stuffy race track slaving over a hot pari-mutuel window.

Undertaker: A man who always puts a customer in his place.

The mistress was on a tour of inspection of the servants' quarters and she came to Mamie's room. "Why Mamie," she exclaimed, "the window in your room is awful dirty. You can't see out of it."

"When I want to look out, ma'am," said Mamie, "I open the window."

45

He's on a busman's holiday . . . and he never drove a bus in his life.

"My name is Cadwalader Birch. Late of Boston, late of the Eastern Line."
"Why not with us now?"
"I'm always late."

The phone rang at the firehouse just as the chief drew to an inside flush. "My factory is on fire!" a frenzied voice shouted into the receiver.
"Why didn't you call us yesterday?" roared the chief. "We were right in the neighborhood."
"It wasn't burning yesterday."
"WHY WAIT TILL THE LAST MINUTE?"

He's a dirt farmer . . . knows more dirt than anybody.

Even descendants of common fishermen can speak of their ancestral hauls.

"I'm an interior decorator. I decorated Morgan's henhouse."
"How?"
"I put a rooster in it."

I earn $50,000 a year and spend $50,010 . . . all my life it costs me $10 a year to work for nothing.

There's trouble at the dairy farm. The milkers are pulling for higher prices.

The poor dejected man seated himself on the park bench and hung his weary head in his tired hands. "Hey, ain't he the man that writes the daily forecasts for the papers?" a cop asked an attendant.

"Yes," said the attendant. "But he ain't lookin' well. The weather hasn't been agreein' with him lately."

I'm a tree surgeon. I leave Kleenex under weeping willows.

"Now, my dear," said Mrs. Hinos, "before employing you, may I ask if you were ever in the hands of the police?"

"Certainly, madam," replied the woman. "I've been a cook for years."

The doctor was very honest. On the death certificate—where it said "Cause of Death"—he signed his name.

I worked for a fancy corporation. They gave me a tall girl for longhand, a short girl for shorthand . . . and a midget for footnotes.

When the doctor sent me the bill I started to boil . . . so he charged me $5.00 more for purifying my blood.

They promoted me to chief clerk. I'd rather have my old job back in petty cash.

It was the middle of the night. Suddenly there was a loud rapping on the doctor's door, followed by a groan. The doctor angrily thrust his head out of the window. "WELL?" he shouted.

"No," moaned the man. "Sick."

I have the best job in town. I work in a bartenders' school. I drink the mistakes.

I work my head to the bone.

A retainer is what you pay a lawyer before he does any work for you . . . similar to putting a quarter in a meter before you get any gas.

"Mr. Kroop," she told her boss, "I like a pat on the back. But not so low."

Janitor: A guy who'd rather sleep than heat.

Sister has a most unusual job. She's professional inspiration for an exposé magazine.

The boss sneaked up on the auditor. "Why aren't you busy?" he demanded.
"—'cause I didn't see you coming," said the auditor.

"What should be done in case of drowning?"
"Have a funeral."

He works in a men's-wear factory. He battens down the hatches on the winter underwear.

Just as the elderly woman deposited a coin in the beggar's tin cup she dropped her handkerchief. He gallantly picked it up and handed it to her. "But my good man," she exclaimed. "You're not blind."
"I know it, lady," said the cavalier beggar. "I'm woikin' fer me brudder. It's his day off."

Father got a job monograming tea bags for wealthy idiots.

"That perfume costs $30 an ounce. Here, smell it."
"Give me fifty cents' worth."
"Lady, you just had fifty cents' worth."

Steno: A girl who can't add but can distract.

"Good lord, man," exclaimed the physician. "You're so anemic. Does your finger bleed when you cut it?"

"Nah," said the patient. "It just hisses and puckers up a little."

Detective O'Sherlock, that master fighter of crime, was being decorated for capturing the impostor physician. "How did you know so quickly that he was a fraud?" the commissioner asked, at the same time pinning the Croix de Copp on his chest.

"Easy," said O'Sherlock. "He wrote too plainly to be a doctor."

After careful, deliberate and expensive examination, requiring the attendance of many physicians and specialists, a special medicine was concocted and prescribed for the wealthy industrialist. The head physician handed the medication to him. "Let me know if this gives you relief," he told the industrialist. "I've been suffering from the same ailment you have and been trying to find a cure for years."

A doctor is the only person who enjoys bad health.

The man called the waiter to him and in a raucous voice said, "I want a chicken smothered in gravy."

"If you want it killed in a cruel way like that," said the waiter, "you'll have to do it yourself."

The two laborers were working as a team driving in heavy pegs for the construction layout. One man held the peg while the other took careful aim and sent the ham-

49

mer flying. Instead of hitting the peg he hit his partner on the head. "Stop fooling around," said the struck man. "The foreman's watching."

Uncle is a bounder in a basketball factory.

"How's your brother?"
"Fin's a bookkeeper in a fish market."
"How's he doing?"
"I can't get close enough to find out."

"Got anything to cure fleas on a dog?"
"Don't know. What's wrong with the fleas?"

Chiropractor: A man who keeps a cold in the head from going into the chest . . . by tying a knot in your neck.

Finklestein was arguing with a salesman.
"I don't want I should buy your eggs," he shouted. "My hotel should burn down and I wouldn't buy them. My wife should die and I wouldn't buy them. My children should choke and I wouldn't buy them."
The egg peddler caught the spirit of the argument and said, "You should go blind and buy a case."
"Listen," cautioned Finklestein, "leave *me* out of it."

A stranger went up to Gimbel and offered to buy the store. Gimbel decided to play along with the gag and asked millions for it. The man said he would ask his wife.
He showed up the next day with the missus and the two of them were taken all through the store. Then they went into a secret discussion in a corner. When the man emerged he told Gimbel the deal was off.

"Why?" protested the smiling Gimbel.

"Because," said the man, "there's no rooms to live in the back."

Peter Minuit had just completed the purchase of Manhattan Island from the Indians and was standing with the sellers on the banks of the East River surveying the purchase.

"Say, wait a minute," he exclaimed. "Isn't that Brooklyn over there?"

"Lissen, wise guy," replied the Indian chief, "for $24 you expect the place to be perfect?"

Two friends met in the garment center and one of them began to complain bitterly about business. "Things are terrible, awful, horrible," he said. "Why I haven't seen things so bad in thirty years. It's impossible that it should get any worse. Not a week passes that I don't lose at least a thousand dollars."

"Then why don't you give up the business?" asked his friend.

"After all," replied the complainer, "a man's gotta make a living."

A successful businessman is one who uses two desks. One for each foot.

She wears expensive clothes and buys new dresses daily. Everybody wonders how she can do it on her boss's salary.

She asked me if I was one of those tired businessmen. And I told her I was never too tired to mean business.

Two garment men were sitting in Lindy's during the slack season.

"Did you hear about Seidman?" asked one. "His place burned down."

"Yeah?" said the other. "He's a nice fellow. He deserves it."

"He is your enemy. He hates you."

"Gee, that's funny. I don't remember ever doing anything for him."

The business wasn't a total loss. The business wasn't that good.

I carry only union matches. They strike anywhere.

The insurance man was explaining the benefits of his policy over those of his competitors.

"If you fall from the eighty-fifth story of the Empire State Building, just for argument's sake, and if you hit the ground, we pay you double indemnity. We pay you $15 a week for as long as you live. And payments start from the time you leave the window so that you're making money on the way down."

The young executive succeeded his father as president of a small railroad. The father had been extremely disliked by the line's employees. One day while the son was on a tour of inspection he stopped to talk with an old workman.

"How do you like our new cars?" he asked.

"Good enough for the rails they ride on," said the old-timer.

"How's the rails?"

"Rotten," said the old man.

The executive became indignant. "I'm your president," he said heatedly.

"That so? Knew your father and he's gonna be president again."

"B-but father's dead."

"I know it. And the road's going to hell too."

Lewis always wrote his name john l. lewis, so strong was he against capital.

Morale was very low at the Gypem Novelty Company, so Mr. Gypem decided to employ a recreation director for the specific purpose of boosting spirit. One day the director assembled all the workers and told them a wonderful new plan.

"When you are working here five years," he said, "you get a beautiful green certificate which says you've given valuable service for five years. When you are working here ten years you get a gorgeous blue certificate which says we appreciate very much the valuable services rendered to the firm during the past ten years. And when you are working here fifteen years you get a badge."

"What does the badge say?" asked one of the men.

"Why—er, the badge says, 'This man has a green and a blue certificate—'"

Berkowitz went to see a lawyer but told him that there would be no fee paid unless the lawyer felt sure there were grounds for legal action. Then he gave the lawyer a detailed account of the trouble.

"Good lord, man, the case is airtight," shouted the lawyer. "The other fellow hasn't a leg to stand on. My advice is $50, and for an additional $100 retainer I'll start suit."

"No," said Berkowitz. "I guess I better not."

"BUT WHY?" demanded the lawyer.

"—'cause," replied Berkowitz, "I gave you the other fellow's side."

"Are you sure Mr. Slutz is out?"

"Do you doubt his word?"

Boss: One who's late when you're early and early when you're late.

Pincus was determined to have a grandfather's clock. He told his wife he would be back in an hour with one. He went out to an auction and came back four hours later. "What kept you?" Mrs. Pincus asked.

"I spent all my time arguing with the auctioneer," he replied.

"For four hours?"

"Yes, but it was only a bluff. Four hours is a pretty good test to see if a clock is working okay."

Hefflefinger was teaching his son-in-law the jewelry business.

"Now this is my best money-maker," he said, pointing to a case of wristwatches. "They cost me $10 and I sell them for $10."

"If they cost you $10 and you sell them for $10, where does your profit come in?" asked the boy.

"That," Hefflefinger replied, "comes from repairing them."

The check was $33.50 for the meal. Margolin picked it up and said, "I'll pay it and you can each give me your share tomorrow."

That night one of the guys sat around the house until 3 A.M., and then called Margolin. Mrs. Margolin picked up the phone. "What's the idea of waking up Margolin at this hour of the night?" she squawked.

"Listen," replied the caller, "with $33.50 to be divided by seven he ain't asleep yet."

Greenberg was telling his friends that he was considering giving up ladies' underwear and opening a two-tier turkish bath. "Upstairs I'll charge a quarter," he said, "and downstairs I'll charge ten cents."

"Why upstairs a quarter and ten cents downstairs?"

"Because," answered Greenberg, "when I get through with the hot water upstairs I'll send it downstairs."

The coal driver made a mistake which so irked the boss that he fired him. "You big stupid Irishman," the boss ranted. "You're dumb. Get your pay and get out."

The driver looked at him and said, "Well at least I learned one thing from working with you."

"What's that?" the boss asked, thinking maybe he acted hastily.

"I learned," the driver replied, "that seven hundred pounds makes a ton."

The two partners were having a wonderful time in Florida when suddenly one of them remembered something awful. "Hymie," he shouted. "I'm awful worried. I just remembered I forgot to lock the safe."

"So what?" Hymie replied. "Ain't we both here?"

I'm gonna change my tailor. He reads too much. Everytime I get a letter from him he says, "On going through my books—"

"This is the fifth time you've been before me."

"I know, Judge, but when I like a fellow I like to give him all my business."

Meadows was a little hard-pressed, what with business so bad he had to give up his expensive store, and his daughter marrying a poor but honest man. So he went to see a man he'd once befriended, Ty Barkowitz the realtor, about renting a cheap place.

"I want $100 a month, Sam," said Ty.

This infuriated Meadows but he thought he'd show Berkowitz up for the cheap bum he was so he said, "I'll be more generous than you. I'll give you $125."

"I'm generous too. You can have it for $75."

"No. I'll give $150."

"No. $50."

"No," roared Meadows, "$175."

"NO, NO, NO," shrieked Ty Berkowitz, wizard real estate man. "I'll give it to you for nothing as long as I live."

"Make it as long as I live."

"Why?" asked Ty.

"Because," said Sam, "I'm gonna take your proposition and when I do you're gonna drop dead."

Sharfman applied for a job with Finklestein. "How much is the salary?" he asked.

"Ten dollars a week," replied Finklestein.

"I'm insulted."

"I'll pay you every two weeks," said Fink. "You won't be insulted so often."

Financier's telegram: WIRE ME HOW CASE CAME OUT.
Lawyer's telegram: RIGHT HAS TRIUMPHED.
Financier's telegram: APPEAL IMMEDIATELY.

A tramp knocked at a door and asked the lady for something to eat. "Yes, I'll give you something to eat," she said. "If you'll chop a load of wood first."

"Madam," retorted the tramp, with dignity. "I asked for a donation, not a transaction."

Turtletaub was explaining to his buddy Jess James the reason for his sudden affluence.

"I sell ladies' stockings. Sometimes if the woman of the house is really interested I put them on for her," he said.

"You must sell plenty that way," Jess commented.

"No," said Turtle, "my legs look lousy in women's stockings."

"Can you act?" asked the producer.

"Can I act?" retorted Taretsky. "Once I died so convincingly on the stage that a man fainted."

"Who was he?"

"My insurance agent."

Fashion note: What the well-dressed man will wear in 1975. The clothes he bought in 1972.

Pickpocket: A garment worker.

Business is so bad the customers are staying away in mobs.

Two partners had come to the parting of the ways over social and business differences.

"You stole my accounts," shouted one. "You crook."

"And you stole my wife," shouted the other. "You horse thief."

Competition in cloaks and suits was getting awful, so this left Pincus with only one alternative. He was moving some old trash from behind the machines, preparatory to spreading the gasoline, when he found an old lamp. He was about to throw it away when he accidentally rubbed the top and a genie appeared.

"I'm a fairy," said the genie, "and I ken grent you vun vish. But I'm varning you, whateva you vish your competitor gets dubble."

"Dot's hokay," replied Pincus. "I vish dot I go blind in vun eye."

The woman handed Schumer ten pennies.

"Excuse me, lady," he said, "but these toys are fifteen cents."

"But I thought this was a five- and ten-cent store," she protested.

"So I ask you," Schumer said, "how much is five and ten?"

Two ex-partners met in Lou Siegel's.

"Hello, Sol," said one. "How's tricks?"

"Fine," said the other. "I'm in a new business."

"What kinda business?"

"The witness business."

"The witness business? What's the name of your place?"

"No Matter What Took Place or What Happened We Saw It, Incorporated."

He told the lawyer, "I have stolen $2,000 from the bank I work at. What shall I do?"

"Steal $3,000 more and bring it to me," advised the lawyer.

The man did so, and after bringing the cash to him the lawyer wrote the following letter, which served to get the man off:

"Gentlemen: Your cashier, Sam Shimmel, took $5,000 from your bank. The hard-pressed family, despite the most desperate efforts, was unable to raise more than $3,000, which they offer if you will not prosecute. . . ."

"I see where your competitor is offering a shave and haircut for only twenty-five cents."

"I'm offering a real bargain. Shave, haircut, shampoo, manicure and shine for fifteen cents."

"Don't you lose money on that?"

"No. I haven't had any customers yet."

"My husband is always bringing home samples from the place and I love him for it."

"My husband brings home samples from the place and I hate him for it."

"And what's wrong with bringing home samples?"

"He works in a burlesque house."

Sign: The views expressed by the barbers are not necessarily those of the management.

We offer this at a wonderful price with no money down. We can do this because we offer no quality and can sell cheap because we are in the low-rent district. Signed: The Smiling Arab, Sahara Desert.

"You're sure you want to be an actor? We may find it necessary to throw you down a flight of stairs into a barrel of water."

"I can stand that. I used to be a collector for an installment furniture house."

Dentist writes patient. "Pay up. After all I enabled you to eat."

Patient replies. "If things don't improve you can have your teeth back."

Clerk: "That coat fits you like a glove."
Sir: "So I see. The sleeves cover my hands."

Lawyer: "When we open the theater let's charge seventy-five cents and cover the seats with plush."
Backer: "No. We'll charge fifty cents and cover the seats with leather."
Producer: "Listen, you two, let's charge twenty-five cents and cover the seats with people."

The man strode into the bank and asked to borrow $50,000.

"Certainly," said the president. "Can you give me a statement?"

"Yes," said the man. "And you can quote me. I'm very optimistic."

"Is your watch on time?"
"Yes."
"How much more have you to pay on it?"

The robbers held up the train and took $200 from the New York salesman, who in turn pulled a gun and took back $4.00 from them.

"Hey, buddy," shouted one robber, "whutza big idea?"

"Well, my friend," replied the salesman, "you certainly ain't gonna refuse two per cent discount on a strictly cash transaction?"

"How do you fill out your form?"

"I eat mashed potatoes."

"Yeah, and the government gets the gravy."

Hymowitz and Kaplowitz decided to dissolve their partnership and go their separate ways. Since each knew the other was intent on starting a new business of his own, a bitter rivalry developed during the last days over who would retain the services of Nathan the designer.

Hymowitz, returning from lunch one day, saw the designer and Kaplowitz talking in Kaplowitz's office. He waited outside until Nathan walked out and then stopped him. "How much did that cheap chiseler offer you?" Hymowitz demanded.

"Why-er nothing," replied the surprised Nathan.

"DON'T TAKE IT," roared Hymowitz. "I'LL GIVE YOU DOUBLE."

The door-to-door salesman was making a pretty good buck until his competitor decided to put only schoolboys on the route. Then business fell off sharply. The salesman pondered the situation for some time and finally hit upon a solution. The next time he rang a doorbell and the party answered he said, "Good morning, madam. I'm working my son's way through college."

Shieppowitz was mad. "I'm gonna sue that low-lifer for label," he ranted.

"You mean libel," corrected his accountant.

"No, I mean label," he repeated. "I make good suits, he makes cheap suits and uses my label."

It was past midnight when the telephone rang in the veterinarian's home. "Are you a dog doctor?" a voice asked.

"Yes," replied the doc.

"If I come over will you bark for me?"

I know a friendly undertaker who closes his letters with "Eventually yours."

Specialist: A doctor who has patients trained to become ill only during office hours.

Shirlee went to the doctor to ask him what to do about her husband walking in his sleep at night. The doctor suggested she put a tub of water by his bed.

When he met her in the street the following week he asked, "Did you adopt my suggestion about curing your husband's walking in his sleep by placing a tub of water by his bed?"

"Yes," she replied. "And it also cured me of putting a tub of water by his bed."

The two men were arguing bitterly.

"I still say doctors should write more plainly," yelled one.

"I disagree with you," said the other. "My doctor gave me a prescription and after I had it made up I used it as a complimentary ticket to the movies for a year, then as a railroad season pass for a year and now my daughter plays it on her violin."

At the last meeting of the American Doctors' Group the main speaker tackled a serious problem. "Gentlemen," he said. "There is a severe epidemic of good health—"

The reporter yelled into the phone to the editor. "This storm is something awful. The wind velocity is almost a hundred miles an hour. The rain blinds you.

The floods are high. Boss, I tell you it's no night for man or beast."

"Great!" shouted the editor. "I'll send two photographers to cover it."

The doctor had prescribed three very strong physics but the man didn't pass a thing. "What's your business?" the doc asked.

"I'm an actor."

"Oh. Here's a quarter. Go eat something first."

The physician was going over his books and found he'd had a terrible year financially. "I had a lot more patients last year," he told his wife.

"I wonder where they could have gone?" she asked.

"We can only hope for the best," he replied.

Surgeon: A large fish.

Dentist: "My good man, you don't have to pay me now."

Patient. "Pay you? I'm counting my money before you give me the gas."

Doc: "You should live to seventy."
Man: "I am seventy."
Doc: "What'd I tell you?"

The reporter had gone to cover the hanging for his newspaper and now he was more than four hours late in returning home. His wife was more than a little suspicious. "What took you so long?" she demanded when he finally came home.

"Well, honey, it's like this," the reported explained.

"The hanging was four hours behind schedule. The sheriff and the condemned man got to talking about their bicycles."

"Now, sir, what is your occupation?" the lawyer asked.
"I'm a piano finisher."
"Do you polish them or move them?"

Two Irishmen were digging a sewer. One was six feet five, the other four feet three. The little one was doing more work than the big one. One day the foreman stopped by and tried to shame the taller one into greater effort. "For shame now," he said, pointing to the smaller man. "He's doing twice the work you are."
"And why not?" asked the six-footer. "Ain't he closer to it!"

Doctor: "I'm about to operate."
Intern: "May I cut in?"

They had installed a new elevator in the prison and upon checking the records they found one of the inmates used to run a lift in Macy's department store. So they gave him the job. One day the warden got in and as the elevator made its initial stop the operator called, "First floor! Shoe repairs, rock-breaking equipment, laundry, license plates!"

Pincus was arrested for speeding, reckless driving, driving without lights and violation of traffic signals. He demanded a trial by jury.
"But you can't win against that in court," a friend advised.
"I know," said Pincus. "I did it on purpose. My

nephew just graduated from law school and this is his first case. I want him to lose so maybe he'll get discouraged and get an honest job."

The pickpocket went to visit his friend, who had just been arrested.

"I had to hire a lawyer for you," he said, "and had to leave my watch with him."

"Did he keep it?"

"He thinks he did."

The judge was dining with the criminal psychologist.

"It's rather odd," said the judge, "but I haven't had a pickpocket brought to the courtroom in months."

"There's really nothing odd about it," explained the psychologist. "Their season doesn't begin until May. In this unseasonably cold climate people don't take their hands out of their pockets until then."

Doctor: A man who's always out for his cut.

Can you imagine a barber trying to shave a woman's chin? All he would have to do is hold the razor to the skin. She'd talk so much the chin would shave itself.

The civil service employee was on the carpet before his supervisor. "I am tired of your tardiness," said the supervisor. "I'm therefore suspending you for a day. When would you like to take the day?"

"I'd like to use it up being late."

The old maid thought she heard a noise so she crept quietly down the stairs, not making a sound, walking on tiptoes. Just as she got to the last step the housebreaker turned and saw her. "Gee, lady," he remarked, "ain't you the quiet one comin' down those steps. You oughta be a burglar."

There was a severe epidemic in town so the doctor, in true medical tradition, worked around the clock converting his kitchen into a temporary surgery. But the crowds pouring into the place to be immunized made it inadequate. The doc took one look at the mob and said, "Some of you will have to be vaccinated in the basement."

Mrs. Gottdough, the town socialite, got up and protested. "I, sir," she said, "will be vaccinated in the arm or not at all."

The man was telling his friend about his robust health.

"Just two years ago the doctor gave me six months to live. Then I went back and he gave me six more months to live."

"How do you manage to keep alive?"

"Every six months I write the doctor for a renewal."

The doctor put down the stethoscope, patted the boy on the back and in a pleased voice said, "Son, you're all right. Blood pressure, chest, eyes, lungs, heart. All in excellent condition. There's nothing I need do for you."

"If that's the case," answered the boy, "gimmie my $5.00 back."

Coal dealer: A man who does business on a large scale.

His brand-new Chrysler broke down in the middle of the night.

"Say, there's a man down the street works at Chrysler's," advised a friendly cabbie. "He ought to be able to help you."

So he took off for the house, woke up the man and explained his troubles.

"But I can't fix your car," protested the sleepy man.

"WHAT?" shouted the car owner. "You work in an auto factory and can't fix one of your own cars?"

"Yeah," replied the auto man, "I'm a bookkeeper."

The woman was driving the doctor nuts with her hypochondria. She kept waking him up in the middle of the night with all sorts of imaginary ailments. One night the phone rang just as the doctor had fallen asleep after a particularly grueling operation.

"Oh, Doctor," shrieked the hypochondriac, "I have frantic desires to jump off high buildings. What can I do to stop them?"

"Madam," said the doc before hanging up the phone, "I suggest you follow your desires."

The man was choking on the chicken bone. He hurriedly called for the doctor, who removed it. "What do I owe you?" asked the man.

"At least half of what you were ready to pay when the bone was still in your throat," replied the doc.

"Are these your witnesses?"

"They are."

"Then you win. I've had them witnesses twice myself."

Arch criminal: One that robs shoe stores.

Crime doesn't pay. Nice hours though.

The lawyer brought her to the courthouse. The only thing she knows how to reach is the judge.

The judge isn't exactly crooked. But he zigzags a little.

Her lawyer is honest, but not enough to hurt the case.

A picture of a jail should be painted on every safe.

The policeman rang the doorbell, not knowing quite how he was going to break the news. The door opened and she stood there gazing anxiously into the law enforcement officer's eyes.

"I'm sorry to tell you this, Mrs. Murphy," he said, "but your husband's new watch is all broken."

"All broken?" she exclaimed. "How did it happen?"

"A piano fell on him."

Then there was the Indian who went to law school and changed his name from Sioux to Sue.

The lawyer was petitioning the court for a new trial.

"Why do you want a new trial?" the judge asked.

"On the grounds of newly discovered evidence, your honor."

"What is the nature of it?"

"My client has dug up $400 I didn't know he had."

"Yo' have been found guilty of the crime of murder by a jury of yo' peers and it is the sentence of this co't that on the fust day of June yo' be hanged by the neck until yo' is dead."

"D-d-d-d-do yo' mean this comin' June?"

"Do you mean to tell me that man strangled a woman in a ballroom with over two hundred couples present?"

"Yes, your honor. Everybody thought they were dancing."

He is in jail on account of a woman. She wouldn't let go of the pocketbook.

Ever since three of his clients were hung he's known as "Swing and Sway with Briefcase O'Shay."

The lawyer was hurt. The ambulance backed up suddenly.

"Don't you know you can't sell insurance without a license."

"I knew I wasn't selling any but I didn't know the reason."

Policemen's Union: Amalgamated Copper.

"You say it was nighttime. You were at least five blocks away and still you saw the defendant shoot Mr. Sharfman. How far can you see at night?"

"I don't know. How far is the moon?"

My son is a brilliant lawyer. He can look at a contract and immediately tell you whether it's oral or written.

"Why did you bring this man in? You say he is a camera fiend, but you shouldn't arrest him because he has a mania for taking pictures."

"It isn't that. He takes cameras."

The crook was complaining bitterly to his companion. "That last restaurant we ate in was terrible," he said. "The meat was left over, the bread was stale and even the coat I walked out with was last year's model."

Where there's a will there's a delay.

The judge stared at the case-hardened criminal. "Because of the gravity of this case," he said, in mellow, earnest tones, "I am going to give you three lawyers."

"Never mind three lawyers," replied the experienced defendant. "Just get me one good witness."

"Now," said the lawyer, "are you sure you told me all the truth? For if I am to defend you I must know everything."

"Yep. Sure. I told yuh everything."

"Good. I think I can easily get you acquitted for you have an excellent alibi that proves you are innocent, beyond a doubt, of this robbery. Now you are sure, absolutely sure, that you've told me everything?"

"Yeah. All except where I hid the money."

He got his client a suspended sentence. They hung him.

It was a famous case in one of the small mining towns. Joe was brought in on an assault charge. The state brought into court the weapons used. A huge pole, dagger, pair of shears, a saw and a gun. Jackson's counsel brought in the complainant's weapons. A scythe, a hoe, an ace, a shovel and a pair of tongs. The twelve men filed in slowly and the foreman read the verdict: "We the jury would give $5.00 to have seen that fight."

"Silence in the court," the judge shouted. "Half a dozen men have been convicted without the court being able to hear a word of the testimony."

Cohen went for his final citizenship papers.
"Where do you live?" asked the judge.
"Who? Me?"
"Yes, you."
"In Delancey Street."
"What do you do?"
"Who? Me?"
"YES, YOU."
"I am a tailor."
"How old are you?"
"Who? Me?"
"NO, ME!"
"Well, Judge, I should say you were between fifty and fifty-five."

The judge was being stern with the prisoner. "When were you born?" he demanded. No reply. "I say, when were you born? WHEN IS YOUR BIRTHDAY?"
"Whadda you care?" replied the prisoner. "You ain't gonna give me nothing."

"Hold up your right arm," the judge said.
"Can't, your honor. Got a shot in it."
"Then hold up your left arm."
"Can't. Got a shot in that one too."
"Then hold up your leg," the judge roared. "No man can be sworn in this court, sir, unless he holds up something."

"You are to give the prisoner the best advice you can," the judge told the court-appointed lawyer just before the recess.

Shortly afterward the court reconvened but the prisoner was nowhere to be found. "Where is the prisoner?" the judge demanded of the lawyer.

"Well, your honor," answered the lawyer, "I found out he was guilty as hell so I told him to scram."

The backwoods judge had a queer habit. Just before passing judgment, he would look in a book which resembled a lawbook but was a Sears Roebuck catalogue.

"For being drunk and disorderly," he pronounced one day, "you are fined $4.79 and two days on the road."

As the prisoner was being led from the courtroom he said to the sheriff, "He sure was tough on me."

"Say, you were lucky," the sheriff told him. "If he had happened to open that book to the plumbing section instead of the pants section you might be working on the roads for life."

The vigilantes found a sturdy tree hanging over a cliff and decided to carry out the law right there. "Hey, wait a minute," shouted the horse thief. "You ain't gonna hang me over that river are you?"

"Yes, we are," the leader shouted.

"Then be sure to tie the rope tight around my neck," the thief said. "I can't swim."

"Honest, your honor, I never stole nothing."

"Your testimony rings with a note of veracity."

"You don't get me, your honor—I swear I ain't lyin'."

"Why are you here?" the reformer asked the prisoner.

"Just run through the Ten Commandments," he replied. "I'll tell you if I missed any."

The victim pleaded with the burglar. "Don't take my watch. It isn't valuable. Its only value is sentimental."

"I'm sentimental," said the crook.

"You mustn't give up hope," the lawyer told his client on visiting day. "Why are you so sure you're gonna be here so long?"

"It's the warden," said the con. "He just had me fitted for a new striped suit—with two pairs of pants."

Detective O'Sherlock, ace of the force, couldn't get over the brazen attitude of the murderer he was hunting. "Imagine," he said, "a guy murdering someone, then not only leaving his fingerprints on the knife in the man's back but also his name and the year he was born."

"Are you sure?" asked the chief.

"Certainly," O'Sherlock replied. "That's what it said on the weapon. Rogers, 1847."

The jailbird was explaining his presence in prison.

"I got here through mistaken identity," he said. "I didn't know he was a cop."

The burglar stuck a gun in the man's back but the man turned suddenly, applied a judo grip and flung him across the alley. Then he pounced on the burglar and began pummeling him. He blackened his eyes, broke his jaw, fractured his ribs and broke his arm. "Gee whiz," the crook finally cried in desperation. "Hey, mister, ain't you never gonna call a cop?"

"Now, Sam, do you solemnly swear to tell the truth, the whole truth and nothing but the truth?"

"Ah does."

"Well, Sam, what have you got to say for yourself?"

"Well, Jedge, wif all dem limitations you jes put on me, ah don't believe ah has anything at all to say."

"I pleads guilty and waives the hearing."

"What do you mean you waive the hearing?"

"I mean I don't want to hear no more about it."

A lady in a state prison asked a convict, "Poor man, why are you here?"

"Because, lady," said the con, "my lawyer inherited $50,000 the day before he made his plea to the jury and he couldn't cry."

Algernon Montmorency needed a reliable law firm to represent him in a case he had pending. So he went out to look for one and soon saw a firm—O'Brien, O'Ryan, O'Hara and Finkelman. He went in to see one of the firm. He was shown to O'Ryan's office and there he had a long talk with him. Finally, Algernon arose and said, "O'Ryan, before I give you the case there is one thing I'd like to ask. How did Finkelman get into this firm?"

"Oh," said O'Ryan, "he represents the finance company. That's the only way we could keep the furniture."

The lawyer approached the jury box and opened an eloquent plea for his client. Dramatically, he said, "Ladies and gentlemen of the jury, I want to tell you about this man. There is so much to say that is good. He never beat his mother, he was always kind to little children, he never did a dishonest thing in his life, he has always lived by the golden rule, he is a model of everything decent, forthright and honest. Everyone loves him and—"

His client leaned over to a friend, not waiting for the

finish, and said, "Whaddaya think of dat mugg? I pays him good dough to defend me and he's tellin' the jury about some other guy."

Someone threw an anvil out of a twenty-story window and hit Boris on the head. He had him arrested. "I don't mind a guy having fun," Boris told the court. "But when he jams a gentleman's hat over his eyes and spoils it that way, then let the law take its course."

A group of visitors were going through the state penitentiary when one of the women stopped to speak to an inmate. "Young man, do you like it here?" she asked.

"Lady," said the con, "if I ever get outta here I'll go so far away it'll take $9.00 for them to send me a post card."

The convict hit another convict over the head with a sledge hammer while breaking rocks. "Can't you tell the difference between my head and a rock?" protested the injured man.

"Say, for sixty days do you think I'm gonna rack my brains?" asked the hammer wielder.

The attorney was briefing his witness before calling him to testify.

"You must swear to tell the truth, do you understand?"

"Yas suh, I'm to swear to tell the truth."

"Do you know what will happen if you don't tell the truth?"

"Ah expects our side'll win the case."

The table of contents of the lawbook reads as follows:

Some lawyers think the art of cross-examination is to examine crossly.

"What crime brought you here?"
"Sneezing. It woke up the gent and he nabbed me."

A police officer arrested a man for speeding, saw him sentenced to six months and as he was being led out of court said to him, "Excuse me, sir, but don't you want to rent your flat while you're away?"

A young man went to a barber shop and bought the barber pole. The cops kept arresting him as he walked down the street, bringing him into the station house each time, until finally the chief sent out a general call to all cops. "For Pete's sake, if you see a guy with a barber pole let him alone. He's all right."

The next morning they discovered every barber pole in town stolen.

The two pickpockets were discussing business.
"Say, where did you get that lovely watch?"
"From my cousin."
"From which cousin?"
"How should I know? I found the watch and in the cover it said, 'In memory of your grateful cousin.'"

The thief would not admit stealing the typewriter so they brought it into the courtroom. "YOU STOLE THIS TYPEWRITER!" shouted the D.A.

The thief stared open-mouthed. "Shucks," he gasped. "Is that what that thing was? Ah thought it wuz a cash register I was haulin' away."

If I was to give you an orange I'd simply say, "I give you this orange." But when the transaction is entrusted to a lawyer he puts down, "I hereby give and convey to you all and singular, my estate and interests, rights, title, claim and advantages of and in said orange, together with all its rind, juice pulp and pits and all rights and advantages with full power to bite, cut and otherwise eat the same, or give the same away with and without the rind, skin, juice, pulps or pits, anything herein before or herein after or in any other deed, or deeds, instruments of whatever nature or kind whatsoever to the contrary in anywise notwithstanding." . . . Then a couple of smart lawyers come along and take it away from you.

The beautiful young showgirl appeared at police headquarters in her scanty costume to report the murder of the famous playboy.

"Who killed him?" the detective asked.

"You can search me."

"Business before pleasure," the detective replied.

"Isn't it true the defendant talks to himself when he is alone?"

"Couldn't say. I never was with him when he was alone."

"I hesitated between this brooch and a beautiful bracelet."

"Why didn't you take the bracelet?"

"They were watching me."

Burglar: A gent who is seeking an opening in the better mercantile establishments.

The counselor was certain that he had caught the witness in a lie and he strove to capitalize on the point. He strode arrogantly toward the witness stand and in a cold, commandeering voice he began to hammer away. "You say that the fence was eight feet high? And you were standing on the ground?" he asked, smiling slyly. "You weren't mounted on a ladder or anything?"

"Yes, sir," replied the witness.

The counselor pointed his finger accusingly under the man's nose and shouted, "Explain, if you please, how you, a man of little over five feet, could see over a fence eight feet high and watch the accused's actions."

"Certainly," said the witness. "There was a hole in the fence."

The accused strode forward. "Your honor," she said, "I wish to plead guilty."

"Why didn't you do so at the beginning of the trial?" the judge demanded to know.

"Because," replied the accused, "I thought I was innocent but at that time I hadn't heard the evidence against me."

The girl was bawling out her boy friend. "You brute," she cried. "You even forgot what day this is."

"Aw," he said. "I didn't forget yer boitday. I even went to the jewelry shop to get you something, but he was still open."

The lawyer had ordered a special suit made to order and when he went for the final fitting he was delighted at the wonderful cut, the marvelous texture of the cloth and the magnificent styling and lines of the design. But when he went to put his money into the pockets he found there weren't any.

"But why no pockets?" he protested to the tailor.

"It shouldn't make any difference," the tailor answered. "Who ever heard of a lawyer with his hands in his own pockets?"

"We don't tell anybody pop is in jail. We say he went to Radio City."

"But he's gone so long."

"We say, long line."

"Stick 'em up," growled the holdup artist.

"You're wasting your time," said the intended victim. "Things are so tough with me I haven't had a nickel in my pockets for a week."

"You think that's tough? You don't know what tough is," the holdup man replied. "I ain't been able to afford bullets for this gun for two months."

The judge was expounding on the problem before the court.

"Cohen claims you owe him $100. Cohen has brought in a hundred witnesses who say they saw him tender the money. Likewise, the defendant has produced a hundred witnesses who swear they saw him pay it back. Now—"

Cohen jumped up indignantly. "Judge, I don't care if I lose. But just to show you what a liar he is, I never loaned him the money in the first place."

If there was anything Butch hated it was that preachin' type of crooks. The kind of guys who would rob a bank or beat their mothers and then go to church to pray that they don't get caught. One day the warden put one of these guys right in his cell and the preacher started preaching right away. "Brother," he said, "lose no time.

Turn to the path of righteousness. We are here today and gone tomorrow."

"Don't kid yourself," said Butch. "I got eight years yet."

The absent-minded gangster came home at 2 A.M., took off his clothes, switched off the lights and hopped into bed. His wife, wakened from a deep sleep, called, "Is that you, dear?"

"It better be," he replied, "or there'll be murder around here."

"My uncle died in the spring and fall."

"How could he die in the spring and in the fall?"

"Warden pulled the spring and he died in the fall."

"I understand you called on the plaintiff," the lawyer stated.

"Yes," answered the witness.

"What did he say?"

The prosecutor leaped to his feet and in a fit of anger denounced the question as false, misleading, tending to incriminate an entirely innocent party, etc. He also accused the attorney for the defense of illegal tactics, being an immoral person, guilty of malicious practices in daring to try to introduce such testimony. He also questioned the legitimacy of the attorney's birth. The defense lawyer sprang for the throat of his accuser and the court attendants subdued the two antagonists but not before they'd bloodied each other's noses and blackened each other's eyes. Then the judge ruled that if the attorney would repeat the question the witness would be directed to answer it.

"I repeat then," said the lawyer, wiping blood from his upper lip. "What did he say?"

"He didn't say nuttin'," answered the witness. "He weren't home."

I don't mean to cast any aspersions on the cops of this fair city but the other night I was riding on a trolley. There was only two other passengers. A man with no arms and a policeman. When I got off someone had stolen my watch.

The man was accused of stealing a watch but there was so little evidence the judge was forced to dismiss the case. The prisoner, however, just remained standing in the courtroom. "I said you're discharged," the judge roared angrily. "You are acquitted. You're free. Get out."

"Excuse me, Judge," the acquitted man replied, "but do that mean I gotta give the watch back?"

The convict was berating his attorney.

"You're a rotten lawyer. All you did throughout the trial was to object. You objected at the wrong time."

"I don't quite understand you," said the lawyer. "Explain yourself."

"Well, when the judge spoke you objected. The opposing counselor spoke, you objected. When the jury found me guilty you kept your big mouth shut. That was the time to do all the objecting."

"Go down in the cellar and steal the coal," the twentieth-century Fagan ordered. "Then bring it up here in the poolroom. If I spot the landlord coming I'll yell 'Greenberg' and you run up empty-handed."

But the landlord fooled them by entering the cellar through a back door and catching Big Stoop. "Drop that coal," the landlord shouted.

"Nothing doing," Stoop shouted back. "I can't drop it until Fagan yells 'Greenberg.'"

The witness was being badgered by the cross-examining lawyer.

"You're sure it was exactly five minutes?"

"Yes, sir."

"I'm going to give you a test," the lawyer said, taking out a pocket watch. "Tell me when five minutes are up."

At exactly five minutes' lapse the witness yelled, "Time's up."

After losing the case the lawyer, being a good sport, walked over to the witness and asked, "How could you tell time so exactly?"

"Simple," was the answer. "By the clock on the wall in back of you."

I was readin' in mah Bible, Judge, when some shootin' begun. One of my gals sed 'twas the Harris boys down by the middle of the pasture. Now, Judge, I didn't mind them Harris boys a-shootin' but I was afraid a stray bullet might hit a calf or one of the kids in the herd, so I picked up my rifle and dropped a few shots down that way and went back to readin' mah Bible. Next mornin' I went down that way and they was all gone 'cept four.

This little Italian man was on the witness stand, where he was undergoing a severe examination by the opposition lawyer to which his lawyer kept objecting. "Don't answer that question," the judge said. And a little while later, "Don't answer that question either."

"Heya lissen, Judge," protested the Italian. "I musta get back to my barber shop. You no wanna heara my story, go home."

WOMEN...*and*...*men*

(The hand that darns the sock is usually the one that socks the husband.)

"I'll make you immortal."

"Please—I'm a married woman."

She's always forgetting. For getting this and for getting that.

Her perfume is nothing to be sniffed at.

My wife is a smart woman. She works for my uncle. Her job is to sit in the car and smile at cops.

Like all women, Fanny thought she had her compensating factors.

"I wrote the company and told them I was going to wear their nylon hose and sent them a picture of me," she told a friend.

"Did they answer?"

"Yes." Fanny beamed. "What is an injunction?"

I've seen her without money many times . . . but never without her appetite.

My wife used to wear a two-way stretch . . . now she wears a four-way droop.

A lot of girls who smoke aren't even lukewarm.

Woman is the last thing God made and he must have made her on Saturday night . . . it shows fatigue.

The phone jangled in the middle of the night, and when the psychiatrist answered, it turned out to be one of his former patients.

"Dr. Gibbemgelt, this is Horace Hortense," said the frantic voice. "I've got to talk to you about my sister. She sits in front of the television set with nothing on!"

"Why doesn't she put something on?"

"She can't. The set's broke."

A woman's motto. You can't believe all you hear . . . but you can repeat it.

She was a woman of few words—but what words.

My wife wrote a book. It's called *What the Well-dressed Woman Will Wear and Whom to Borrow It From.*

Women are like champagne. The older they are the better they get. Like my wife. She's fermenting.

Her doctor has her on a diet. Only three males a day.

"I'll wind up an old maid."

"Let me go with you. I never saw anyone wind up an old maid."

She always gets a seat on the subway. When she comes in all the men get up and go into the next car.

She learned to make love by mail. They just buried her letter carrier.

My girl is like a revolving door. She goes around with anybody. She doesn't care whether the food is good—as long as the prices are high. She waits until the orchestra is playing good and loud—so I can't hear what she orders. We all live and learn. She just lives.

She can't resist a man in uniform . . . she got arrested today.

The dumb chorus girl was invited on an "outing"—so she decided to shop for some luggage. "Have you any overnight cases?" she asked the store clerk.

"Yes'm," said the clerk.

"Then give me seven of them," said the girl. "I'll be gone a week."

"Did I take you unawares?"

"Why, Mr. Smith!"

The boy and girl were passing when they bumped their lower extremities. "Oh," said the boy. "Pardon me."

"Oh my, yes."

"Mine too," said the boy. "But nevertheless, pardon me."

She was known as the virgin queen . . . she was always on the verge.

"My wife never wears a dress more than one day."

"My wife buys her dresses on approval too."

The man reported his wife missing and now a detective was at his home to get a complete description. "Can you tell me the color of her hair?" he asked.

"I'm not sure," he replied. "She disappeared right after a beauty parlor appointment."

Gossip: "You must have missed a great deal by not marrying."

Old maid: "Only the ceremony."

There's a girl with plenty of S.A.—summer asthma.

When a woman gets to be forty she stops patting herself on the back and starts patting herself under the chin.

Irving wanted to be a sportsman so he decided to take up deep-sea fishing—and—being very confident of success he decided to take the missus along. They weren't at sea five minutes before seasickness laid him out for the day.

"I see your husband is a poor sailor," the captain said to Sadie.

"He certainly isn't," she answered haughtily. "He happens to be a rich dress manufacturer."

She stands in front of the mirror for hours and admires herself. She calls it vanity. I call it imagination.

"This hat makes you look ten years younger."

"How old are you?"

"Twenty-nine."

"I mean without the hat."

There's an old saying, "Silence is golden"—that's why so many married men are prosperous.

Women can get more dirt out of a telephone than out of a vacuum cleaner.

My uncle was a shoe manufacturer but he went broke. He forgot to mark the size tens down to size six double A.

My girl is sports-minded. Passing out twice an evening is par for her.

Women's noses are the same size as men's . . . yet they get along with handkerchiefs one fourth the size.

Why is it that a woman will wear a riding habit when she wouldn't think of getting on a horse? A golf outfit when she doesn't know how to play? A bathing suit when the sight of water makes her seasick—but when she puts on a wedding dress she means business!

My wife is so thin—when she closes one eye she looks like a needle.

"My picture doesn't look a bit like me."
"You ought to be grateful."

Her mouth is so big . . . it takes two men to kiss her.

Trouble turns a man's hair gray in one night. Vanity turns a woman's hair any color in one minute.

The wife of the deaf and dumb man talks so much—he can't get a finger in edgewise.

The best thing about women smoking is it gives a man a chance to say a few words now and then.

Ulysses was telling his friend Homer about the swell time he had in the park the previous evening.

"I went there with this luscious dame," Uly said. "What a face, what a figure and she was crazy about me. On the way over I bought some red and black gum drops. When I got there I lit a lantern—"

"What?" interrupted Homer. "You were with a luscious babe and you lit a lantern?"

"Sure," replied Uly. "How else could I tell which were the red and which were the black gum drops?"

Even an old battle ax isn't so dull once she gets an edge on.

About the only time the average woman is a good listener is when money talks.

"Officer, this man is annoying me."

"But he isn't even looking at you."

"I know. That's what's so annoying."

She hides her age better than a torn-up birth certificate.

A girl who is built like a house has a good excuse for getting plastered.

She doesn't mind him talking in his sleep . . . but it bothers her when he just chuckles.

"You seem to like his attentions. Why don't you marry him?"

"Because I like his attentions."

She had just returned from her honeymoon and the girls asked her about the biggest thrill of marriage.

"Well," she said. "It was thrilling when Seymour took me to the license bureau. The wedding ceremony was a thrill. Signing the hotel register mister and missus was a bigger thrill." She paused and sighed. "But the biggest thrill was thumbing my nose at the house detective."

Twenty years ago the girls never thought of doing the things they do nowadays . . . that's why they didn't do them.

I knew her when she was a mere slip of a girl and she's slipped a lot since.

Legs like hers were few and far between.

He was somewhat appalled to call upon the lady and find her all prepared to go out—wearing a sweater.

"Tell me, dear," he said. "That V on the sweater. Does it stand for victory?"

"Oh, no," she said. "Virtue. It's an old sweater."

One of the girls had just returned from a winter vacation in Florida. When she left the room the others got busy admiring her.

"How healthy she looks," said one.

"Yes," agreed another. "Isn't it unbecoming."

Fine girl. She knows a lot of important people. She's friendly with every house dick in the business.

She was one of the bags thrown overboard at the Boston Tea Party.

She's a bedutante.

She's only kind to her inferiors . . . when she can find them.

Her hair is titian—imi-titian.

She's determined to mate good.

Wife: The one who introduced the monologue into conversation.

A woman never knows how young she looks until she has her portrait painted.

They were having a terrible battle. It raged far into the night and finally he couldn't take it any more so he adopted the position of "peace at any price."

"I was wrong," he repented. "Now does that satisfy you?"

"NO!" she shouted. "You must admit I was right."

My girl is so old she doesn't celebrate her birthday . . . she just knocks wood.

I call my girl "Serial"—because she quits when I get to the most interesting parts.

Some girls are like bathtubs . . . they acquire one ring after another.

She looks as if she was knocked down by a motorist . . . or picked up.

She was only a drill sergeant's daughter . . . but she knew when to call a halt.

She's so perfect even practice can't make her.

When a girl tells you she's insulted on the streets three or four times every day it's hard to tell whether she's bragging or complaining.

"He says I'm the nicest girl in town."
"Why don't you go with him any more?"
"I don't want to disappoint him."

Old maids: Uncalled for packages.

She was going to have her face lifted but then she found out the price—so she let the whole thing drop.

It is said that there are over ten thousand young ladies studying law in this country. They probably all hope to become mothers-in-law.

She's a bargain hunter. She married her husband because he was 50 per cent off.

Junior came running into the house. "Mommie, Mommie, the garbageman is here," he called.
"Thanks for telling me," she said, patting his little head. "I have a cold and would have missed him."

She just had her hair washed . . . I saw the laundry tag sticking out.

My hair will be white as long as I live . . . and hers will be black as long as she dyes.

God gave her her face . . . but she picked her own teeth.

"Darling, may I hold your hand?"
"Why? Are you frightened?"

It was the age-old battle of the sexes—but this time on a so-called intellectual level. "Do men go to heaven?" asked the lady professor.

"Why yes," replied the visiting lecturer.

"I never saw a picture of an angel with a beard."

"True," agreed the speaker. "They all get there by a close shave."

Her name was Virginia. They called her "Virgin" for short . . . but not for long.

Most girls today have a keen sense of rumor.

"Will you be true to me when I'm gone?"

"Yeah—but don't be gone too long."

A widow knows all about men . . . and the only men that know about her are dead.

A honeymoon couple traveling the Midwest were surprised to see an Indian carrying her baby in front of her. "How come she carries her papoose in front of her instead of in back like all the other squaws?" they asked the chief.

"Last year we were in Australia," said the chief. "She saw a kangaroo and never got over it."

A woman is the only creature who would think of wearing a hunting suit to set a mouse trap.

Busybody: A woman who's been married four or five times.

She did a terrific rhumba. Learned it on the farm when she was a little girl. Drove a tractor with a loose seat.

"Were you ever bedridden?" they asked the old maid. "Yes," she replied. "And once in a sleigh."

She has a past . . . and it financed her present and future.

She had a lovely figure . . . but no one could meet it.

Many a girl who spends all day in a swimming pool can put up an awful argument about dishpan hands.

"Would you like a small diamond or a large rhinestone?"
"I'd love them, George."

The longshoreman came down to breakfast, tasted his bull's-eyes and then flung them into his wife's face. "A man wants fresh eggs with his bacon," he roared.
"All right, dearie," she cooed. "Cackle a bit while I run down to the grocer's."

She stepped out of the gorgeous new Cadillac. Terrific body lines. The car wasn't bad either.

If you want to know why they're called the opposite sex, express an opinion.

She's a sweet little innocent thing . . . but she loves her hootch.

"Give something for juvenile delinquency."
"I already gave three sons to reform school."

My wife's hair is like a mop. But she doesn't have to worry. She doesn't know what a mop looks like.

She knows so little and knows it fluently.

Her nose was like an interesting book . . . it was red to the very end.

Two old maids were watching a parade when one of them suddenly began to cheer vigorously. She waved her handkerchief, stamped her feet and clapped her hands. Then she turned excitedly to her friend and said, "I love soldiers."

"Aw, go on," said the other. "You say that every war."

She couldn't take the rounds of café society any longer —so she hung up her bottle.

The two maiden ladies were thinking back. "As a girl," said one, "I had four sweethearts."

"All tolled?"

"No. One kept his mouth shut."

She says she's thirty-three . . . and there are very few people alive to contradict her.

Dubin, the accountant, had always impressed the theory of economy upon his wife, Doreen. Now he was very ill and rather than hire a nurse she was caring for him. Slowly she filled the tablespoon with prescribed liquid and held it out to him. "I won't take it," Seymour shouted. "It tastes awful."

"But, sweetheart," pleaded Doreen. "You can't die and leave all this expensive medicine wasted."

"If you wish to attend the party meet us at the Waldorf-Astoria."

"The party is at the Waldorf-Astoria?"

"Not exactly. We meet there and go two blocks away to the party."

Divorcée: A woman who gets richer by decrees.

She pencils her eyebrows . . . she has to draw the line someplace.

A man is as old as the women he feels.

Women never lose their temper . . . they always have it.

She belonged to the cream of society . . . now she's gone through the separator.

She believes in every man for herself.

The most pitiful case in psychiatric history concerns the two-faced woman who talked to herself and tried to have the last word.

She has dice eyes . . . all she has to do is roll 'em to make her point.

Mr. and Mrs. "Bring 'em Back Alive" Berkowitz were on a safari in Africa. Berkow decided to hunt some big game. Slowly and stealthily he crept through the underbrush, his gun poised for quick and efficient action. Carefully he focused the tiger in his sights and was about to pull the trigger when he felt a tap on his shoulder. It was the missus. "Don't waste a bullet on him, darling," she whispered. "He hasn't got the right expression for a rug."

She went with a sculptor till she found out he was kissing the models and chiseling on her.

"Did you hear about the girl in the cotton stockings?"
"What happened to her?"
"Nothing."

When a woman wants a man to listen to reason she wants him to listen to her.

She's not so old, she just has an old-looking face. Her mother was frightened by a room full of antiques.

Gossip: A woman who can start a scandal quicker than a mink coat.

"Darling," said the affectionate husband, "I've insured myself for $50,000 so if anything happens to me you will be provided for."
"Good," said the affectionate wife, "now you won't have to call the doctor every time you feel sick."

"You always cook more than we can eat."
"How could I economize with leftovers if I didn't?"

She wasn't married because of the ancient law of supply and demand. What she was supplied with there was no demand for.

Her age is her own business, but she's been in business a long time.

The woman was complaining to her lawyer. "For three weeks I didn't know where my husband was spending his evenings. Then one night I went home—and there he was."

"I lost a lot of weight this winter."
"I don't see it."
"How could you? I lost it."

My wife went to a monster sale. Bought two monsters.

She's not hard of hearing . . . she's hard of listening.

The girl was giving an account of her blind date with the gentleman. "When he looked at me," she reported. "He said BOO—"
"Did he frighten you?"
"Well, it was about even."

She has antique jewelry. She got it when it was new.

"You don't shrink from kissing do you?"
"If I did I'd be skin and bones."

"You know, dear," said the beleaguered husband in an attempt to assuage his bewildered wife, "I've been thinking over our argument and—well—I've decided to agree with you after all."
"That won't help you a bit," she replied. "I've changed my mind."

"Your husband has a new suit."
"No he hasn't."
"Well something's different."
"It's a new husband."

"My boy friend is one in a hundred."
"How do you keep him from finding out?"

Women: They start shooting from the lip.

She met the most wonderful man. It was a case of wink, blink—and mink.

Women are the weeper sex.

Her figure speaks for itself. It did a lot of ad-libbing in the wrong places.

"Did you ever hear me speak?"
"I never heard you do anything else."

Dumb? She thinks *Harper's* is a periodical devoted to music.

Where would woman be without her finery? In the bathtub.

She's a debutante . . . came out in 1934 and hasn't been home since.

"No man ever touched your heart, young lady."
"Well, it's the only thing they didn't."

"You've got a good lawyer to take care of the estate?" asked her mother.
"Oh—don't talk to me about lawyers," she said angrily. "I've had so much trouble over the property—sometimes I wish Frank had never died."

She is very mature . . . in fact she's past that.

Statistics show that women live longer than men. Paint is a good preserver.

It's the woman who pays . . . unless she has everything charged.

Any time you see a woman in an evening gown you know she's open to criticism.

"She looks the same as she did twenty years ago."
"Sad isn't it."

There is nothing better in the world than the love of a good woman . . . unless, of course, it's the love of a bad woman.

"She looked like she was made for the dress."
"She shoulda held out for a fur coat."

A woman is only a woman . . . but a good cigar is a smoke.

"You are asking me if I'm a good cook?" said the wife of the traveling salesman to her neighbor. "Why my Joe is just crazy about the pot roast I make. When he comes in from the road that's the second thing he asks for."

Linguist: A man who has mastered every tongue but his wife's.

You can never tell about women . . . even if you can you shouldn't.

Yetta was one of the new rich and she didn't hesitate about letting her friends know. One day she got a jeweled wristwatch and when one of the girls asked her the time she said, "It's exactly two emeralds past the diamond."

One woman talking is a monologue. Two women talking are a catalogue.

Reformers say the more jewelry a woman owns the wilder she gets. Still, many a girl has been tamed by a diamond.

She lay back on the couch and began to tell the psychiatrist about what she'd done the past few weeks. "I bought a rabbit," she revealed, "and fed it to my husband every day for dinner."
"What did he say?"
"He didn't say anything," she said, surprised. "He just looked at me with his big pink eyes."

She calls her husband "Henry." He's the eighth.

Myth: A woman who hasn't got a husband.

She should have lived in the Dark Ages. She looks terrible in the light.

The seven ages of woman . . . right age and six wild guesses.

"Have you a gentleman in your room?"
"Just a minute, I'll ask him."

The woman went into the gun department. "I want to buy a revolver," she said. "It's for my husband."
"Did he tell you what kind to buy?" asked the clerk.
"I should say not," she replied. "He doesn't even know I'm going to shoot him yet."

Women remind me of angels. They are always up in the air, have few clothes . . . and are always harping on something.

"I believe in higher education for women."
"I believe in short skirts."
"Why?"
"I believe in higher education for men."

You can't tell about a woman these days. If she looks young—she's old. If she looks old—she's young. If she looks back . . . follow her.

She never needs a permanent wave. Her skin is naturally curly.

There are seven ages of woman. The baby, the girl, the teen-ager, the young woman—the young woman—the young woman—the young woman.

She believes in suing her wild oats.

"I think there's a man under the bed."
"You go look. I've been fooled before."

He was wooing her ardently. "Your cheeks are so rosy," he declared.
"My cheeks belong to you," she whispered.
"Your lips are like rubies," he said.
"My lips belong to you, darling—just you," she breathed. "But when you get to my eyelids—they're Max Factor's."

I call my sugar "Candy"—because she's built like a peanut cluster.

"I trapped these furs myself," said the woman—explaining her sudden fashion. "My husband talks in his sleep."

She's a vegetarian. She goes out only with men who have plenty of lettuce.

"I understand your husband has gone at last."
"Yes. And I hope he hasn't gone where I know he has."

She's a terrific housepeeker.

Last week my girl was a redhead, this week she's a blonde. Next week she's gonna be a redhead . . . she has a convertible top.

The women were busily tearing apart one of their beloved friends. They tore and tore and tore, until finally one of them couldn't stand it. "These things are untrue," she protested.
"But, darling," protested the ringleader. "I remember the incidents as if they really happened."

A gentleman is a man you don't know very well.

"I admit I won't see twenty-two again."
"You wouldn't recognize it."

She's a blueblood . . . it shows right through her tattooing.

An old maid is a woman whose father didn't have a gun.

As Confucius said—and she was there when he said it.

She had thick black hair, but she wore long sleeves so it didn't show.

"I did something last night that I've never done before in all my life."
"I can't imagine what it is."

It was so cold her tooth was chattering.

A smart girl is one who knows she can get more from Santa if she leaves her legs in the stockings.

Daughter of a flapper: A zipper.

My aunt is an old maid and she loves to go to the picture shows. An usher walks her to her seat and it's the only chance she'll get to walk down the aisle with a man.

She was so tired she could hardly keep her mouth open.

Grass widow: A woman whose husband died of hay fever.

"Why, darling, you look lovely. How old are you?"
"Twenty-eight."
"You don't look it."
"Certain people think I'm older than twenty-eight."
"Who?"
"My ma and pa."

"I just despise that Jim. I'm going to the party with him."
"If he's so obnoxious to you why do you go with him to the party?"
"I have to. It's at his house."

She may have been all the world to Henry—but to me she was just a passing fanny.

Girls used to wear seven petticoats and never thought of taking a drink . . . now they down seven drinks and you learn the naked truth.

Nobody seemed to notice Mabel's new rock, so she decided to subtly call attention to it. "Oh dear," she sighed. "I'm so warm in my new ring."

"Aren't you afraid the hot climate in India might disagree with your wife?"
"It wouldn't dare."

A wife was the first person to find double use for a rolling pin.

She gave me her hand, her lips, her heart . . . I was doing piecework at the time.

A pretty girl is like a malady.

"She's thirty-four. I went to her birthday party."
"Were there thirty-four candles on the cake?"
"There were on the piece I had."

Women are the salt of the earth, that's why they drive men to drink.

A girl can talk rings around a jewelry store.

They call her "Cigarette Lighter"—a little juice and she's well lit.

Heaven protect the working girl and heaven protect the man she's working.

I call her "Flour"—because she's been through the mill.

The judge was very stern with the woman. "You are the wife of this man," he said severely. "You knew he was a burglar when you married him?"

"Yes," she replied. "I was getting old and had to choose between a burglar and a lawyer."

She was one of the only girls I ever loved . . . but I can't remember which one.

The modern girl likes to wash her face and neck.

The USO was holding interviews for select hostesses. "Can you entertain soldiers on leave?" asked the director.

"Well," said the pretty thing, "when they're with me I let them do anything they—"

"NO—NO—NO—!" shrieked the man.

"That's what I say"—she shrugged—"but it don't do any good."

Many a saint has a homely face to thank for her halo.

Generally speaking women are generally speaking.

She had been dangerously ill . . . but is dangerously well again.

Old maid: An unemployed back-seat driver.

Give a woman an inch and she thinks she's the ruler.

There is only one thing in this world more aggravating than a woman who gets noisy when she's mad . . . that's one that gets quiet.

"May I see you pretty soon?"
"Don't you think I'm pretty now?"

She was beautiful from head to foot but she certainly made a mess of the stuff in between.

Nature hasn't been kind to her but she makes up for it.

There was something dove-like about her. She was pigeon-toed.

The new 1976 bathing suit. Take a piece of thread . . .

"Nobody would suspect you were mother and daughter."
"Are you knocking me or boosting mother?"

Give a girl enough rope . . . and she'll ring the wedding bell.

She's been married ten years and still in love . . . but her husband doesn't know who it is.

If you really want to know a woman's bad points—praise her to another woman.

The woman was excited. "I'm going down to the theater," she told her brother. "Vic Mature is appearing in person. I'm going to go backstage and wait for him and when he comes out I'm going to throw myself on him."

"Now, Shirlee," protested her brother. "Men like Victor Mature like women who play hard to get."

"If I get a man like Vic Mature I don't wanna play hard to get," she rhapsodized. "I just wanna play."

When an old-fashioned girl sees any night life she sprays insect powder on it.

She has nice even teeth . . . 1, 3, 5 and 7 are missing.

"Men don't interest me. I've said no to many of them."
"What were they selling?"

I made up my mind to stay home but it was too late. She'd made up her face to go out.

"He knows her past."
"She told him everything!"
"What courage!"
"What a memory!"

She hates to go to her husband's office. It burns her up to hear them calling him boss.

The woman, whose latest boy friend was inclined to weight, was telling her friends about their courtship. "I've been seeing a lot of him lately," she said. "It's practically impossible to see all of him."

"He dresses nattily."
"Natalie who?"

She left for the movies in such a hurry she hardly had time to put the dirty dishes in the oven.

There's a girl who will do things someday, she just did me.

She was rejected so many times her hope chest developed a cough.

The woman was happily showing off her new mink coat. "It was nice of your husband to buy you that fur coat," said a friend.

"He had to," replied the woman. "I caught him kissing the maid."

"How dreadful. Did you fire her?"

"No." She smiled. "I still need a new hat."

Her fortune is in her face . . . she had her nose fixed.

Women always look at themselves in the mirror—from the front. They ought to try backing up to a mirror sometimes. You don't always meet people, you gotta pass people too.

"I know what you're thinking of."

"You don't act it."

Although they'd been divorced the couple maintained a pleasant relationship. He kept coming to her for companionship and she kept coming to him for money. One day she pulled a surprise. "Honey," she said, "the judge that granted our divorce wants to marry me. What's your opinion?"

"He didn't hear all the evidence."

Nagging woman: Her fate is familiar.

Many a girl is like an electric iron . . . she begins warming up when there's a new attachment.

Fine, cultured woman. She wouldn't say anything to your face that she wouldn't say behind your back.

She had a schoolgirl complexion—it looked like it was expelled.

She went shopping for a gift for her husband. After looking over men's jewelry, golf clubs, sportswear and watches, she decided he had all those things. So she hit upon the idea of getting him an ashtray.

The clerk showed her several dozen but nothing pleased her. Finally she pointed to a large ashcan and asked the price.

"But, lady," said the clerk. "That's no ashtray. That's an ashcan."

"That's all right," she replied. "My husband is very near-sighted."

When a woman gets a man on the spot she usually takes him to the cleaners.

He talks like a book, but she can shut him up easily.

"I've been going with him for three years."
"When are you thinking of marriage?"
"Constantly."

Woman: One who mistakes rouge for the fountain of youth.

She had so many flowers on her hat two funerals were following her.

The perfume was so dangerous . . . she wore it only when she was alone.

A girl who looks like a dream usually gives a guy insomnia.

"I've been asked to marry a thousand times."
"Who asked you?"
"My mother and father."

Women make the best wives.

The centenarian was reminiscing (must have been a woman—men don't live that long). "I remember when I was a young upstart of eighty," she said. "I wish I knew then what I know now."

A woman's face is her fortune only when it draws a lot of interest.

She went out with her husband last night—it was cheatless Tuesday.

The lady was a little bashful about telling the new male clerk what she wanted exactly, so she decided to be somewhat esoteric.
"I want something that stretches and snaps," she confided.
"Sorry, lady," said the clerk. "We don't sell turtles."

She kissed him with thick glasses on. She felt as if she were window-shopping.

The only way a girl can keep her youth these days is to watch him all the time.

The doctor told her to ride a bicycle and get a figure like Lana Turner's. She did. Now she has a figure like Lana Turner's bicycle.

The way she keeps her eyebrows takes a lot of pluck.

She was only a preacher's daughter but I wouldn't put anything pastor.

Emily Post: A branch of the American Legion.

She's so good-looking that a blind man gave her a seat in a crowded car.

My wife thinks she's changed. She's always talking about what a fool she used to be.

"Do you prefer talkative women or the other kind?"
"What other kind?"

It isn't true that a woman always has the last word. Sometimes she's talking to another woman.

She had one of those one-in-a-million figures. Luscious, well-developed, neat with the perfect contour. But despite all these gifts she developed a neurosis about Peeping Toms.
"What measures do you take to avoid this calamity?" asked her psychiatrist.
"Well, I keep the shades down, I bar the windows and I always undress behind a screen."
"How do you keep the boys from peeking through the keyhole?"
"I leave the door open."

She went to finishing school. When she gets a man he's finished.

She came in carrying a tremendous package. "What did you buy?" hubby asked.

"I don't know what it is," she replied.
"Then why did you buy it?"
"The man said you can't get 'em any more."

My girl comes from a tough neighborhood. They couldn't afford a nutcracker. They'd just stick the nut in her eye and tell her to wink.

Woman: A human gimmie pig.

Girls who eat a lot of sweets will soon develop larger seats.

"You can't get it for love or money, right?"
"I don't know. I tried only money."

He's her white-haired boy. She turned it white.

Beautiful girl: Something to look forward to and backward at.

The only girl who thinks beauty contests are on the level is the winner.

During the war they tried to make a date for her with the gardener's son. "I wouldn't go out with him in a million years," she ranted.
"But," explained her friend. "He's the only man left in town."
"My," she sighed. "How time flies."

She couldn't keep her ears off her.

The old maid sighed when she died, "Who said you can't take it with you?"

She has a million dollar smile. She smiles only at guys who have a million dollars.

Womanhood: One of the louder figures of speech.

Her thirtieth birthday isn't far away. Only six years ago.

"I love Columbus."
"You should. He brought your parents to this country."

Wave: A sailor that gets liberty but won't give any.

She reached the take-it-or-leave-it stage: sixty-four trying for thirty-two.

My girl was scared by the Book of Genesis—all them begets.

The two female writers were running neck-in-neck for the coveted honor of female writer of the year. At long last the decision was reached and the runner-up was asked to make the presentation. When they were on the stand the victor asked, "How do you feel standing next to me?"
"Very young," said the vanquished.

Don't forget to tell everybody it's a secret.

When she was a kid in school all she thought about was boys. She's over that now. All she thinks about is men.

She's so cold she has arctic circles under her eyes.

The Kat Klub was meeting to honor one of their members who had made a trip to Europe. "Tell me the scandal while I was away," said the adventuress.

"Darling," said the president, "there *was* no scandal while you were away."

They didn't know Jane to speak to, only to talk about.

My girl has two loves. She's in love with love and crazy about money.

The girl was complaining to her mother. "I had to change my seat five times at the movies."

"Some man annoy you?"

"Yes," said the girl. "Finally."

The modern girl isn't as she is painted, but she certainly is painted.

She's quick on her feet—you should see her in Gimbels' basement. But she's no bargain.

"It is your civic duty to volunteer for jury duty," said the famous lawyer.

"But the jury can't talk," protested the woman. "I'd rather be a witness."

"If a person was born in 1898 how old would they be today?"

"Man or woman?"

She holds her age well. She's been twenty-nine for years.

I got hoarse listening to her talk.

"Darling, we're invited to a cocktail party."

"That's nice. Who are we going to be under the table with?"

She went crying to mother. "Mother, oh Mother, he's a terrible brute."

"What did he do this time?" mother asked.

"Well, when he came home this evening dinner wasn't ready and when he asked me why I said, 'Can't you see my voice is husky?' And then he said, 'If I got as much exercise as your voice I'd be husky too.'"

Smart girl. Her motto. "United we stand, provided we fall."

She's a draftsman. Every time I make plans she draws the line.

"My cooking left my husband cold."

"You divorced him?"

"No. I buried him."

Gossip: A woman of affairs.

I told her I couldn't marry her, I wasn't even making expenses. She said I should marry her anyway, she'd make expenses.

"Say the two words that mean heaven or hell to me."

"Shoot yourself."

Men who go out on the loose frequently end up tight.

"This year the government allows you $600 for your wife."

"I'm gonna turn her in before the price goes down."

"I'm reading a sad book. *Forever Amber*."

"That's not a sad book."

"It is at my age."

"Someone wrote her a poison-pen letter and frightened her. So she asked me if I'd sit with her. We'd sit around and smooch for weeks because she said she was afraid. Now she says she isn't afraid any more."

"What are you going to do?"

"Write another letter."

"I lost my wife in a fire. Her dress caught—"

"Burned alive?"

"No. Luckily the firemen arrived on time and she was drowned."

He knew he had to, but he didn't quite make it. He made a Z line for the door.

The sailor had a tattoo of an anchor on his chest. Now it's on his stomach. He dropped anchor.

The handsome, well-dressed man handed the poor beggar a five dollar bill. "Here, my good man," he said, "eat your fill and there's enough there for a drink or two."

The beggar entered Tony's restaurant, where he ate the biggest dinner of his life and then topped it off with a bottle of wine and a big tip to Luigi, the waiter. "Ah," said the handsome, well-dressed stranger, "it's a good world. Everyone is happy. The poor beggar because he is no longer hungry, Tony because he has made a big sale, the waiter because he has received a nice tip. And me? . . . I'm happy too, because the bill was counterfeit."

He: "You must marry me. I love you. There can be no other."

She: "But I don't love you. You must find some other woman, some beautiful woman."

He: "But I don't want a beautiful woman. I want you."

Husband: A man who was once in love.

Pallbearer: A man who gives a friend a lift.

"We have to teach this girl right from wrong."
"Okay. You teach her right."

He's nursing a grouch. His wife is sick.

Song title: "I Want a Girl Just Like the Girl That Turned Down Dear Old Dad."

The super-duper salesman had accomplished a near miracle. He had sold an icebox to an Eskimo. One day, while in town, he bumped into the customer once more. "How's the refrigerator I sold you?" he asked.

"Swell," said the smiling Eskimo. "But the old lady hasn't got the knack yet of chopping up the ice square to fit them little trays."

It was his first day in the Army, being among the first men to be called to the colors in the new draft. "Please get to the mess hall on time," said the sergeant. "And please be sure to rise early. And remember, if you please, the proper attire which constitutes the uniform of the day."

The next day the sergeant came in and roared, "Hit the deck, you slobs, get over to the slop hall for some mess and put on dungarees for latrine detail."

"But, Sergeant," pleaded the draftee, "yesterday you were so nice."

"Yesterday," roared the sergeant, "we were taking pictures for *Life* magazine!"

The young man had just proposed marriage to his lady love and she had turned him down. "If you don't marry me immediately," he threatened, "I'll go to the lake, cut a hole in the ice, dive in and drown myself."

"Why this is April. The ice won't cover the lake for eight months!"

"Okay, then I'll wait."

Louise's boy friend is either a lousy speller or he's mad at her. He just sent a valentine and left out the "I."

Finger was startled to see the nonchalant way Shimmel was taking the fact that his lady love was seen with another man.

"You said you love her and yet you saw her with another man and you didn't knock the guy down?"

"I'm waiting."

"Waiting for what?"

"Waiting to catch her with a smaller feller."

"Hi'ya, beautiful," the marine called.

"I bet you're calling me that because I spent six hours in the beauty parlor."

"No. Because I spent six months in the Solomons."

Long hair makes men look intelligent. But when found on their coats it makes them look foolish.

He has everything a woman admires in a man . . . charm, personality, a sense of humor and suede shoes.

Her face was like a beautiful poem. I don't know which line I liked best.

"She's the salt of the earth."
"Can't say much for her shaker."

She was only the optician's daughter. Two glasses and she made a spectacle of herself.

The district attorney was cross-examining the murderess.

"And after you had poisoned the coffee and your husband sat at the breakfast table partaking of the fatal dosage didn't you feel any qualms? Didn't you feel the slightest pity for him knowing that he was about to die and was wholly unconscious of it? As you sat there didn't you feel for him at all?"

"Yes," she answered. "There was just one moment when I sort of felt sorry for him."

"When was that?"

"When he asked for the second cup."

He had married her after knowing her only two hours, and now he was having his regrets. "You were so affectionate and loving before we were married," he lamented.

"And how would you know?" she snapped.

"I saw you with other men."

His wife was brooding all day and Seymour couldn't stand it. "What's wrong, sweetheart?" he asked.

"That terrible Doreen Dubin next door has a hat exactly like mine," she replied, dabbing away an angry tear.

"And I suppose you want me to buy you a new one?"

"Well," she said, "it's a lot cheaper than moving."

The girl was anxious but the boy was nervous.

"What would you do if I kissed you?" he asked.

"I'd call my brother," she said.

"How old is he?"

"Two and a half."

She always has her own way. She writes her diary a week ahead of time.

According to historians women used cosmetics in the Middle Ages . . . and today women are using cosmetics in the middle ages too.

"Does your wife drive the car?"

"No. It looked this way when I bought it."

Women and telephones repeat what they hear . . . but the telephone repeats it exactly.

They call my girl "Hotel Towel"—because she's been in many a salesman's grip.

The engineering firm had advertised for a secretary with engineering experience and this tall, beautiful, blue-eyed blonde walked in and asked for the job. "Can you read a blue print?" asked McBridge.

"Certainly," she replied. "I can read any color print. Especially if it's in English."

"The girl I was out with last night was touching thirty-one."

"Touching it? She was beating the heck out of it."

She was a fictitious character. Fictitious means made-up.

Becky was tired of Sidney's habit of oggling curvy women, so she warned, "I'll wear my low-cut gown next time and show you a thing or two."

Alimony: If you don't pay it in due time you do time.

The marriage broker was hard of hearing and had to rely on his assistant during the interviewing of prospective brides. His first question always pertained to age.

"I'm young," said one applicant. "In the early twenties."

"What'd she say?" he asked his aide.

"She said she was young in the early twenties," he replied.

She was married at an early urge.

The burglar was caught in the old maid's room. "Please let me go, madam," he cried. "I ain't never done nothing wrong."

"Well," she replied, "it's never too late to learn."

She does settlement work. Her lawyer sues and she gets the settlement.

Ginsburg had been hearing stories about his wife's behavior but had done nothing about it. One night he returned home and found her sitting on the lap of her lover.

"SARA!" he roared angrily. "Company or no company, supper's got to be ready on time."

The murder trial had reached the highest point of tension and the beautiful blonde hung her head and squirmed under the cross-examination.

"I repeat my question for the fourth time. Where WERE you on the night of December 15?" the D.A. bellowed.

"Oh—I—I cannot tell you."

"YOU MUST TELL US."

"All right. I—I was home working out a simple cross-word puzzle."

"Why are you ashamed of that?"

"Oh, it's terrible. A beautiful dame like me, wasting a night on a crossword puzzle."

Intuition: Feminine radar.

Three girls were arrested for soliciting and a peddler, newly arrived in this country, was arrested for peddling without a license. They were brought before the court.

"What do you do for a living?" the judge asked, pointing to the first girl.

"Your honor, I'm a model," she answered.

"Thirty days," was the sentence. Then he turned to the second. "What do you do for a living?" he asked belligerently.

"Your honor, I'm an actress."

"Thirty days." Then he turned to the third girl. "What do you do for a living," he demanded.

"To tell you the truth," she answered, "I'm a prostitute."

"For telling the truth," he said, "I'm going to suspend

sentence." Then he turned to the little immigrant peddler. "And you," he said, "what do you do for a living."

"To tell you the truth," the peddler said, twisting his ancient cap in his hands, "I'm a prostitute also."

The lawyer was advising his pretty client.

"When we go to court I want you to wear a short skirt."

"But they're not in style," she protested.

"Do you want to be acquitted?" asked the lawyer. "Or do you want to be in style?"

The girl was so dumb she should have been beautiful.

Women are like ocean vessels. When you meet them they are shipshape, but once they're yours they come apart at the beams.

She didn't go out with boys until she was three . . . her parents were very strict.

"When do you use a waterless cooker?" asked the home economics teacher.

"When you don't want to cook water," Brighteyes answered.

"You asked me for an honest answer," said the beauty counselor.

"Yeah," she replied. "But you didn't have to tell me the truth."

There was a sale on nylon stockings and a tremendous line formed at the counter. One man was standing in line for an hour and making no headway. He kept being pushed and shoved farther and farther back. He finally got mad and began to push and claw his way forward.

"Can't you act like a gentleman?" asked one of the customers.

"I've been acting like a gentleman for an hour," he replied. "Now I'm going to act like a lady."

It is becoming difficult to be wicked. There are so few really beautiful women.

The banker's show-girl wife was preparing to leave him. "But why?" he protested bitterly. "Haven't I given you everything you want?"

"Not everything," she said. "My new boy friend has gotten what you got, only twenty years sooner. *He* can give me everything."

"Her figure's like a figure 8."
"How's mine?"
"You made yours the hard way. Two 4's."

New Year's Eve: When a wife sits up till twelve for the New Year to come in . . . and till four for her husband to come in.

Two chorus girls were engaged in the usual discussion, men.

"I was out with a big sport last night but all his money was tied up."
"Where?"
"In his handkerchief."

The doorman saw the wealthy young playboy enter the show girl's apartment and, knowing he was a good tipper, decided to wait until he came out to hail a cab for him. Much to the doorman's surprise the playboy came out of the apartment after spending only five minutes inside. When the cab came the doorman held the door open for the young man and said, "Good night."

"Not necessarily," replied the playboy.

The traffic cop stopped the woman. "Here's my driver's license and picture," she said coquettishly.

"You know something," replied the cop. "This is one of the finest, most realistic pictures I've ever seen. I'm glad to see you ain't one of those vain women who have the photos retouched to remove all the lines in their face."

"Sir," she replied icily, "you are looking at my thumb print."

"Don't be discouraged, Lulu," said Lulu's mom, "in this world there's a man for every woman. It's a wonderful arrangement."

"I know, Mamma," said Lulu. "I don't want to change it, I just want to get in on it."

Two friends had been traveling in India and told the couple they'd brought them one of the most unusual kinds of mystic gift. They then produced two small bottles of clear fluid and told them that if either one cheated the liquid would turn black.

The following summer the wife went away on a vacation and while she was gone one of the friends sneaked into the house, put black ink into one of the bottles and placed it behind a picture.

The wife returned and one day while cleaning came across the bottle of black ink. She hurriedly emptied it and filled it with water.

In the old days a siren was a girl who lured men to the rocks. Today she lures rocks from the men.

She belonged to the horsey set. Especially her teeth.

"Do you smoke?" he asked. "No," she said. "Do you drink?" he asked. "No," she said. "Do you neck?" he asked. "No," she said. "What do you do that's naughty?" he asked. "I tell lies," she said.

Love comes only once to every woman . . . but that doesn't prevent her from getting married three or four times.

"The batter stuck to my pan," the wife sobbed.
"I thought you looked better today," replied her husband.

Gordon was going to driving school and the instructor was briefing him on the type of question he might be expected to answer in the oral examination. "Now, Herb," said the instructor, "if your wife were driving ahead of you and she put her hand out and gestured with the index finger toward the approaching corner, what would it mean?"
"It would mean the window's open."

"Have you entertained my proposition," the boss asked his new secretary.
"No," she said. "But your proposition entertained me."

The lawyer was explaining why he lost the case even though he was representing a very pretty woman. "She sat on the witness chair, raised her skirts and the chair looked like it had six legs."

"Do you know that girl?"

"No, but her face sounds familiar."

"Nice young girls shouldn't hold a man's hands."

"Nice young girls have to hold a man's hands."

An old maid in silk underwear is like malted milk in a champagne bottle.

The poor woman was dejected. She had just lost her seventh boy friend in seven weeks and she was sure it was because of her aging complexion. Still she did not have the nerve to undergo plastic surgery. One day she met a friend who told her about a new type of cosmetic that was so wonderful it could take the wrinkles out of prunes. Happily the woman skipped down to the drugstore and bought a case of the stuff. It didn't do her complexion any good but now she has the smoothest prunes in Flatbush.

I got even with that lawyer who blackballed me at the club. His wife came to me to see about divorcing him and I praised him so highly she decided to stick.

I'm hungry for the beautiful girls . . . but the beautiful girls are too hungry for me.

The old maid went to the doctor and told him she had a recurring dream every night about a young handsome man who wanted to flirt with her and the dream was keeping her awake. The doctor prescribed an extra-strong sleeping pill.

A few days later she was back in the office again. "Don't tell me you aren't sleeping these days?" said the doc.

"Oh, I'm sleeping fine now," she replied. "But to tell you the truth I certainly miss that young man."

Nothing annoys a woman more than to have friends drop in unexpectedly and find the house looking like it usually does.

She's been on a diet for three weeks and all she's taken off is her hat.

All a dame has to do is go to court, fill her eyes with tears and the jury wipes them away with your bankbook.

Women would never make good convicts. They believe in starting a new sentence before they finish the old one.

The chorus girl was explaining why she hadn't marched down the aisle yet. "I ask him why we don't get married and he always says *mañana*. That's Spanish for money you know."

She was only a typesetter's daughter, but she knew her p's and q's.

Fine feathers do not make fine birds, but they can make a girl feel like a chicken.

Divorcée: A woman who takes her man for better or worse but not for good.

Figures may not lie—but girdles keep a lot of them from telling the truth.

If men dressed like girls . . . women would turn around and look too.

To an actress bad publicity is when all the newspapers come out and her name isn't in them.

"You men are all beasts."
"What are you here for?"
"I love animals."

"They just arrested a girl for walking the street in a no-piece bathing suit."
"What did they do to her?"
"Nothing. The judge is holding her for further examination."

My girl friend is so bowlegged when she sits around the house she sits around the house.

The district attorney had the pretty redhead on the stand.
"I want you to tell the court where you were on the night of April 9."
"I'll agree to tell you," she said, "if the judge will tell where he was the same night."
"What have the actions of the judge on that particular night got to do with the case?"
"Nothing," she answered. "But I like a little gossip just as well as you do."

Pedestrian: "You must have been driving carelessly."
Woman driver: "I am a careful driver. I've been driving for eight years."
Pedestrian: "Lady, you got nothing on me. I've been walking for forty-eight years."

Prior to World War II the Brownsville section of Brooklyn was undergoing a cleanup of the notorious

"Murder Incorporated" gang. For weeks all the New York newspapers carried pictures of the killers on their front pages. One day a woman was riding home on the IRT subway when she unfolded the evening paper and there on the front page was a story and picture of Abraham Lincoln.

Another woman, reading over her shoulder, said, "He looks like a familiar face from Brownsville. How many did he kill?"

"How much is that bag?" Mrs. Epstein asked.
"Twenty-five dollars," said the salesgirl.
"I'd like to exchange it."
"But you haven't bought it yet."
"I know. But I'm sure I'm not going to like it."

Mrs. Edgar Allen Pincus was trying very hard to bargain with the salesclerk. "Madam," he said. "This is not Saks New York. This is Saks Beverly Hills."
"Oh my goodness," shrieked Mrs. E.A.P., "I knew I got off at the wrong station."

"Is your wife having any success in learning to drive the car?"
"Well, the road is beginning to turn when she does."

A hen party is where everything is torn apart but the chicken.

Lawyer: "Didn't you suspect burglars had been in the house when you saw all the drawers pulled out and the contents scattered all over the floor?"
Woman: "No, I just thought my husband had been looking for a clean shirt."

She had long black hair running down her back. Too bad it wasn't on her head.

Old maid: "I hate to think of my youth."
New maid: "What happened?"
Old maid: "Nothing."

"She looks better than he does."
"That's 'cause her mustache is neater."

My new girl belongs to the 400. She's one of the zeros.

The best way to approach a woman with a past is with a present.

When Mrs. Brown arrived home with her latest purchase it turned out to be a very expensive Dior creation. "Where am I gonna get the money to pay for it?" Brown demanded.
"Darling," said the missus, "you know I'm not inquisitive."

"I've got tickets for the theater."
"Good, I'll start dressing at once."
"Please do. The tickets are for tomorrow."

The scantily clad southern girl was brought into court, where she got very flip with the judge, who admonished her for not dressing sufficiently and fined her $5.00 for contempt of court. When asked what the fine was for, she replied, "Fo temptin' the co't."

The woman called to complain of a robbery.
"There is no honesty these days," she cried. "My maid

ran off with three of my best dresses. The ones I smuggled through customs from my trip to Paris."

Pinup: A girl whose body usually goes to her head.

She's the life of the party line.

A woman stands a better chance of catching a man if she keeps her trap closed.

Chorus girl: A girl old men are always poking funds at.

She has so many cavities she talks with an echo.

A famous playboy had a date with Peggy Hopkins Joyce but his car broke down on the way. So he wired her the following: CHANGING TIRES WILL BE HALF HOUR LATE DON'T MARRY ANYONE TILL I GET THERE.

She knows the meaning of the golden rule . . . get all the gold you can.

Old maid's prayer: Now I lay me down to sleep . . . darn it.

She was only the dentist's daughter, but she ran around with the worst set in town.

Ladies generally shop in couples. When a woman has money to spend she loves to take a friend along to see her spend it.

Mrs. McGirdle didn't quite know how to speak to a military man. So when General MacArthur addressed the bond rally she walked up to him, stared at the twenty-five rows of ribbons and decorations and said, "I take it you've been in the war?"

She's an old-fashioned girl. She takes the pipe out of her mouth before pulling the nightgown over her head.

Katz's wife was driving along in her usual manner, knocking over lampposts, hitting every tree in sight, smacking every parked car, making the pedestrian run for his life and—being a very safe driver—driving through every safety zone. When she was finally stopped by a traffic cop she had knocked down, he demanded, "Let's see your license."

"You mean," she asked, "with that kind of driving they'll give me a license?"

Flirting: Wishful winking.

Two Boston women were in California talking about the unusual heat for the wintertime. "It's never like this in Boston," remarked Mrs. Van Knich.

"Of course not," answered Mrs. Shlumpper. "But you must remember we are three thousand miles from the ocean."

A mother, unable to find a baby-sitter and being a strong music lover, decided to take the child to the concert hall where a famous symphony was to be played. She warned the little girl to sit quietly. After two long-drawn-out movements the child turned to her mother, who was applauding hysterically, and asked, "May I scream now?"

KIDS...childhood... school

(Children are the light of the house, but when you have half a dozen of them it's time to shut off the light.)

It was a happy reunion between old friends. "We've known you for ages, haven't we, Jack?" the girl said as her brother nodded.

"Remember how we used to romp together when we were children?" her brother added.

"Yes," Jack said nostalgically, "you two are my old pair of rompers."

The children of today are spoiled. They get everything they want and don't know the meaning of need. They take everything for granted. They not only don't know what it means to be cold at night but now when they go to sleep they even have electric blankets. Today the kids don't say tuck me in, they say plug me in.

When I was a kid I lived in such a tough neighborhood we used to play cops and robbers with real cops. When I ran away from home my father sent me a telegram: DON'T RETURN AND ALL WILL BE FORGIVEN.

Most kids eat spinach only so they'll grow up to be big and strong enough to refuse it.

"I never heard such cussin' since the day I was born."

"I'll bet there was a lot of cussin' the day you was born."

"Now, Johnny," said the teacher, "if the phone were to ring in the middle of the night at your house, what might it mean?"

"The bill is paid."

To some children the greatest seafood ever is salt-water taffy.

The baby decided it was gonna have a bottle or bust.

The kid was with Santa Claus. "I wanna have a train, a six-gun, an erector set, a chemistry set, a cowboy suit, a bicycle, a scooter, a catcher's mitt, a set of soldiers, a toy garage with cars and trucks and a heavy crane—"

"Okay," laughed Santa. "I'll look in the book and see if you were a good boy."

"Never mind looking in the book. I'll settle for a pair of roller skates."

The child was explaining why he preferred to sit in the rear seat of the last row in the classroom. "Sitting there I get last chance at a question. By then it's almost impossible to guess wrong."

In school I had to stand face to the wall. Not because I was bad . . . because I was ugly.

The young child prodigy drew a masterpiece of the Holy Family. Only he added a fourth to the group. There was the Christ child and Joseph and Mary. "Who in the world is the fourth person?" asked the theological expert.

"That's the baby-sitter when Jesus' mommy and daddy wanted to go out," he explained.

"I posed for talcum powder ads when I was a kid."

"With that face?"

"The face had nothing to do with it."

"That bulldog looks like Aunt Minnie."

"Don't say such things."

"Aw—the bulldog can't hear me."

Billy was bad in class so the teacher decided to use the psychology of personal competitiveness to get him to improve. "You must study harder," she said. "How would you like to stay back in this class another year and have little Joan go ahead of you?"

"Oh," replied Billy, "I guess there'll be other Joans."

The kids were bragging about the accomplishments of their respective fathers. "My old man was the first man to fly ten thousand feet with a stick in his hand," boasted Butch.

"Oh, he was a flyer?"

"No. The poolroom blew up."

"You have an awfully good stomach, haven't you, Mamma?"

"Why do you say that?"

"I heard daddy tell my nurse you swallow everything he tells you."

Mary was complaining to Jim across the dinner table. "What a day," she said. "Baby got his first tooth, took his first step, fell and knocked out his tooth and then said his first word."

While mamma and papa Schultz were reading the language daily Benjamin was reading a fairy tale to his

138

baby sister. "And mamma bear said, 'Who's been eating my porridge?'"

"See," said mamma. "We ain't the only ones dot got cockaroaches."

"How old is he?" asked the clerk, pinching the nurse on the cheek.

"Six months," she said, pinching him back.

"Talk yet?"

"No."

"Boy baby, eh?"

A child was being examined to test her reliability as a witness.

"Do you know anything that is in the Bible?"

"I know everything."

"What?" the judge exclaimed in astonishment. "Tell us some of the things that are in there."

"Well," she said, "there's a picture of sister's beau, one of mother's recipes for tomato ketchup, a curl of mine and the pawn ticket for daddy's watch."

In my third year in school I won the Academy Award for playing hooky.

"Keep your kid off the streets. There are lots of crimes committed in the streets these days."

"Yeah? By our kid?"

"Willie," shouted his mother, "two pieces of pie is enough for you."

"That's funny," said Willie. "You want me to eat properly and you won't let me practice."

As the hero in the play slapped the heroine a small voice in the audience was heard to ask, "Mother, why doesn't she hit him back like you do?"

"How long have you been here?" asked the lawyer of the new office boy.
"Six weeks."
"And you don't like the law business?"
"Naw. It's no good. I'm sorry I learned it."

I came from a very tough neighborhood. When other kids were rubbing off the blackboards we were rubbing out the teachers.

"What did the Prince of Wales say in 1894?"
"Daddy."

We were so poor when the wolf came to the door . . . he brought his own sandwiches.

His parents never refused him anything. When he'd ask for $5.00 his mother would go right down to the basement . . . and print him one.

I was the spit-oon image of my father.

When I was in the sixth grade they were very tough on me. They asked me to count up to ten . . . from memory.

Teacher used to tell us about bees and flowers. Bees carry pollen from flower to flower. I tried it once . . . it ain't much fun.

In my neighborhood when a debutante had a coming-out party . . . it was held in a freight car.

As a kid the rabbits loved to play with me . . . until I had my two front teeth fixed.

We lived in a tent when I was a baby . . . so my head grew to a point.

The man lay on the couch while the psychiatrist took notes relative to the id balance. "When I was fifteen years old," said the man, "I got my first lesson about women."

"What happened then?"

"I went to my cousin Effie's sweet-sixteen party. It was a long trip and I had to stay overnight. Aunt Caroline gave me the room next to Effie's and, at night, when I was getting ready to undress I turned the lights out and tiptoed over to the door and peeked through the keyhole."

"And what did you see?"

"Nothing. Her eye was in the way."

My early struggles started when mother tried to wash my ears.

"Do you like Tootsie Rolls?"

"Naw—I don't go out wit goils."

Mormon: One of those people who ain't very smart.

"An anecdote is a tale," said the teacher. "Now, Sidney, use it in a sentence."

"I tied a tin can to the dog's anecdote."

On my block when the cats got hungry they hijacked a cow.

Eternal triangle: Something that babies wear.

"Where can I get hold of your sister?"
"I don't know. She's ticklish."

The kids were boasting about their respective fathers. "My daddy bathes twice a week," said Henry.

"That's nuttin'," said Butch. "My daddy bathes three times a week."

"Oh yeah," said Percivale, not wishing to be out-daddied. "My daddy keeps himself so clean he never has to take a bath."

I was late for school only once. That was when the patrol wagon came for daddy . . . and I wanted to see him off.

He had an unforgettable childhood . . . his father played cornet.

There was an unfortunate accident in his childhood. He was born.

As a kid they kept him in the refrigerator to keep him from getting spoiled.

Anyone in my old neighborhood with teeth and ears was a sissy.

Butch was one of those potential delinquents who they talked into going to the settlement house for music lessons. The teacher was a great psychologist. She knew just how to get along with kids like him, and at the same time make the lessons interesting. She sat Butch down for his first lesson.

"The white keys are lower down," she said cutely. "Black keys are higher up. White—basement. Black—attic. Play first in basement—then attic."

"Hey, what da hell do I gotta do," yelled Butch, "carry the piano all over da house to play it?"

Wonder what momma stork tells baby stork when it asks where it came from?

Baby's going to be an auctioneer when he grows up. He just put uncle's watch under the hammer.

"There you go tracking mud all over the house. Didn't I tell you to wipe your feet before you came in!"

"Oh, nobody's blaming you, Mom. You did all you could."

A cow is an animal that lays milk.

The boy came skipping into the house with a big lollipop in his hands. "Where did you get it?" his mother asked.

"I bought it with the nickel you gave me."

"The nickel I gave you was for Sunday school."

"I know, Mom," said the boy, "but the minister met me at the door and got me in free."

Mother used to warn me not to tell tales out of reform school.

"Now, William, what do you know about Eskimos?"

"I eat their pies."

As a kid, uncle couldn't afford a telescope . . . that's why his eyes pop.

I was so ugly they had to diaper my face.

When my brother was born, mom looked up his birth certificate . . . to see if there were any loopholes in it.

The kid opened the door to let Mrs. Van Noseair in.

"I heard my father say you were stuckup," he greeted her. "How much did they get?"

"Mommie," said the little boy. "You still burned up about my pranks?"

She smiled. "Well," she said, "I guess I have cooled down a bit."

"Well, you're gonna be burned up again. I just set the living room on fire."

I was in school so long the principal had to frame me to graduate.

"Say, Daddy, do you play billiards with the grocer?"

"No. Why?"

"I heard mommie tell him yesterday that she would give him his cue when she saw you coming."

If I don't find my little boy I'll never be happy again. He's got my pipe.

The neighborhood was so tough the mothers had to play strip poker with the kids to get them to undress for bed.

First kid: "I don't like you any more."

Second kid: "Why?"

First kid: "Cause when I hit you on the head with a mallet you make faces and cry."

"You don't seem to like the new governess," his mother said.

"I hate her," screamed the kid. "I'd like to grab her and bite her on the back of the neck like daddy does."

Do you know what happens to little boys who tell lies? They ride for half fare.

"What comes before six?"
"The milkman."

The revenue man stopped the little hillbilly boy. "Son," he said, "I'll give you a dollar if you take me to see your father."

"I'll take you," agreed the little boy. "But you'll have to give me the dollar first."

"No," insisted the revenuer. "When I get back I'll give it to you."

"Look, mister," said the kid. "If I take you to my old man's still you ain't comin' back."

My sister got a bundle of joy from a football player . . . now they have a bouncing baby ball.

Book title: *The Child Is Born . . . or . . . Each Dawn I Diaper.*

"I matched pennies and won thirty-five cents, and you say I'm dumb."

"I mean in school."

"This *was* in school."

The kid eats all day . . . we practically inherited a famine.

Father was helping Sonny with his lessons. "Daddy," said Sonny, "I read in school that animals have a new fur coat every winter."

"Be quiet!" father warned. "Your mother's in the next room."

Randy was learning fast from his daddy. "Yesterday I killed three female and two male flies," he told the teacher.

"How did you know they were males and females?"

"Well," said Randy, "three were on the mirror and two were on the cigar box."

You can lead a boy to water . . . but you can't make him wash his neck.

Billy became a famous congressman. He has his Uncle Zeb to thank for teaching him all about politics. One day Billy was inspecting a litter. "Uncle Zeb," said Billy, "what kind of pups are these?"

"Democrats," said Uncle Zeb.

"You told me last week these pups were Republicans."

"That was last week, Billy," replied Uncle Zeb. "This week they got their eyes open."

Children's clothes will stay clean for several days . . . if you keep them off the child.

The woman offered to care for the eight-year-old daughter of her next-door neighbor. She arrived in time to prepare breakfast, laying a generous helping of bacon and eggs in front of the child.

"Mother always has hot biscuits for breakfast," said the eight-year-old.

So the woman, anxious to oblige, hurried into the

kitchen and quickly prepared a plate of hot biscuits, which she laid in front of the girl. "No, thank you," she said.

"But I thought you said your mother always has hot biscuits for breakfast?" asked the surprised woman.

"She does," said the child. "But I don't eat 'em."

With children it's the same as brides . . . everything happens the second year.

"I did my good deed for today, Mom. I put a tack on the teacher's chair."

She was horrified. "You consider that a good deed?" she scolded.

"Sure. Everybody in the class hates him."

I fell from the crib when I was a babe. But I was lucky . . . I broke the fall with my head.

He was a bad student . . . but a whiz at recess.

The kid walked into the darkened room and threw the light switch. Immediately sister's boy friend leaped from the couch.

"Whatta you doing?" asked Junior.

"Nothing," said the boy friend.

"Then how do you know when you're finished?"

"What's your son going to be when he graduates?"

"An old man."

We didn't live on the wrong side of the tracks. We were so tough we lived in the middle of the tracks.

"Daddy, who did you say gave me that bike for Christmas?"

"Santa Claus."

"Well, he was here this morning and asked for another installment on it."

They were showing wedding pictures of father and mother. The one in the middle was me.

The truant officer spotted the schoolboy coming out of the picture show. "Have you missed school lately?" he asked politely.

"Not a bit," replied the boy.

When he was born they called him "Webster" . . . no words could describe him.

I watched so much television, in my ABC's I always say H-I-J-K-L-S-M-F-T.

Clarence was one of those real tough kids. "I'll give you a book," said the teacher, trying to get his interest.

"That's okay," said Clarence.

"How about—oh—let's see. *Little Women?*"

"That's even better."

"We were so poor I didn't have pants to wear."

"Not even jeans?"

"Hers wouldn't fit me either."

My first girl had pop eyes. Well, her eyes didn't exactly pop. Her forehead receded a little and made it look that way.

I always look stern. Ma was frightened by the rear end of the Staten Island ferry.

As a baby I was unusually strong. So much so that my folks would tie me to a bed when they went out. I'd wait a half hour . . . then me and the bed would go to a picture show.

Then one day I went to school. Couldn't get a table at the poolroom.

The little boy decided to run away from home. But after wandering for two hours he came home. Nobody paid any attention to him. The kid wandered aimlessly about the house hoping for some sign that would indicate his absence had been felt. Just as he was about to give up, the family pup wandered in. "Hey, Ma," shouted the boy. "Is this the same dog you had when I went away?"

I was so big as a baby that when I was born the doctor was afraid to slap me.

As a child I was very young.

I looked like my mother was frightened by everything.

I had so many teeth missing . . . I was the only kid in school who could stick his tongue out without opening his mouth.

Solly watched her mother remove the cream from her face.
"What's that for, Mom?" he asked.
"That's to make me beautiful."
"Didn't work, eh?"

"I told you not to swallow," roared the dentist. "That was my last pair of pliers."

Little Irving's dog was run over and he mourned for days and days. "Oh come now, Irving," said his father. "You didn't carry on this way when grandma died."

"Yeah," cried Irving. "But I didn't raise grandma from a pup."

When I was a kid I was so thin . . . the teacher kept marking me absent.

"Sure my face is clean, Mom. Just look at the towel."

When I was a kid they used to shoot vitamins in my arm every day. By the time I was fourteen I was all shot to health.

Pious: Full of pie.

"Mommie, why am I so skinny?"

"Don't worry about it, dear. When your father was born he weighed only four pounds."

"Really? Did he live?"

Junior pondered the problem for some time and finally decided to query his mother about it. "Ma," he said. "Papa got a red nose from drinking, didn't he?"

"No," she replied. "It's the cold winter weather that makes it so red."

"Well you better dig up another answer," said Junior. "I'm gonna ask you the same question next summer."

My kid has sensitive ears. He screams every time I pull 'em.

The kid saw snow for the first time. "Look, Ma," he shouted excitedly. "See what Duz is doing now."

My girl writes me every day but her letters smell of shaving lotion. That's 'cause her mother licks the envelopes.

The tough kid was getting an eye examination in school. "Read what you see on that chart," said the teacher.
"Okay," he said, "I read it."
"Read it aloud."
"Whatsa matter?" he asked. "Can't *you* read?"

Sister wanted to be alone with her beau but little brother kept hanging around. "He's not very s-m-a-r-t," spelled sister.
"No," agreed her beau. "He looks like a little d-o-p-e for a fourteen-year-old."
"It's okay with me if you want to go to the movies," said little brother. "You don't have to spell it."

"Johnny, go wash your face and neck."
"Neck who, Ma?"

When I was a kid I came from a tough neighborhood. I had eight notches on my bean shooter.

That was one of her father's jokes. She's one of her mother's.

The woman returned to the department store. "Those trousers you sold me were not Sanforized," she told the clerk. "I washed Willie's pants and they shrunk so, the child could hardly walk. What am I going to do?"

"Try washing Willie," suggested the clerk. "Maybe he'll shrink too."

My baby brother was sent from heaven . . . they must like it quiet up there.

"Look out for worms in apples," said the teacher.
"Let them look out for themselves."

Johnnie and Horace watched the stout lady get on the scale, place her coin in the slot and wait for her correct weight. But the scale was broken and it registered only sixty-five pounds. "Gosh," exclaimed Horace, "she's hollow!"

My folks can never forget my birthday. I was born between the second payment on the radio and the seventh on the automobile.

"Mommie?" whimpered the cute little youngster. "Do you love me?"
"Yes, darling."
"Then why not divorce daddy and marry the man in the candy store?"

"Why, son, when I was your age I was lucky to get ice cream once a year."
"Now's your chance to make up for lost time."

The class assignment in composition was to write about something unusual that happened during the past week. Little Irving got up to read his. "Papa fell in the well last week—" he began.
"Good heavens," shrieked Mrs. Kroop. "Is he all right now?"

"He must be," said little Irving. "He stopped yelling for help yesterday."

The father and son checked into the cheap rooming house. "Don't be afraid, son," father said after they'd turned out the light. "The angels are watching over you."

"I know," said the kid. "Two of 'em just bit me."

On my block the goldfish get out of their bowls and chase the cats up the alley.

"How about a date sometime, kid?" he asked the high school girl.

"I can't go out with a baby," she sneered.

"Oh," he gasped. "I didn't know."

He had an extremely high IQ when he was five . . . but luckily he grew out of it.

As a kid, father talked me into running away from home.

I ran away from home—and mother couldn't find me. She didn't look.

The teacher wrote on the blackboard, "I ain't had no fun all summer." "Now, Sidney," she said. "What shall I do to correct this?"

"Get a boy friend."

When the circus came to town little Seymour went into the tent to see how the performers live. He found the superstitious trapeze performer weeping. "I broke a mirror," he told little Seymour. "I'll have seven years' hard luck."

"Aww . . ." pooed little Seymour. "Them things don't mean nothing. My aunt broke a mirror and didn't have seven years' hard luck."

"Really?"

"Nah. She died the next day."

"Teacher, is it correct to say I watered the horse when I give it a drink?"

"Yes."

"Then I've just milked the cat."

"Why didn't you laugh at daddy's joke, Herman?"

"I'm in the fourth grade now."

"Now, Junior," said the teacher, "a little birdie told me that you swear."

"It musta been one of them damned sparrows."

He grew up. What other way could he grow?

Mother never saw me before I was born. Wonder how she recognized me?

"Pop, can I have an ice-cream soda?"

"Shut up and drink your beer."

The kid stood on the sidelines watching the parade and bawling.

"Listen, stupid," said his mother. "You're never satisfied. You've been kicked by the general's horse, stepped on by a colonel, shoved by a major—and you're crying."

They called me "Meatball"—when I was three years old my old man dropped me in the gravy.

My neighborhood was so tough Santa came up from the sewer.

I was born on the sidewalks of New York . . . my folks couldn't afford a hospital.

"Little boy, what game do you like to play?"
"Jacks."
"Jacks?"
"Yeah. Jacks or better."

Bright child. He learned to talk before he learned to walk. He was fourteen at the time.

I came from a real tough family. The menfolk used to eat their meat raw . . . then sit on the stove to barbecue it.

When I was four years old I had a swell-looking nurse. I could hardly wait for next week—'cause she said she liked older men.

I came from a real tough neighborhood. When we saw a cat with a tail . . . we knew it was a tourist.

The minister was preaching to the young congregation. "One boy chose the wicked path of crime and ended in a cell—while the other became a great lawyer. Now, what can the difference be between those two brothers who, together, embarked upon life's stormy seas?"
"Easy," said Herman. "One got caught."

I'm very sentimental about that appetizing aroma that used to come from the kitchen. Mother was boiling laundry.

"Look, mister," the guard said angrily. "Put a nickel in the slot for the kid. He walked under the turnstile."

"Whatta you want from me?" the father shrugged. "Can I help it if he's stubborn?"

I gave mom my pay envelope every Saturday night. At the end of the year she'd have fifty-two envelopes . . . I had all the money.

"Go to the kitchen and cut yourself a piece of cake."

"I don't want any cake."

"Then go in the kitchen and just cut yourself."

I did nothing when I was a kid. I knew what I wanted to be when I grew up—and I practiced for it.

I was never kept after school. I never went.

I played hooky from the fourth grade . . . so I could cast my first vote.

The teacher had a simple diet to keep us kids quiet. Cookies and chloroform.

Mother made me stop kicking the man. I had my new shoes on.

He was born of poor but unusual parents . . . they kept him.

Children never bother to write a letter all year 'round —but on Mother's Day they send her a wire . . . and scare hell out of her.

I was born with a silver spoon in my mouth. Now every time I go into a restaurant . . . I try to complete the set.

"I wear this dress to teas," said the old maid aunt.

"Aww—g'wan," said little nephew. "At your age who you gonna tease?"

"I've had this mustache since I was two years old."

"How can you have a mustache when you're only two years old?"

"I hadn't learned to shave."

I made mother jealous . . . she used to look at other kids and get jealous.

I've had gray hair since I was born. Mother put talcum powder in the wrong place.

He came up from the gutter . . . and is he homesick.

The kids at boarding school thought they'd have a little fun so they dumped the coffee into the cook's boots. Nothing was said so after a week one of the boys got curious. "Did you find out who put the coffee in your boots?" he asked.

"No," said the cook. "But I know who drank it."

The child was like a bungle from heaven.

"All right, wise guy," said the principal. "What's the name of your parents?"

"Ma and pa."

When I was small I had so many freckles the mosquitoes used to go crazy trying to find a place to bite.

What has a thousand legs and can't walk? Five hundred pairs of pants.

He grew up so fast that at the age of four his mother was kept busy cutting up his trousers to fit his father.

I came from a real tough neighborhood. When we'd go to Sunday school the beer was the only thing in the joint with a collar on.

The kid looked like he hadn't tasted food since they broke him of sucking his thumb.

When I was a kid mother was near-sighted. She put my pants on the wrong end. It was five years before I saw the light of day.

When I was young I carried a blackjack . . . in my pencil box. I won the Academy Award for playing hooky.

I was born in 1995 . . . that's the room right next to 1996.

I was born in London. It was so foggy . . . I was ten years old before I met my mother.

There are two schools of thought. The day school and the night court.

It was the day of the big oral exam and teacher was testing Herman. "If one horse runs one mile in a minute and a half and another horse can do the same distance in two minutes, how far would the first horse be ahead if they ran a race of two miles?"

"Listen, teacher," said Herman. "My old man told me never to have nothin' to do with horses in any form."

"Goats' milk makes you young," said Henry's mother, trying to get him to drink some.

"Yeah?" questioned Henry. "I saw a goat four years old with a beard."

When I was three years old I was repaint man for a hot tricycle ring.

I was the only kid in school who could put a curve on a spitball.

Butch raised his hand. "Teacher," he said. "A bee is stinging me."

"Get up quickly," ordered the teacher.

"No," said Butch. "I'm hurtin' her as much as she's hurtin' me."

Every time somebody came over to see us mom used to want me to wash up. I gave her some time. Company or no company I wasn't gonna have my face washed with spit.

My people had no money so I was born at home. After my mother saw me she went to the hospital.

"Son, when I was your age I got only fifteen cents a week. Do you know how I got along?"

"You stole."

On my block the kids used barbed wire for dental floss.

Tough? All my tattooing was done by a stone mason.

When she was a kid her ears were so long—mom and dad had to hide her during rabbit season.

If she was ever kidnaped they could ransom her with a phone slug.

They do everything fancy today. They don't call girls Helen any more—now it's Helene. And a good old name like Shirley is changed to Shirle. No wonder my folks named me Butche.

When I was born my parents weren't discouraged. They had five more kids.

Santa Claus: Daddy when he's working.

The guests were all seated, patiently waiting for the dessert that would top off the excellent dinner—when from the front of the house the little boy's friends called him to come out and play.

"Sorry, fellas," he yelled back. "I can't come out now. It's my turn to help mother count the spoons after the company is gone."

Children. No mother should be without them.

Teacher made me say five hundred times "I'm a bad boy." But I got even with her. When I got home I said five hundred times "No I ain't."

Willie was watching his father put bands around the trees.

"What's that for, Daddy?" he asked.

"That's to keep bugs from crawling up the trees," his

father explained. Just then a man walked by with a mourning band on his sleeve.

"Daddy," said Willie. "What's to keep them from crawling up his other arm?"

Seymour's mommy was a widow lady—and now there was a gentleman calling on her regularly who wanted very much to have Seymour like him. "What's your opinion of me?" the man asked one night when they were alone.

Seymour thought awhile and then replied, "I ain't talkin' till after Christmas."

Those pants stuck to him through thick and thin . . . and he ain't gonna let them down now.

I was born . . . now they can't blame things on other kids.

Banana? I know how to spell it . . . but I don't know when to stop.

She nodded to the minister as he passed. "Mother," asked Junior, "who's that man?"

"That's the man who married me," mother replied.

"If that's the man who married you," said Junior, "what's daddy doing at our house?"

Papa just told me about the time he was a soldier in the war. Wonder what they needed the other soldiers for?

The kid bawled and bawled and bawled. "Dad and ma won't take me to the movies tonight," he told his aunt, between waterfalls.

"But don't cry so," pleaded auntie. "Do they ever take you when you cry like that?"

"Sometimes they do and sometimes they don't," said Junior. "But it ain't no trouble to yell."

He was a surprise to his parents . . . they expected a boy or a girl.

"Will dessert upset me tonight," asked little Herman, "or is there enough to go around?"

He wasn't really a juvenile delinquent. He was merely an active, precocious boy with homicidal tendencies.

I have a terribly heavy beard. I take after mother.

When I was a baby—though father was a streetcar conductor—it was mother who made the change.

On the day of my birth mother wired everyone . . . apologies.

"Son—I'd rather you fail in school than cheat."
"If that's what you want I guarantee results."

The boy stood there crying. "Shame on you, Tommy," said mother. "You're too old to cry."

"Yeah?" said Tommy. "Well, I'll betcha I'm too young to get what I'm crying for."

The child knelt at his bed to say his prayer. Mother, waiting in the hallway, called, "I can't hear you."

"Sorry, Mom," said the little boy. "But I wasn't speaking to you."

"Mamma," the child called from the alleyway. "Papa isn't like other men is he?"

"Why do you ask?"

"Because instead of waiting for the elevator like other people he just went down the shaft without one."

"And now little fella, what does your mother want for Christmas?"

"Alimony."

"I can speak Italian," the kid told the teacher.

"All right," she said. "Say something in Italian."

"Onea, twoa, threea, foura," said the kid. "Then it changes when it comes to five."

"Well, say five in Italian."

"Twoa and threea."

"What is the crack of dawn?"

"That's what mamma gives papa when he comes in."

A great many children have been lost lately. They get lost running around trying to find their mammas.

Bobby's daddy marched him out to the woodshed. "I don't mind whippin' much, Pa," said Bobby. "But at least tell me what it's all about."

"I'll tell ya," pa replied. "It's because you are at the bottom of the class."

"Aww Pa," moaned Bobby. "It makes no difference whether one's at the top of the class or at the bottom. They teach the same at both ends."

"Punctuate this sentence," said the teacher. "Mary walked down the street."

"I'd make a dash after Mary."

When he was born his father gave him a funny look
. . . and he's had it ever since.

Whack—whack—whack went the strap. "I hope you
see I'm doing this for your own good," his father said.

"Sorry, Pop," bawled Herman. "My eyesight ain't that
good."

"You should hear what father said."
"What did he say?"
"I'm not supposed to know them words."

The dog chewed a big hole in an expensive rug, and
daddy, in a rage, called for the dog catcher's wagon. No
amount of arguing on Donny's part could convince
daddy to let the dog stay until he said, "Daddy, I'm posi-
tive I can train him so he'll lay over the hole nearly all
the time."

Some men make their mark in the world, while others
learn to write their names.

The young student walked into the library and spoke
to his father. "Pop," he said, enthusiastically, "I've got
great news for you."
The father smiled and asked, "What is it?"
"Remember you promised me $5.00 if I passed in
school?"
The father nodded.
"Well," said the son, "I'm sparing you that expense this
year."

"You've been learnin' for seven years now and you can
count only up to ten. What will you be in life if you
continue this way?"
"A referee."

The teacher was questioning Johnny. "If a number of cattle is called a herd, and a number of sheep a flock, what would a number of camels be called?"

"A carton," he replied.

"How is it you extracted a watch from that man's pocket without his knowing it?" asked the judge.

"My fee is $5.00 for the full course of ten lessons, your honor."

My son will go to college. I want him to start out in life with the same handicap other boys have.

"Do you think your boy will forget all he learned in college?"

"I hope so. He can't make a living necking."

It was open school week and the proud mother was speaking to the teacher. "My child is a genius. He has many original ideas hasn't he?"

"Yes," replied Mrs. Hough, "especially when it comes to spelling."

Professor: "I take great pleasure in giving you eighty-one in mathematics."

Student: "Why don't you make it a hundred and really enjoy yourself?"

Most of the professor's research work consisted principally of hunting for his spectacles, and today was no exception. Having misplaced them before entering the restaurant, he asked the busboy to read the menu for him. The boy tried hard and then said, "No, sir, I can't read it either. Guess I'm as dumb as you."

"Doesn't that boy swear terribly?"

"Naw, he knows the words all right, but he don't put no feeling into 'em."

Teacher: "What countries are on the other side of the Jordan?"

Student: "That depends on what side of the Jordan you are on."

It was the beginning of the new college term and the professor was asking perfunctory questions of the literature class to determine the general advancement of the students.

"Are you acquainted with Shakespeare?" he asked the college football hero.

"Not personally," was the reply, "but he's a great friend of my brother's."

The professor was annoyed. "Why Shakespeare has been dead for more than three hundred and fifty years," he said angrily.

"He has?" exclaimed the athlete. "Say, won't my brother be surprised to hear that?"

To be college bred means a four-year loaf, requiring a great deal of dough, as well as plenty of crust.

"I want to take my son out of this lousy college."

"But he's at the head of his class."

"That's why I think this is a lousy college."

The keeper of the celestial gate was on duty on admittance day. Suddenly there was a knock at the gate.

"Who's there?" he called out.

"It's me," a voice replied.

"Enter." Then there was another knock. "Who's there?" he called again.

"It's me," said another voice.

"Enter." There was another knock and again he called, "Who's there?"

"Tis I," was the reply.

"Darn it," said the keeper. "Another one of those danged schoolteachers."

"When the teacher asked a question I was the first to raise my hand," he told his father.

"Why didn't you get better marks?"

"Because by the time I got back to the room somebody had already answered the question."

My son is quite a wrestler. He wrestles with big shots. He writes me from college that the dean had him on the carpet the other day.

"You is a pronoun."

"You is?"

Inspired by: Polite form of saying "swiped from."

The young girl, having gone to college, was now ashamed of her immigrant father. "You have no savoir-faire," she said.

"WHAT!" he exclaimed angrily. "I HAVE NO SUB-WAY FARE?"

"Why didn't you get a hundred per cent?" asked the disappointed mother.

"I had a period upside down," explained the annoyed son.

Percivale was standing on the campus looking very dejected.

"Didn't you make the debating team?" asked a solicitous friend.

"N-n-n-no," replied Percivale. "They s-s-s-said I wasn't t-t-t-tall enough."

MANNERS...*tact*... *diplomacy*...*etiquette*... *mores*

(Never throw cigar butts in urinals. They get soggy and are hard to light.)

"I won't offer you a drink, Mrs. Brown, because I know you're the head of the Temperance League."

"Oh no. I'm president of the Anti-Vice League."

"I knew there was something I shouldn't offer you."

Weissman had a very good season the year before and had moved to a very high-class neighborhood. One night, while entertaining, the guests spoke of Mozart. "Oh yes," said Mrs. Weissman, "I saw him on the number five bus with his wife. They were going down to the beach."

There was an embarrassing silence and finally the guests left.

"Haven't I told you when you don't know what you're talking about to keep your big mouth shut?" yelled Weissman.

"But what did I say that was wrong?" cried the protesting missus as she dabbed away a tear.

"Look, stupid," he replied. "You've been here long enough to know the number five bus does *not* go down to the beach."

"It is the duty of the court to charge that the warden of the state penitentiary shall closely hold you in confinement until the thirty-first day of August next, when, between the hours of sunrise and sunset he shall put you to death by the electric chair. And may the Lord have mercy on your soul."

"May I ask a dyin' favuh of the co't?" the prisoner queried. And when given permission said, "I ain't got no quarrel with da date. I kin git all mah worldly affairs settled between now and den and make my peace wit da Lord. But I fails to see the point keepin' me settin' in dat chair from sunrise plum till sunset."

The man was seated in the cafeteria, when a woman and two children sat down with him and began to eat. Suddenly the man belched.

"Sir," said the woman haughtily. "Are you in the habit of doing that before *your* children?"

"Well, I'll tell you, ma'am," he replied. "There are no rules in my house. Sometimes I go first, sometimes they go first."

"And now to make the longer story short," said the speaker.

"I'm afraid it's too late for that," whispered the host.

Letter: I shall expect you at my office at 3 P.M. to explain why you are running around with my wife.

Answer: Dear Sir: Your form letter received and contents noted. I shall be glad to attend the gathering.

Ashtray: A place to put ashes if you haven't got a floor.

"Now, Mrs. O'Grady," the attorney asked, "you say your husband never said a kind word to you since you were married? Are you sure of that?"

"Come to think of it," she replied, "once in a while he did say, 'You're a foine one.'"

"You simply can't go," implored the spinster. "It's raining. You must stay for dinner."

"It ain't raining that hard."

"Who's that awfully ugly-looking woman?"

"That's my wife."

Would you say there was something wrong with this note?

"It was nice meeting you for so short a time."

She watched the young man have his soup with the wrong spoon, grasp the utensils with the wrong fingers, eat the main course with his hands and pour tea into the saucer and blow on it.

"Hasn't watching your mother and dad at the dinner table taught you anything?" she asked.

"Yeah," said the boy. "Never to get married."

I knew about etiquette when Emily Post was a stump.

Nothing on the dinner satisfied the woman. She kept complaining constantly. Finally she sent for the manager. "Sir," she said, "that fish does not look good."

"Madam," replied the manager, "if you were as dead as this fish you wouldn't look good either."

The man failed to tip the Irish doorman so he stopped him and said, "If you be losing your purse on the way home, sir, remember, you didn't pull it out here."

The warden was very apologetic to the prisoner. "I'm terribly sorry, but it seems we've kept you here a week too long."

"Aw—that's all right, Warden," said the convict. "Just take it off the next time."

Finklestein had attended Cohen's twenty-fifth wedding celebration and had horrible memories of the event. The following year he and his wife were invited to the twenty-sixth wedding celebration and he decided to avoid a similar catastrophe.

"Look," he warned the missus as they were leaving the house, "when we get there start eating right away because they don't coax at Cohen's parties."

The fighter had a good chance to capture the championship if he trained diligently but he couldn't break the habit of indulging in New York night life. Finally his manager was forced to lay down the law. "Either you quit the night life until after the bout," he ordered, "or I'll cancel the bout on the grounds that you're out of condition."

The fighter agreed to behave himself and all went well for about a week. Then the manager found the fighter sneaking into camp at four in the morning. "Well, what's your alibi this time?" the manager asked in disgust.

"I heard a noise," the fighter explained, "so I got up to investigate."

"Yeah, well how come you're all dressed up in a tuxedo?"

"I thought it might be a lady burglar."

"I'm sorry," said the bored young lady when the bore asked for another date. "I can't see you Sunday, I'm expecting a headache."

The area had been hit with an epidemic of robberies perpetrated by the notorious gentleman burglar. One night Sadie woke and shook Hymie. "Hy, there's a burglar in the house," she said.

"There is not," Hy said sleepily. "Go back to sleep, stupid."

Just then a man sprang from inside a closet. "There is too," he declared. "Now apologize to the lady."

Shnookyville was suddenly on the map. Reporters from every major newspaper in the country were covering the trial. The wire services were well represented as were the radio and television networks. The boy was being tried for the crime of chopping down his parents with an ax and then shooting his sweetheart, after which he broke her mother's leg and drowned her father and two brothers. The judge, looking over the crowd, thought saying a few words would be expected of him.

Looking over his glasses he clucked a few times and said, "Now look here, son, you know you ain't been actin' right."

Goldberg and his rich friends were on the French luxury liner and he wanted to show them how smart he was by ordering from the foreign-language menu. The waiter was astounded but went to fill his request and came back with a whole roast pig with an apple in its mouth. Goldberg snatched the fruit from the pig's teeth.

"You know," he said, smiling to his friends, "it's a funny thing, but this is the only way I like apples."

To sing is human . . . to forgive divine.

I caught a very aristocratic moth. It will eat holes only in full-dress suits.

"Do you think if I have a slice of onion with my hamburger that I'll get heartburn?"

"For a lousy quarter you get a hamburger, not medical advice."

You can always tell a high-class restaurant by the quality of its napkins. They're usually made of the finest grade paper.

His suit looks like a million dollars. All wrinkled and green.

Goofy: "You can lose all your worldly possessions and still remain a gentleman."

Goofier: "Well, I challenge any guy to lose his pants and remain one."

Success formula: Be nice to people until you make a million. After that people will be nice to you.

Madam: "Now, Ling, after this when you enter my bedroom, please knock. I might be dressing."

Ling: "Me no need knock. Me allays lookee in keyhole flirst."

"There are only three possible verdicts," the judge informed the jury. "Not guilty, which means the accused is innocent and will go free; guilty in the second degree, which means the accused will face life imprisonment; or guilty in the first degree, which means the death penalty."

The jury retired to render its decision and was out an overly long time so the judge sent an attendant to see how things were going. The attendant returned a short time later. "How are things going in the jury room?" asked the judge.

"They report that they are standing ten to two, your honor."

"For which verdict?" asked the judge.

"I can't be sure, your honor," the man replied, "but as I was leaving they were taking up a collection for the prisoner's widow."

Gantzmeyer had his restaurant renovated and decided to run it very high-class. So when Shlumpfelder came in and took his jacket off he decided to upbraid him. "You can't take your jacket off in here," Gantzmeyer ranted. "What would they say if you did that at the Waldorf?"

"They'd say," replied Shlumpfelder, "where do you think you are, in Gantzmeyer's?"

Kravets and the missus were stuck. They'd just received an invitation to a very high-class wedding but couldn't figure out the meaning of the abbreviation RSVP. "If only our son, the college grad, was here, he'd know," sighed Mrs. Kravets as she kissed her husband good-bye.

She pondered the problem all day and finally in a moment of triumph called Kravets at the shop. "Darling, I've figured it out," she shrieked. "RSVP means Remember Send Vedding Present."

Never speak French in front of children.

"Remember," shouted the director, "act natural at all times. Okay. Roll 'em."

The crowd started moving and everything seemed to be going fine when the director suddenly yelled, "Cut!" Then he walked over to one of the actors. "Don't tip your hat as you pass her," he instructed.

"Why shouldn't he?" asked the actress.

"Because," said the director. "He's supposed to be your husband."

He had the manners of a gentleman. I knew they didn't belong to him.

"Pardon me, lady, have you got this dance?"

"No, I haven't."

"Then hold this cigarette for me."

Always say pistachios . . . it is impolite to say nuts.

Some people believe everything you tell them . . . if you whisper it.

"I'd like to die by poison."

"I'd like to be killed by kindness."

"It's easier to get poison."

The woman had her arms loaded with bundles and for twenty minutes she stood in the subway car. Suddenly she felt someone tap her on the shoulder. It was a seated gentleman. "Watch out at Forty-second Street, lady," he said. "That's where I get off."

"Got a match, Tom?"

"No. But I got a lighter."

"How'm I gonna pick my teeth with a lighter?"

It is not generally considered proper for the hostess to wear a T-shirt while serving tea.

My uncle is 200 per cent a gentleman. He even tips his hat when he passes the tomatoes.

All night long the dowager was trying to play up to the professor but could get no response. When they sat down to dinner she managed, by special maneuvering, to be seated next to him. But she couldn't get a rise out of him. "You don't talk much do you, professor?" she remarked.

"I speak only when it's important, madam," he replied. "Would you please pass the meat?"

"That's no way to insult guests."
"Do you know a better way?"

The man was in the turkish bath when he looked up and saw someone stealing his clothes. He took off after him with only a felt fedora for cover. As he turned the corner he bumped into two girls who looked at him and burst into laughter.

"If you were ladies," he said angrily, "you wouldn't laugh at a man in my circumstances."

"And if you were a gentleman," said one, "you'd raise your hat."

Hollywood people have the worst manners. I don't like the way they treat visitors. For one thing, they threw me out.

My girl's father is a high-society guy. He has the crap-game privilege at the Metropolitan Opera House.

Uncouth: Lacking in couth.

A gentleman is a person who never insults anyone intentionally.

If you drop a fork it's a sign company's coming . . . if a fork is missing it's a sign company's going.

Nice girl. She takes after her mother . . . but her mother takes first.

Never break your bread or roll in your soup.

Chew tobacco only when you wear a brown suit.

"Come out sometime with your wife and meet my wife."

"I haven't any wife."

"Well, come out anyway and meet the maid."

When I was in Hollywood, Ava Gardner asked me out four times . . . I was in her home at the time.

The after-dinner speaker stopped in the middle of his speech to lean over toward his host and remark, "It seems everybody in the audience has coughs."

"Them ain't coughs," said the host. "Them's time signals."

What does one send to a sick florist?

"Can you tell me which way to Sixth Avenue?"

"I'm afraid not," said the cop. "It would mean I should have to point."

Never take a gentleman's hat and coat . . . while he's looking.

The business associate was showing the guest through his home. "I spent a lot of money on my place," he said. "I want to make it fit for a gentleman to live in."

"Ah," said the guest, "you are going to rent it, eh?"

My family acquired polish by drinking it.

I'd seen better conversations in alphabet soup.

As usual, the woman was the last to arrive and quite tardy at that. "I beg your pardon for coming so late," she told the host.

"My dear," said the gentleman. "No pardons are needed. You can never come too late."

"Suppose you were in my shoes. What would you do?"
"I'd shine 'em."

She dropped her handkerchief but I didn't pick it up. I use Kleenex.

Never use profanity at the laying of a corner stone . . . even if they lay it on your foot.

If you don't go to folks' funerals you can't expect them to come to yours.

They were playing a word game. The word she had to guess was "negligee."

"What do you put on when company comes unexpectedly?" her partner hinted.

"A pot of coffee," she replied.

I avoid all formal affairs because I don't like to wear tails. They are so lumpy when I stuff 'em in my back pocket.

My girl likes flowers. So I sent her a package of seeds.

"I didn't see John at the dance last night but I hear he acted the part of a thoroughbred."

"What part?"

It was one of those fancy cocktail parties and the two women sat in the corner taking in the sights. "That guest there is one of the handsomest men I've ever seen," whispered one.

"He's not a guest, he's the butler," whispered the other.

"How do you know?"

"Can't you see he knows how to act in society."

When attending cocktail parties of long duration it is advisable to sit down and take a load off the floor.

Always fold your napkin . . . if you expect to get it into your pocket.

"Who is that terribly homely man sitting over there?"

"That's my brother."

"There is not the slightest resemblance."

It makes no difference which side bread is buttered on . . . eat both sides.

The lady had just purchased one of those world-wide-reception portable radios and was strolling down the street when a gentleman approached, tipped his hat and said, "Pardon me, madam. Don't look now, but your antenna is dragging."

Profanity saves many a gentleman from a nervous breakdown.

When visiting at a person's home for the first time, do not spit haphazardly. The floor might leak.

"Meet my pater."

"Happy to meet the pater of my termater."

It is not good manners to add cream and sugar to your coffee . . . after you've poured it in the saucer.

"Take a chair."

"I will on my way out."

The people were lined up for blocks to get tickets for the hit show. The tall, aristocratic, formally dressed gentleman turned to the little man behind him.

"Listen," said the little man. "I'm going across the street to get some cigarettes."

"My good fellow," said the gent, "that is no reason to slap me on the back."

"I didn't slap you," said the little man. "I just made a big chalk mark on your back so I wouldn't forget my place."

If it weren't for toothpicks some people wouldn't know what to do after dinner.

I kiss your hand, madam . . . a second choice of course.

"I'll never invite him to my parties again. Last time he did something I didn't like."

"What was that?"

"He came."

My girl is very refined. She drinks her hootch with a spoon.

If you get sparks out of your knife and fork . . . you are eating too fast.

This great dame stood nervously in front of the puddle. "Spread your coat for me," she ordered her escort.

"I will not," he replied.

"Raleigh spread his coat for a lady," she reminded him.

"He can afford it," said the man, "with that big tobacco business he's got."

"What keeps those strapless gowns up?"

"A city ordinance."

Suggested speech for guest of honor at $100 plate dinner:

"I have just been informed that you paid to get in here and I got in for nothing. Suckers."

The well-dressed, very elegant-looking man was approached by the beggar, who was the opposite in appearance: shabby, ill-smelling, stooped and unclean. "Can you spare twenty cents for coffee?" asked the bum.

"Coffee's only a dime," corrected the gent.

"I know," admitted the bum. "But won't you join me?"

Diplomatic note: If I don't get in touch with you in a couple of days please show me the same consideration.

An after-dinner speech for meritorious occasions:

"I shan't spend a whole evening talking about the shortcomings of our guest of honor when it will take me only two minutes to talk about his accomplishments."

The Secretary of the Navy should be addressed as Your Warship.

He looked askance . . . and that is the most terrible way a person can look.

The lady was one of the new rich and, not wishing to appear a snob, invited her old friends to the house. She was now taking them on a tour of the establishment and had reached the room where they would dine that evening. "These knives and forks are solid silver," she said. "Even the chains they're fastened to have real emeralds."

Manners will never be observed until someone invents self-winding spaghetti and invisible toothpicks.

"How long may one use a tea bag?"
"As long as one gets rusty water."

The trouble with night clubs is, the tables are reserved but the guests aren't.

Women should be handled with kid gloves . . . and silk stockings.

"Mrs. Swathington was terribly ashamed when she had a party and there were thirteen at the table."
"Is she superstitious?"
"Yes. That's why she had only twelve of everything."

The lady dropped her handkerchief . . . it was wrapped around a can of beer.

My club is so exclusive . . . they won't let the members in.

"Did he do something to help the party?"
"Yes. He went home."

Politeness is like an air cushion. There may be nothing in it but it eases the jolt.

When sandwiches are served it is not proper for the hostess to shout, "They're free."

"Isn't my face familiar?"
"It's trying to be."

The women left the room when they started to tell dirty jokes. They didn't want the men to hear them.

I'll never go to auntie's house for dinner again. They use forks to dig into the food. Look at my hand.

She's easy on the eyes . . . but her manners are hard on the eyebrows.

"Why don't you take your handkerchief all the way out of your pocket when you use it?"
"That ain't my handkerchief. That's my shirt tail."

She's about five feet tall but looks six feet . . . with her nose in the air.

It's bad manners to dip your bread in gravy . . . but it's good taste.

"Who do you think you're pushing?"
"How many guesses do I get?"

The party was breaking up. "How do I get to the station from here?" asked the guest.
"Do you have a car?" queried the host.
"No."
"Then you'll have to walk."

We wish to invite you to the wedding of our daughter Bertha . . . but no one will have her.

She holds her nose so high in the air, there is always an inch of snow on it.

The lady was talking to the bore. "I'm inviting the king and queen to my party," she said.

"But you don't know them," he insisted. "Why don't you invite me?"

"You'd come."

DRINK...water...liquor ...beer...and sundry liquids

(I get drunk on water, as well as on land.)

I was a successful young executive. On the way up. Well thought of by my superiors. Then my career hit a bottleneck.

The judge was inclined to be lenient with the drunken man.

"I'm going to release you in your own custody," he said. "You see I knew your father."

"Shay ain't dat shumptin'," said the surprised drunk. "Sho did I."

I seen ya been drinkin', Ma . . . yur lipsitck's on the trough.

The man stood at the bar for hours telling the bartender about all his great exploits. "Now," said the bartender, "supposing you tell me something you can't do."

"Well," said the man. "For one thing—I can't pay the check."

Uncle Ephra bought some cotton candy at the fair. Musta got mixed up when he ate it. When he got home his shirt was gone.

Women are the spies of life.

". . . so there I was standing at the bar."

"Standing?"

"Yeah. It was early in the evening."

The only thing that ever sobered him up was the check.

I nearly got drowned on Broadway. I fell in a manhole.

Lulu and Bill lived above the saloon with their eight kids. One day they had an argument over who would take the kids down, and Bill, as usual, lost. He started carrying them through the bar past a drunk, one by one. When he'd carried the sixth one down the drunk turned to the owner and gasped, "Holy smoke, he must have a nest up there."

A man is never really drunk if he can lie on the floor without holding on.

"Would you like a room with running water?"

"Hey, whaddaya think I am? A trout?"

My uncle and aunt are good housekeepers. They even like their whiskey neat.

"You say you were drunk only once and it made a wreck of you?" asked the doctor.

"Yes," said the patient. "I got married while I was drunk."

"What do you say to a couple of martinis?"

"I never speak to them."

The cops walked over to the man lying on the beach. "We're looking for a drowned man," they said.

"You don't shay," said the surprised drinker. "Whatcha want one for?"

"Who was that lady I saw you with last night?"
"That's what's puzzling me too."

She's a girl with old-fashioned ideas . . . and has the hangovers to prove it.

"Charlie asked me to stand up for him."
"I hope you made it."

Nobody drove me to drink . . . but they had to drive me back.

The boy was graduating from college and he decided it was time he knew the truth about who his father was. "Well, son, it's like this," began his mother. "In a certain town, there's a certain bar. In that bar is a certain man—"
"Father?"
"I'm not certain."

I always drink better when I think.

Mickey Finn: A Tenth Avenue Ovaltine.

As a young man I was misled by a chaser . . . someone hit me on the head with a soda bottle.

"Shay, whosh at guy?"
"Where?"
"Thanksh."

Famous last words: That's the last time I tell a bartender anything.

For a hangover take the juice of two quarts of whiskey . . .

"Your father made it and you want me to drink it?"
"Yes. He'll be hurt if you don't."
"Okay. But have some sand ready to kill the taste."

Here's looking at you . . . which is why I need this drink.

Uncle is so henpecked. At his house the champagne bottles go "mom" instead of "pop."

Coquette. A small Coke.

Chief Trainwhistle came to town and met a blonde. All night long, while making the rounds, she kept calling him Chief Trainwhistle. After the fifth stop he said, "You don't have to call me Trainwhistle. Just call me Toots."

She's mine till breath do us part.

Champagne: Bottle of wine that gets excited like seltzer and costs like diamonds.

There's a mistake in daughter's letter. She said they were living in Rye . . . should be on Rye.

"You expect the court to be lenient because you've been brought in on drunk and disorderly charges twenty times?"

"Yes, your honor. I want to be treated like a steady customer."

Doctor told me to wear a nightcap . . . but the ginger ale gets in my eyes.

The near-sighted drunk walked over to the bar. "Who're all your friends?" he asked.
"Those are my golf clubs," explained the driver.
"Oh," said the drunk. "I was wondering what they were all doing in one seat."

Mother was Irish and proud of it. Father was Scotch . . . and fond of it.

There's nothing wrong with rolling in the gutter . . . it keeps one off the streets.

"Lishen," said the lush to the cop. "I got a hot tip for ya. I know who drank Beethoven's fifth."

We had an uncorking good time.

The cop was on the witness stand.
"I could see him in the middle of the road on his hands and knees."
"Your honor," interrupted the lawyer. "Just because a man is in the middle of the road on his hands and knees at midnight is no sign that he is drunk."
"What the attorney says is quite true," agreed the cop. "But the defendant was trying to roll up the white line."

Uncle does setting-up exercises every night. He goes into a saloon where they set 'em up.

Anywhere but home, James.

I did a Walter Raleigh for the lady. I spread my coat in the mud. I was in it.

The man called the stationmaster. "I left a bottle of Scotch on the train this morning," he said. "Was it turned in to the lost and found department?"
"No," said the master. "But the fella who found it was."

It was a great party while I lasted.

The two drunks stopped in front of the theater. "Whosh playin'?" asked one.
"Lillian Russell, the American diva," said the other.
"Great," said the first. "I love them American swimmers."

"How'd you like a little chaser?"
"Fine. Bring 'er in."

She was very sophisticated. She told me she was gonna stay on the wagon.

The man was struggling to carry the big grandfather's clock. Just then a drunkard walked by, watched him for a few minutes and said:
"Take my advish, mishter. Get yourshelf a wrisht-watch."

Foam sweet foam.

I haven't had a wink of food or a bite of sleep.

"I'm going home from a New Year's Eve party."

"Why, New Year's Eve was eight months ago."

"Yeah? I thought it was time to go home."

A bum got a quarter from a passer-by. He was very hungry so he thought he would buy himself an apple to subdue his hunger and keep the rest for a drink. But one apple didn't satisfy him so he bought a second and then a third, and finally, with his last three pennies, he bought a plum, which satisfied his hunger. "What a fool I've been," he muttered. "Why didn't I buy that plum first— then I would have had enough for a drink."

"Say, that drunken fellow back there looked just like you."

"Lettsh go back. Maybe it wuzsh."

"Pssst—hey, babe—wanna drink?"

"Swine."

"No. Applejack."

"Wonder if I'll drink in the next world."

"Don't know. But I'm sure you'll smoke."

Uncle went to the blood bank and made the only donation with a head on it.

"I shay, Offisher, how far ish it to Canal Street?"

"Twenty minutes' walk."

"For you (hic) or for me?"

Mrs. Giltedge insisted that hubby accompany her to the concert. But long about the middle of the program he disappeared and she didn't see him again till breakfast time. "Where did you go during intermission time last night?" she demanded.

"Out."

"Out where?" she asked angrily.

"Out cold."

"How did you get yourself into this horrible inebriated state?"

"Just worked my way from bottom up."

She used to be a fortuneteller in a bar. She went around reading olives in martinis.

"Where's the antifreeze?"

"Here. Shall I stop the car?"

"No. I'll drink it this way."

"What day ish today?"

"Wednesday."

"Boy am I late."

Jimmy Morgan had been accused of selling liquor illegally and the prosecuting attorney was trying to make Mike, a teamster, admit he had delivered the contraband to the accused.

Mike gave testimony to the effect that he had delivered to Morgan some freight and part of the freight was a barrel but what was in the barrel he did not know.

"Don't know?" shrieked the prosecutor in disbelief. "Wasn't the barrel marked?"

"Yes, sir."

"Then how dare you tell the court that you don't know what was in it?"

"Because, sir," Mike calmly replied, "the barrel was

marked 'Jimmy Morgan' on one end and 'Bourbon Whiskey' on the other. Now how the devil did I know which was in it?"

"How about a drink, toots?"
"I'll have you know I'm a lady."
"I'll simply have to get over this habit of judging folks by first appearance."

"How did you get married?"
"I just sobered up and there she was."

I had a great time at the party but nearly caught cold lying there with nothing but a thin table over me.

Patrick was brought before the court, accused of peddling a bottle of liquor without a license. "Look at this man," his lawyer said to the jury. "Do you honestly think if he had a quart of whiskey he would sell it?"
The jury took one look and found him not guilty.

The bartender looked up and saw a pink elephant, a green rat and a yellow snake at the bar. "You're a little early boys," he said. "He hasn't come in yet."

The aristocrat stumbled into the low-down saloon quite by accident. The waiter brought him a menu and asked, "What is your wish?"
"Uh—I left my glasses home," replied the aristocrat.
"We furnish glasses," the waiter informed him. "But you can drink it out of the bottle if you want to."

"What'll you have to drink?"
"Water."
"You can wash up later. What'll you have to drink?"

"Drinking makes you look beautiful."
"I don't drink."
"I do."

She drank so much she got weak in the nays.

"What made that red mark on your nose?"
"Glasses!"
"How many?"

The farmer was a little high and one of his neighbors approached to inquire about an unusual procedure he was following. "Why," asked the neighbor, "are you feeding milk to a cow?"

"Because," said the farmer, "I wanna make sure it's clean so I'm running it through twice."

"You're an awful son. You've forgotten me on Mother's Day."

"Sho what? A herring lays a million eggs a year and nobody remembers her either."

"Shall I get you an hors d'oeuvre?"
"No thanks. I'm on the wagon."

"Gimmie a fifth of milk."
"Milk don't come in fifths."
"Oh, I forgot."

The bull ran at me with a snort. And believe me, I could use the snort.

The two explorers were discussing their plans.
"I'm taking along a gallon of whiskey in case of rattle-snake bites. What are you taking?"
"Two rattlesnakes."

My buddy gets pickled so often they call him "Cucumber."

Pat slipped and fell four stories. He awoke and found the doctor holding out a drink of water for him. "Begorrah," Pat exclaimed. "How far must a man fall before he gets whiskey?"

The drunk walked into the drugstore. "Shay," he said, "have you shomething for my head? Itsh shplitting."

The clerk sold him an ice bag. Two hours later he came back, this time all bloodied and cut. "Lisshen," he shouted, holding up the ice bag, "ain't you got shumptin' elsh? I'm havin' a hellava time getting my head in it."

Father came in late last night, rammed into the garage doors, pulling one right off. It's a good thing he didn't have the car.

Man: "You come to my restaurant, order a glass of water, drink it and then calmly walk out?"

Scotsman: "What do ye expect me to do, man, stagger out?"

Two drunks registered at a hotel and asked for twin beds. However, in the darkness they both got into the same bed. "Hey," yelled the first drunk, "they gypped me. There's another man in my bed."

"There's a guy in my bed too," called the second.

"Let's throw 'em out," called back the first.

A terrific wrestling match ensued and finally one drunk went sailing out of the bed. "How'd you make out?" the drunk on the floor called.

"I threw my guy out," the bedded drunk replied. "How about you?"

"He threw me out."

"Well, that makes us even. Get into bed with me."

Jenkins was an ideal husband when he was sober but a terrible man when he was drunk. Finally, after a real doozy of a bout, the missus hauled him into court. The judge, sizing up the situation, was inclined to be sympathetic. For after all here was a man who would never run afoul of the law were it not for the evils of drink.

"Why do you drink so much?" the judge asked.

"Well, Judge, it's like this," Jenkins answered. "My blood is turning to water and I have to drink a quart of whiskey every day to keep it from freezing."

The judge smiled knowingly. "Now, my good man, how long can you go without drinking?"

"About four blocks," replied Jenkins.

"Now in this play you drink yourself to death."

"Can I start rehearsing now?"

The old army general was telling his grandchildren about the harrowing experiences of warfare in India.

"Ammunition, food and whiskey had run out and we were parched with thirst—"

"Wasn't there any water?"

"Sure, but it was not time to be thinking of cleanliness."

Dr. Stitchem was trying very hard to convince Percy that he should give up drinking.

"Ever notice a cactus plant?" he asked the boozer. "If you pour water around its roots it thrives, turns greener and grows bigger. Take the same cactus plant. Pour vile liquor on it and what happens? It shrivels, it shrinks, it dies. Doesn't this teach you anything?"

"Yes," said Percy. "If you want a cactus growing in your stomach drink water."

Mike told Pat he was going to a wake, and Pat offered to tag along. On the way Pat suggested a nipper or two and they both got well sloshed. As a result Mike couldn't remember the address of the wake. "Where is your friend's house?" Pat asked.

"I forgit the number but I'm sure this is the street."

They had walked along for a few minutes when Mike squinted at a house that he thought was it. So they staggered in but the hall was dark. They opened the door and discovered a living room, which was also dark except for the faint glimmer of candles sitting on the piano. They went down in front of the piano, knelt and prayed. Pat stopped long enough to look at the piano. "Mike," he said, "I didn't know your friend, but he sure had a fine set of teeth."

"Who is the best lawyer in town?"
"Henry Brown when he is sober."
"And who is the second-best lawyer in town?"
"Henry Brown when he is drunk."

The officer was suspected of being drunk and rowdy. One night they brought him into the station house with his uniform completely disheveled, his coat ripped down the middle and his badge missing. "Where's your badge?" the precinct captain roared angrily.

The cop stroked the empty chest. "The wife's using it to pin clothes on the baby," he said.

The Irishman was brought up before the judge.
"Why were you drunk?" the judge asked.
"I was on a train with bad companions. Four teetotalers."

"They are the best company you can have."
"I don't think so. I had a bottle of whiskey and had to drink it all by meself."

I'll never go near a bar again . . . the television burns my eyes.

"What induced you to steal this case of whiskey?"
"I was hungry."

Last week I went into a dry goods store . . . it is very seldom that I got into a dry goods store.

Father has a new position . . . he is now standing up.

Gasoline and alcohol don't mix . . . but try drinking it straight.

The wolf wasn't doing too well. After she'd downed her eighth drink he asked, "Don't you ever feel your liquor, honey?"
"Of course not," she said. "Why should I get my fingers wet?"

I couldn't understand how that girl drank so much liquor. I finally found out in an ordinary arithmetic book. It said one gal is equal to four quarts.

"Shey, lishen, bartender, can you imagine anyone going to sleep with their shoesh on?"
"Who does that?"
"My horse."

The modern debutante no longer comes out . . . she's carried out.

It was his first date with her, and it was a blind date. So he went into the bar for a little encouragement. Then he proceeded to her home.

They sat in the parlor for a while and then she said, "All my other boy friends bring candy when they come."

"Zshat so?" said Happy. "I don't shee ya passing none of it around."

Two buddies used to meet every day and walk to every saloon in town. "I read in the papers that if all the saloons in the country were set end to end they'd reach from New York City to Chicago," one said.

"Wow," said the other. "What a walk!"

"Uncle fell down the stairs with two quarts of liquor."
"Did he spill it?"
"No. He kept his mouth shut."

He was bitten by a snake. I gave him whiskey. I didn't cure him . . . but he died happy.

I ordered a banker's cocktail for her. One drink you lose interest . . . two drinks you lose principal.

"Oh dear. I told you to beat the eggs till stiff."
"I am."

Grandfather lost two front teeth trying to drink out of a flask . . . while falling downstairs.

One lung said to the other, "This is the stuff I was telling you about."

"My cat can say his own name," said the drunk.
"What's his name?" asked the bartender.
"Meow."

I found $5.00 . . . just smell my breath if you don't believe me.

The tough guy sauntered into the dimly lit saloon. "Is there anybody here called Donovan?" he snarled. Nobody answered. Again he snarled, "Is there anybody here called Donovan?"

There was a moment of silence and then a little fellow strode forward. "I'm Donovan," he said.

The tough guy picked him up and threw him across the bar. Then he punched him in the jaw, kicked him, clubbed him, slapped him around a bit and walked out. About fifteen minutes later the little fellow came to. "Boy, did I fool him," he said. "I ain't Donovan."

Milk. That white stuff without the head.

The man asked the bartender to suggest a drink. "Rum flip," said the bartender. "It has sugar, milk and rum. The sugar gives you energy, the milk strength."

"What does the rum give you?"

"Ideas about what to do with the energy and strength."

Drinking doesn't drown your troubles . . . it just irrigates them.

A drink in time . . . is fine.

Whiskey may not cure the flu . . . but it fails more agreeably than most things.

Pop always was nosy. And when the new neighbors moved in next door he stood by the window and studied every piece of furniture that went into the place. There wasn't much, only a load of beer barrels.

"Begorrah, Kathy," he called. "They're having the place nicely furnished next door."

Waiter: "Order, please."
Drunk: "Whatzamatter, I ain't makin' noise."

Water is the curse of bathtubs.

Two pints make one quote.

Father saw a sign that said "Drink Canada Dry" . . . so he went up there.

The doctor put Pat through a lot of tests because of a paralysis in his legs. "Look, Doc," said Patrick. "Place a glass of whiskey on the table over there. If I don't make it I'm helpless."

Uncle invented a cocktail shaker with built-in fire extinguisher. When you get lit you can put yourself out.

Our butler drinks too much . . . sort of an old family container.

Dignity is something that can't be preserved in alcohol.

The two men walked quietly up the pathway, each supporting the other. "Lishen," the host advised. "When we get inshide pay no attenshun to the man in the housh."
"Whoizsh he?"
"We don't know."
"Then how doezsh he happen to be living with you?"
"He wuzsh there when we moved in."

Uncle drinks anything. Right now he's under the influence of lacquer.

"I ain't thought of a glass of beer in three days," said the recuperating Bowery man.

"Of course not," said the doctor. "Your mind in on higher things."

"No, Doc," said the serious man. "I ain't thought of the dollar drinks either."

"You got a helluva nerve," roared the female souse at the tavern owner. "Who ever heard of telephone booths for men only."

"Down with Liquor" was father's motto . . . he downed more liquor than anybody else.

The drunk walked out of the tavern and noticed an Italian man roasting a turkey in a rotating roaster. "You won't get a dime from me, ya bum," said the drunk. "I can't hear any of the tunes and it smells as if something is burning inside."

I like that saloon. Every time I get drunk they lay me in the street. Only place I know where they give curb service.

. . . and to pass the time away we all took mickeys.

At Christmas uncle acted like a child . . . he always hung himself up to get filled.

Reminiscences of youth. Father used to take me to the pubs with him. I was too young to drink . . . so he spun me around on a stool. It was okay . . . until he got one of his friends to hold my head.

I'm on the wagon halfway . . . cut out the chasers

We played house. I was the walls and got plastered.

There's so much alcohol in my system . . . I signed the pledge two years ago and my breath still smells of liquor.

Georgie was sitting home, polishing off the case of beer and watching a television show, when the announcer came on and gave the following commercial:
"When you see a beautiful girl you don't notice her beautiful form, you don't notice her beautiful face, you don't notice her beautiful legs. The first thing you notice is her hat—"
"Hey listen," interrupted Georgie. "The kiddies are all in bed. Let's give the right answer."

The reporter was a little high when he called the office.
"City desk speaking," he heard.
"Yeah?" he was astonished. "What drawer?"

I picked up my mail . . . so it wouldn't get broken.

Poor Aunt Sadie. Got drunk one night, fell in a barrel of Jergen's Lotion . . . and softened to death.

He breathed on the back of her neck . . . and bleached her hair.

My family distills Bullfrog Gin. Drink a little, hop a little and croak.

"Now you went and ruined my watch," she complained to her bar companion. "Here it says three o'clock in the afternoon and I know perfectly well it's three o'clock in the morning."

In my club, members are not responsible for guests left over thirty days.

Always start the evening off with a whiskey glass full of water . . . that will take care of the chasers.

He wasn't born . . . he was squeezed out of a bar rag.

Grandfather never had his suits cleaned . . . he had them distilled.

I don't know whether the party's being given or thrown. Them that's given ain't much fun.

After one drink he felt ten years younger. After the second drink he felt like a new man. After the third drink he felt like a baby . . . and crawled all the way home.

"Then you dare to say that this gentleman was drunk!" the attorney yelled at the policeman.
"No, sir," said the cop. "I simply said he sat in his car for three hours in front of an excavation waiting for the light to turn green."

There's a new drink advertised in all major railroad stations: Traveler's Aide.

I'm wearin' a T-shirt . . . but I ain't drinkin' tea.

"Going out tonight?"
"Not completely."

MONEY ... rich people ...
poor people ... credit

(I wasn't affected by the crash of '29. I went broke in
'28.)

"I would like to teach you that there are lots of things more important than money."

"I'll buy that."

Pawnbrokers live off the flat of the land.

Pincus and Lefcourt had a very good season so they decided to take their wives out for a good time. The night of the outing the women really looked the part. They wore long flowing sable coats, dresses of imported mink, and each wore rings totaling twenty-five carats. Five carats for each finger.

"Let's show everybody how rich we are," Mrs. Pincus said. "Merscen darling [his real name was Max], when we get to the restaurant order the most expensive thing on the menu and order it good and loud so that everybody can hear."

When they got to the restaurant the waiter handed the menu to Pincus. But it was printed in a foreign language. This didn't stump him very long. "Waiter!" he shouted like he meant business. "BRING ME FIFTY DOLLARS WORTH OF SALAMI AND EGGS!"

Montgomery thought he pulled off a major business transaction when he sold his bicycle until the government stepped in with the bill.

"Just because I sold a bicycle for $6.00 I got to pay the government $5.59," he protested to the collector.

"The government needs the money to pay the Army, the Navy and outfit the Marines. They have to pay senators and congressmen, and with the Russians acting up they need every penny in case of war."

"Hey," said Montgomery, "it's a good thing I sold that bicycle."

Some people turn black and blue from overeating. They eat more than they can pay for.

I never did too well on the market. When I bought stocks to go up, they went down. When I bought them to go down, they went up. It's a good thing for me they couldn't go sideways.

"I found a rare coin."
"What others are there?"

Googleman was having trouble with a customer.
"How much is that scarf?" the customer asked.
"Ten dollars."
"Why, I could buy my wife a pair of shoes for that."
"Yeah, but how would a pair of shoes look around her neck?"

They call it "the Rainbow Room"—'cause when you get the check your face turns color.

"I can hear your radio as if it were in my room."
"Then will you help me make the monthly payments?"

"You are the worst man who ever came before me. You beat a poor old man to death for the few dollars he had saved."
"Sounds like me. When was this?"

"I make a hundred dollars a day."

"Honest?"

"What's the difference?"

The meek-looking man had been hauled into court and now he stood shamefully before his attorney to explain his dilemma. "I was arrested for resisting an officer."

"Resisting an officer!" the lawyer cried in disbelief.

"Yes," said Mr. Meek. "I offered him five and he wanted ten."

Two garment cloak and suiters were sipping champagne in Nedick's and complaining about the fortunes of life. "When the breaks go against you they're awful," said one. "The stock market cleaned me, then my father died and today my boy broke a leg."

"You think you got trouble?" consoled the second. "I just bought a suit with two pairs of pants and burned a hole in the coat."

The telephone jingled late at night in Blumenthal's home and when he answered his old friend Ginsburg bellowed, "Sol, you've got to help me immediately. It's a terrible emergency. I need $50 very badly."

"Quick, Molly," Blumenthal shouted to his wife, "look in the files under 'G' and see why I'm sore at Ginsburg."

"I insist this must be a very healthy town. Why, there's only one undertaker," said the real estate agent.

"So why is he so rich?"

"I am beginning to think my lawyer is too interested in seeing how much money he can get out of me."

"Why do you say that?"

"Just listen to this. 'Bill: For waking up at night and thinking about your case. $5.00.'"

"You have known the defendant how long?"
"Ten years."
"Tell the court whether you think he is the type of man who would steal this money or not."
"How much was it?"

There's so much inflation now there's no money in money.

Vacation: After a couple of weeks of it you feel good enough to go back to work and so poor you have to.

"I could go to the bank and get the money out."
"Why don't you?"
"I'm afraid they'll catch me."

"Give till it hurts."
"Here's a quarter."
"You can't stand much pain."

He who steals my purse steals IOU's.

Most credit houses won't take a penny down. It's not enough.

Joe Frisco had just finished talking to the income tax collector who told him he owed the government $40,000 when he met an actor friend who appeared worried. "What's wrong?" asked Joe.
"I gotta pay the government $135."
Turning to the tax collector, Frisco said, "Put that on my tab."

"How is it you can't get a lawyer to defend you?" the judge asked of the prisoner.

"As soon as they found out I didn't steal the money they wouldn't have anything to do with me."

A policeman was called before a jury to explain how he had managed to bank $10,000 in two years out of a $140 a week salary.

"How many winners did you pick to make up your $10,000?" the judge asked.

"None at all, your honor. I never gamble."

"Then how do you account for it?"

"I saved it out of my toothpaste money."

"My watch costs $500."

"What's its movement?"

"To and from the pawnshop."

Tramp: "You haven't a dime for a cup of coffee, have you?"

Banker: "You've been speaking to my friends again."

Counterman: "Why do you stand behind that cheapskate every day and take his seat?"

Witnit: "I don't know the man but every time I sit in his seat I find money under the plate."

Since he was dealing with an Oklahoman, the real estate agent felt he could really make a killing. "We want $50,000 for this lot," he said, figuring his sucker carefully.

"Fine," said the Okie. "Now tell me, how many barrels of oil does it produce a minute?"

"Does your husband worry about the grocery bill?"

"No. He says there is no sense in both him and the grocer worrying about it."

The chorus girl was really peeved at her banker boy friend. "You dirty cheapskate," she shouted. "I tried to hock the jewelry you gave me and they offered me $4.00 for the diamond ring, the diamond necklace, the diamond brooch and the diamond bracelet."

"You must have gone to a fraudulent pawnbroker, my dear," protested the banker. "Why I paid $4.00 for the necklace alone."

"So it's Thanksgiving. What have I to be thankful for? I can't even pay my bills."

"Be thankful you're not one of your creditors."

The rich old couple was sitting in church when the collection plate came around. "Don't put in more than a quarter," advised the old lady.

"Look, Prunella," said her husband. "Andrew Carnegie gave over half a million for his seat in heaven. John D. gave over a million. Where the hell do you think I'll sit for twenty-five cents?"

Such weather we're having. One day rain, one day snow, one day wet, the next day sunny. It's getting so a fellow doesn't know what to hock.

Remember, you may not have time to count it on Judgment Day.

He's settling all his debts. He came around and picked up all last year's IOU's. Then he issued new ones, with interest.

Her husband is rich and old. That's a great combination.

I helped the old man with his taxes. I looked over his shoulder and every time he was gonna write down the truth, I reminded him.

Charity begins at home and ends up at the Waldorf Astoria or Commodore hotels.

I asked my father-in-law the $64,000 question. Loan me $64,000.

The man checked into the hotel, went to his room and was about to turn in for the night when he remembered that he'd forgotten something. He called the desk and asked, "How much is this room costing me?"
"Thirty dollars a day," said the room clerk.
"WHAT?" shrieked the flabbergasted man. "Then I demand you send up another Bible."

I went to visit rich friends. They served nothing but money. I bit into a bad fifty. They told me to try the fives. They're softer.

Money brings only misery. But with money you can afford it.

We had a sinking fund. It just went down for the third time.

Breadwinner: You gotta win it, it's too high to buy.

They had a swimming pool with coffee. When they dunk, they dunk.

There is nothing my wife can't do with a half a buck that she couldn't do with a million dollars, only she'd look better doing it.

These days a person can't afford to make a living.

I lost all my money. I'll just have to roll up my sleeves and get a cheaper table at the 21 Club.

Things are so bad the crooks are using second-hand blackjacks to cut down the overhead.

The IRS took everything but they let me keep mother.

January: The month we hear the echoes of Xmas bills.

Sister is looking for a kindly, elderly, successful man, preferably way up in the higher age bracket.

The stockbroker fell hopelessly, madly, passionately in love with the chorus girl. He decided to buy her a little something to demonstrate his feelings. "I want to see a ring," he notified his jeweler.
"What kind?"
"Oh, nothing expensive," said the broker. "Something where I'll only have to miss a hundred and fifty lunches and forty-five dinners."

Anybody with $50,000 can always find a bargain.

I invited her to come up and see handwriting on the wall . . . I'm too poor to have etchings.

My face is my fortune. I pay no income tax.

It costs the rich so much to live they can't afford to have children.

A visitor to the Hollywood studio asked the producer about a single dollar hanging in his office, suitably framed. "Oh that," said the producer. "That's the buck we've been passing around here for years."

I've been broke so long, I can't get used to money. When I buy a suit I have them put a patch in it.

Things are bad with Mr. and Mrs. Newbucks. She's wearing last year's jewelry.

Two millionaires were discussing their personal buying habits.
"I like to shop at Lord & Taylor's. They're very reliable," said the first. "I tore my coat on a nail in front of the store and they immediately gave me $10."
"Really?" gasped the second. "Do you think the nail is still there?"

My wife gave me a check for a large sum—all made out and ready to sign.

I'm saving my money for a rainy day—that's why my checks are made of rubber.

I'm in the upper brackets. I stole $100,000 from my last employer.

I like fancy things, like monogrammed aspirin tablets.

"I had a five dollar bill in this dictionary. Now it's gone."
"Did you look under the V's?"

I didn't get a tax refund. They just sent me a bridge they couldn't find a river for.

What a snob. She's out in the garden allowing the flowers to smell *her.*

Income tax: To have and have not.

He insulted me because I owed him money. I immediately gave him my personal check. That was a quick comeback.

She's so snooty that she sends her garbage out to be gift wrapped.

The insurance man rapped lightly on the door and the widow opened it ever so slowly, her black garb sharply contrasting with her pale white features. She ushered him into the living room, where two cups of tea were poured. They sat in silence until the man dug into his portfolio and in a quiet voice said, "Everything is in order, Mrs. Krup. Here is our check for $50,000."

She stared at it. "Fifty thousand," she muttered. "Fifty thousand for a life full of goodness, love, faith and charity. You know"—and here she stopped to dispatch a mournful tear—"I'd gladly give half of this back to have George alive today."

I'm as sound as a dollar. Ever go to the grocery store with a dollar?

Sign at entrance to Tax Bureau: "Watch Your Step" . . . and at exit . . . "Watch Your Language."

There are enough karats in her bracelet to keep a family of rabbits eight years.

"I spent a fortune for this—$8.50."

"Eight-fifty is a fortune?"

"I had only nine dollars."

We have the highest standard of living in the world, too bad we can't afford it.

The big crowd gathered on the Coney Island beach and watched the man apply artificial respiration to the heiress he'd just rescued. Her parents broke through the crowds, joyful at seeing their daughter alive and well. "Mamma," said the old man. "Give that fella a dollar. He saved her life."

"But, Papa," protested the girl. "I was half dead."

"All right," papa said. "Give him fifty cents."

He's a very wealthy man. He goes begging with two hats.

The judge was very easy on him. After all, he was just any other ordinary twenty-year-old boy with $74 million.

Debutante: A tomato with plenty of lettuce.

"I'm prepared to pay you $15 a week."

"It didn't take much preparation."

"The salary he wanted wasn't too bad," one partner told the other. "But the expenses were awful."

"What'd he want?"

"A thousand dollars a week and carfare."

Charity may be deducted from income tax. The catch is it must also be deducted from income.

I got what no millionaire's got. I got no money.

This luscious, fancy society dame took a liking to my Uncle Herman. So she invited him out to her estate. Right after dinner she snuggled up to him and, pointing to a kind of a private room, said, "Shall we have our coffee in the library?"

"Nahh," said Uncle Herman. "I don't like to read when I'm drinking coffee."

"Give me ten cents for coffee."
"I only got ten pennies."
"Okay. I'll have drip coffee."

It's the woman who pays and pays, but look whose money she uses.

"What makes you so uneasy?"
"Easy payments."

The gossip reported to the millionaire on the activities of his spouse. "While you were away I saw a tall dark man kissing your wife."

"Did he wear glasses and button shoes and have a mustache?" he asked.

"Yes," she replied.

"That was my iceman. He'll kiss anybody."

"Where did you get that medal for playing checkers?"
"I bought it."

Speaking of operations, what this country needs is a good five cent scar.

"I know a man who made $50,000 and paid only $29 taxes."

"I'd like to see him."

"Why go all the way to Atlanta?"

The two commuters struck up a conversation on the economic situation of the country. "It's hard to collect money," said commuter A.

"How do you know?" asked commuter B. "Are you a collector?"

"No," said A. "But lots of people have tried to collect money from me lately."

"What is a debtor, Pa?"

"A man who owes money."

"And what is a creditor?"

"The man who thinks he is going to get it."

My fiancée is so wealthy the rings under her eyes have diamonds in them.

Song title: "I'd Rather Be a Millionaire in New York Than a Poor Man Anywhere Else."

"Are you still living within your income?"

"No. It's all I can do to live within my credit."

Paradise: Where the only government collection agency is the Department of Sanitation.

There's a pound of gold in every ounce of philosophy, but the banks won't cash it.

A deficit is what you've got when you haven't got as much as you had when you had nothing.

Rich? He has bank accounts named after him. I put a drip pan under his vault.

A philanthropist is a man who gives away what he should be giving back.

More rabbits than people have made their million.

Broker: A man on the right end of a telephone.

"What's the latest report on the ticker?"
"Doc says not to worry. It's just gas."

The wealthy old liver-upper was on his deathbed, broke.
"Funny," he whispered to his nurse. "Fifty years ago I arrived here with $5.00. Why have people accused me of being a spendthrift? I still have $5.00."

Women spend money like it's going out of style.

All work and no play makes jack the dull way.

During the Depression it was common to ask your broker, "Who was that lady I saw you jumping out the window with?"

Real swell wedding. They threw puffed rice.

Women are the quickest to learn the three R's. This is R's, that's R's, everything's R's.

"Just burned a hundred dollar bill."
"You must be a millionaire."
"Well, it's easier to burn 'em than to pay 'em."

This is the story of two young boys. Brought up in the same neighborhood, attended the same schools, basked in the same environment. One became rich. The other stayed as he was. The poor one didn't want to make money like the rich one, he preferred working for it.

The stockholders of today are the stowaways of tomorrow.

Talk about the high cost of living, the only thing that comes down now is rain . . . and that soaks you.

Memo to a rich relative: It is easy to borrow an electric fan on a cold day.

The first thing people ask about a man who amounts to something is "How much is the amount?"

You can't take it with you, but you can get better accommodations where you're going.

The greatest extravagance is a fancy funeral.

He's rich. He's got gold in California, silver in New Mexico, but the lead is still in the same place.

Her face is her fortune. One of those fortunes that are made overnight.

Rigid economy: A dead Scotsman.

"I need some extra dough for my hobby."
"What's your hobby?"
"Eating."

There was a time when you had to be a drunk to be a success—now you have to be a success to be a drunk.

If you're rich you can get a room. If you're filthy rich —you can get a room and bath.

April 15 should be called tax-giving day.

He's so rich he puts one set of suits away for the moths.

"Would you help a fella in trouble?"
"What kinda trouble you wanna get in?"

Gold is a basic metal—without it you can't get to first basic.

That Treasury Department gave me plenty of headaches about my taxes last year. But I got even with them this year. I didn't sign my name on the return, let them guess who sent it in.

When they took out his appendix he left a tip on the operating table.

Uncle's a great guy. He took me and my girl out till all ours—till all ours was gone. Then he had to spend his.

It was one of those society marriages. They had more in preferred than in common.

"This is a remarkable policy," said the insurance man. "If you keep up the payments until you're ninety-five you get $10 a week for life. What's more, and get this, if you are killed in a buffalo stampede on Friday between

5 and 6 A.M., you collect double indemnity. What's more —and listen to this—no matter where, when or how you die, provided you don't commit suicide on Thursday, you get $200."

"The policy's no good."

"But why?"

"How can I live on $200?"

Money don't go as far as it used to, but at least it goes faster.

During the Depression, Irving spotted Sol walking down the street. "Hey, Sol," he called. "What're you doing?"

"I'm walking down to the office to save a nickel."

"Why don't you walk down Fifth Avenue," advised Irving, "and save a dime."

"I saw a suit that had an $8.00 price tag on it."

"That ain't expensive for a suit."

"The tag was $8.00. I don't know how much the suit was."

A half dollar is no longer a tip. It's an insult.

Her clandestine lover suddenly noticed the urn on the fireplace mantel. "Wh-whose ashes are those?" he gasped.

"My husband's."

"Dead?"

"No. Stingy."

He stretched a million into a shoestring.

California bankroll: Two dollar bills wrapped around an orange.

Don't make fun of the rich. You may be rich someday yourself.

At the March of Dimes I spoke three hours—had to give 'em the dime anyway.

Two bums were seated on a park bench stealing food from the pigeons. "Say," said one. "If you suddenly found a million bucks would you lend me ten thousand?"
"That depends," said the second. "What security you got?"

Bank: A paper house.

I took a suite at the Waldorf. The man at the counter made me put it back.

The woman's head on silver dollars corroborates the fact that money talks.

I just don't know my own strength when it comes to squeezing a penny.

Man who has income pays income tax. What's the outcome? No income.

"You're a great movie star. If we give you $10,000 will you endorse our cigarettes?"
"For $10,000, provided I don't have to smoke them."

My girl's father is very rich. He has a first mortgage on a flower pot in Florida.

"You've owed me $5.00 for a year."

"What's your hurry? I'm not through with it myself yet."

I took her to an afternoon movie. She got only a buck on her ring.

Money talks—mine only stutters.

The two men stood on the lonely lighthouse. Through the fog they could see a small boat making its way toward them, with a lonely occupant. Suddenly a squall lifted the craft and tossed the man into the water. They sprang into action. Hurriedly they launched their own craft and fought their way through perilous and treacherous waters to reach the man. At last they got him aboard.

"It's a good thing you rescued me," the dripping man said gratefully. "I was coming out to see you about your income tax."

I had a very good season. I owe more taxes this year than last.

My brother found a way to save his money. He uses mine.

Labor unions make no attempt to raise the wages of sin.

Married men tremble at the outcome of their income.

It's better to give than to receive. But where's the profit?

Sandy and Mike were out hunting when they were

both startled by a wolf howl. "I'll bet you a dollar you can't go out and kill that wolf," Sandy said.

Mike took him up on it and ten minutes later came back with the carcass of a dead wolf. That night, just as they were about to turn in, another howl pierced the night.

"Gimme back my dollar," said Sandy. "You killed the wrong wolf."

"Why shouldn't I be happy?" said the businessman. "I have an auto, a house, a wife and three kids, all in my own name."

Anyone with two of my checks never need fear a rainy day—he has an excellent pair of rubbers.

The snobbish woman was describing her European tour.

"I went over on the *Elizabeth*," she said.

"So did I," said her friend.

"Yeah," said the traveler, "but you should have seen the upstairs."

After careful deliberation the committee for keeping the swanky residential section swanky decided to let the dress manufacturer move into the area. One night the chairman passed by and he saw the manufacturer carrying out the ashcans.

"You," he berated, "a rich man. Putting out your ashcans."

"You're right," agreed the dress man. "After this I'll have my wife do it."

I made so much hush money, I had to whisper my bank deposits.

He got his LL.D. from Harvard, his Ph.D. from Yale and his C.O.D. from Macy's.

He's richer than me for only one reason—he has more money.

I walk in the middle of the street. I owe people on both sides.

Money isn't everything. You get the same results with a checkbook.

"I got the first dollar I ever earned. I framed it."
"How much you got now?"
"Fifty cents. I hadda pay fifty cents for the frame."

Perfume is priced by the dram. There are also special prices for people who don't give a dram.

Fancy broad. She wore a mink toupee.

The automotive industry is the only honest business in the country. They tell you the prices in advance so you can arrange a bank loan in time.

Ye olde Scotch proverb: No matter how much you applaud a jukebox, you gotta put another nickel in for an encore.

The millionaire was born in a log cabin—mahogany logs.

I don't like money, but it quiets my nerves.

Since they couldn't get the goods on the notorious bootlegger they decided to use the old tax gimmick to put him away. But Al was smart. He decided to answer all their questions.

"You made $4 million last year?" asked the investigator.

"Sure," said Al. "But I had a lotta expenses."

"Expenses?"

"Yeah, I pay $30 a dozen for bullets. I buy them at Saks."

"But why such expensive bullets?"

"I shoot a nice class of people."

Rough year. I made more money than I could afford.

I'm suspicious of any business that pulls down the shades at three o'clock in the afternoon.

She buries her money. She can't take it with her so she's sending it on ahead.

I did so bad last year, I didn't have to borrow to pay my taxes.

My brother makes better bills than the government. George Washington looks ten years younger.

The dress manufacturer could not produce his books —the walls were freshly painted.

He's been spending money like water—now he's trying to float a loan.

They're so rich they have an electrician come in every morning—to plug in the toaster.

Many a politician is born with a silver foot in his mouth.

TRAVEL...geography... history...vacations and tourists

(In England they've been changing the guards for two hundred years. Guess they aren't big enough to change themselves.)

A vacationer on a dude ranch is called a tenderfoot . . . though that's not the place where he's tender.

In Russia the most popular game is Truth or Consequences. You tell the truth or you go to Siberia.

Columbus was right. He discovered dry land.

When Montgomery got to Paris he was determined to see if the French women were all they were cracked up to be. He approached a girl in a restaurant and, not being able to speak French, drew a picture of two bottles. She nodded, so they had wine. Then he drew a picture of a knife, fork and a chicken. She nodded again, so they had dinner. Along about this time the girl felt she ought to do something for him so she drew a picture of a bed. "Gee whiz," gasped Montgomery, in absolute astonishment. "How did you know I'm from Grand Rapids?"

"I just found out why the Scotch bagpipes make a Scotsman brave in war."
"Why?"
"He'd rather die than have to hear them."

New York is better to live in than Los Angeles. When it's cold in New York you can go to Florida. But when it's cold in Los Angeles where can you go?

If a man born in Poland is a Pole, is a man born in Holland a Hole?

The bore was being the death of the party. He kept talking about a sea voyage to Europe, which interested no one. "The waves were fifty feet high," he said. "I was at sea thirty years ago and never saw them that high."

"Well," said one guest, "waves are much higher now than they used to be."

The seaman was taking his examination for a higher grade.

"Now, Summerville," said the inspector, "you are quartermaster on duty at night. Your ship is tied up at the wharf on the Rhine. You see a figure crawling and stumbling toward your ship in the dark. What do you do?"

"Why I 'elps the skipper aboard, sir."

"Did you have any trouble with your French when you were abroad?"

"No. But the French did."

These cigars were exported from Cuba. Well, they weren't exactly exported, they were exiled.

The new World's Fair is going to be the most modern. Instead of pressing a button to open it they're gonna pull a zipper.

"I'm going to Texas, where men are men and women are women."

"You should fit in some place."

Two American soldiers were in England, where they were having trouble with the British pay-phone system. One of them went into a booth that had the customary dialing buttons A and B. He pressed one button and just then a V-bomb exploded nearby, leveling the entire community. As the soldier came stumbling out of the wreckage of the booth he said to his buddy, "Honest, Joe, all I did was press button A."

The missionary was captured by cannibals and placed into a pot to cook when the chief appeared and began to talk to him in perfect English. The chief explained his mastery of the language by relating that he'd gone to Harvard.

"You're a Harvard man?" said the missionary. "And you still eat your fellow man?"

"Yes," replied the chief. "But now I use a knife and fork."

When the Scotsman inquired as to the cheapest way to sail the Atlantic the travel agent decided to humor him a bit. "You can go first class for $200, second class for $150, third class for $75. And you can swim alongside the boat for $3.98 plus tax. Now which will it be?"

"What kind of food do they throw overboard?" asked the Scot.

Three Chinese sisters who aren't married: Tu Yong Tu, Tu Dumm Tu and No Yen Tu.

"Didn't I meet you in Miami with your husband?"
"No. With yours."

"We're living in a better neighborhood now."
"So are we."

"Have you moved too?"

"No. We're still living on the block you moved away from."

Two Indians were on top of a mountain sending smoke signals. Suddenly there was a tremendous atomic explosion and the smoke hurled skyward for miles. "Gee," muttered one. "I wish I'd said that."

The foreign diplomat was unable to speak English. When the lunch bell rang at the United Nations Assembly he stood behind a man at the food counter and heard him order apple pie and coffee. So he ordered apple pie and coffee too. For the next two weeks he kept ordering apple pie and coffee. Finally he decided he wanted to try something else so he listened attentively while another man ordered a ham sandwich. "Ham sandwich," he said to the counterman.

"White or rye?" the counterman asked.

"Ham sandwich," the diplomat repeated.

"White or rye?" the counterman asked again.

"Ham sandwich," the diplomat replied.

The counterman grew very angry. "Look, Mac," he roared, shaking his fist under the diplomat's nose, "do you want it on white or rye?"

"Apple pie and coffee," answered the diplomat.

Scotsman: A man who stays home and lets his mind wander.

A couple of travelers found themselves detained at a village inn and inquired whether there was any amusement to be had at the establishment. "Oh, yes," replied the waiter, "we have a billiard room."

At their request the travelers were conducted there and

found a musty old room with an inferior table that had seen better days. A set of balls was in the middle of the table. They were of uniform dirty color and were as worn as the green cloth that covered the board.

"But how do you tell the red ball from the white?" asked one of the visitors.

"Oh," was the reassuring retort, "you soon get to know them by their shape."

A camera addict went big-game hunting in Africa. One of his companions was chased by a lion and fled for camp with the animal breathing down his neck. As he neared the encampment he heard a shout and looked hopefully toward the thicket whence it came, knowing it was probably his salvation. The camera fiend came bounding out. "Hold on there," he yelled. "You're too far ahead. I can't get you both in the picture."

I never realized what wonderful friends I had until I sailed for Europe. Then three of my buddies came to see me off. They brought candy, cigars and liquor. And when the boat left the pier there they were eating, smoking and drinking.

I like the open road . . . but not the open plumbing.

Park Avenue: Where men live after they rise and women after they fall.

There is irrefutable proof that Revere was a woman. Only a woman would stay up all night to hear gossip and then run around telling everybody.

"Get any French francs?"
"Yeah. But they're not as good as our hot dogs."

238

When I was in New England I slept in a room Washington slept in, but his name wasn't spelled out in full on the door.

This country is getting so it isn't a safe place to die in.

Joan of Arc: Noah's wife.

Or—as the yacht owner said when his wife unexpectedly came aboard—"Through these portholes have passed the most beautiful girls—"

European history is where one day the people sit on the throne and the next day they're thrown on their seat.

During the war the butcher asked the ladies not to bring their fat cans in on Saturday.

Eskimo: One of God's frozen children.

"I came from Texas, where men are men and women are women."
"We have the same arrangement in Kansas."

When I was abroad I stayed at a Marshall Plan hotel. You pay and hope for the best.

Song title: "An Irishman May be Head of the Firm but He'll Always be an Erin Boy at Heart."

Two Englishmen met in London. "I say, Derrick," called Quincy, "how are you, old chap?"
"Fine. Just fine," said Derrick. "Lots doing. Business grand, children fine, weather pleasant and all that sort of balderdash."

"Jolly good. Anything else?"

"Let me see—oh yes—buried my wife."

"Really?"

"Had to. Dead you know."

"Did you learn any Spanish in Mexico?"

"No. But I picked up a little Cuban one night in Havana."

The steward had run room service for the man all evening without any form of compensation. He finally decided to shame the man with a direct approach. "You ought to give me a tip," the steward came right out and said. "Why the champion tightwad on this boat gives me a dime."

"Yeah?" said the man. "Meet the new champ."

In London a guy sneaks up to you and shows you some hot pictures of the sun for a quarter.

He was a tired Englishman. Didn't even give me that pip, pip stuff. He was too pooped to pip.

The drunk chinned up to the ticket clerk's window. "Shay," he said, "how fasht can I get to Chicago?"

The clerk pointed down the line. "This train goes to Chicago in five minutes," he said.

"I'll take it," replied the drunk. "Thatsh great time."

In Hawaii they do a striptease that takes fourteen hours. They take off one straw at a time.

They thought the picture of me was taken outside a Paris sidewalk cafe, but it was furniture.

I just got a letter from a girl in Kansas. I can't see her for dust.

The woman was nervous. She had a vacation coming up and was afraid to ask anyone where she should go.

"In Texas everybody's a gentleman."
"Really? No ladies at all?"

A politician is like Columbus. He doesn't know where he's going, how he's gonna do it all on borrowed money.

My wife is a poor sailor. She gets seasick when she opens a box of salt-water taffy.

Washington was father of his country. I wonder when Martha had time to make all that candy.

"What is the diet of these New England people?"
"Fish, mostly."
"I thought fish was a brain food. These are really the most unintelligent-looking persons I've ever seen."
"Just think what they would look like if they didn't eat fish."

The professor was listening to a student expound on Darwin's theory. "Darwin says we descended from monkeys. My grandfather may have been a gorilla," he informed the class, "but it doesn't worry me."
"Perhaps not," agreed the professor. "But it must have worried your grandmother."

She was Miss America at sixteen—there were very few Americans then.

Next year on the Riviera prices will go down so that the poorer millionaires can go there.

Russian: A man who sits on nothing and dances.

They excavated the thumb of a million-year-old woman. If they look farther they'll find a million-year-old man under it.

Americans will go anywhere but to the rear of a bus.

I had a very large room in London. I'd sit at my desk and, on a clear day, I could see the bed.

Things are so bad in Spain the gigolos are dancing with each other.

It was during World War II that a British housewife went crying to mother. "Dennis is a brute," she wailed.
"What is it this time, daughter?" The old lady was getting used to these things.
"We went out last night," she wept. "And he didn't even notice my new gas mask."

"So you're the chief of police of this wonderful, quaint little town. I'm so pleased to know you. I wonder if I could shake hands with the fire chief."
"Sure. Just wait till I change hats."

"Why do you look at me so intensely?" asked the missionary of the witch doctor.
"I'm the food inspector."

A small town is where there's nothing doing every minute.

I know why Washington stood up in the boat. Every time he sat down they'd give him an oar.

It was a surprise party for one of the girls in the office who was leaving to get married. Most of the other girls wanted to know if the prospective groom was a man of means.

"Well," said the bride-to-be, "he surprised me by saying we were going to spend our honeymoon in France."

The gals tittered excitedly. "How did he spring it on you?" they asked anxiously.

"Well, we were discussing it," she replied, "when he said as soon as we were married he would show me where he was wounded in the war."

Anything in a man travel brings out. I found that my first day at sea.

"Quick operator, send an SOS—"
"How do you spell it?"

Foreign exchange is at a low rate. This goes for opinions as well as money.

Southern dance: A homosexyouall.

When uncle was traveling in Switzerland all the townspeople came to see him. The St. Bernards were out of brandy.

Two cannibals talking:
"Who was dat lady I seen you out wit last night?"
"Dat was no lady. Dat was my lunch."

Free speech isn't dead in Russia—only the speakers.

"Where were your forefathers born?"

"I only got one father."

"Your business?"

"Rotten."

"Where is Washington?"

"He's dead."

"I mean the capital of the United States."

"They loaned it all to Europe."

British chocolate rationing: One ounce per person, per week, perhaps.

My uncle is a Scotsman. He runs his toothpaste tube through a wringer, but my aunt has hers run over by a trolley.

Franklin was all excited about electricity, but they soon made light of it.

Pawnees: A tribe that ran hockshops for Indians.

"Why were you thrown out of the Navy?"

"Some visitors asked me where the crow's nest was, and I pointed to the captain's cabin."

The shrewd businessman was on a trip through the Middle West and looking for souvenirs to bring home to his friends. He spotted an old Indian with loads of painted jugs and colorful blankets.

"How much?" he asked, pointing to the lot.

"Hundred dollar," said the Indian.

"Nothing doing," said the businessman.

"How much you give?"

"Twenty-four dollars."

"Listen, wise guy," said the Indian, "bargains like Manhattan Island you don't get no more."

The present condition of China: cracked.

I come from a small town. They won't allow you to use electric razors there. When you plug 'em in all the trolley cars stop.

Half a loaf is better than no vacation at all.

Indians did not invent the whooping cough.

Capital idea: An idea thought up in Washington.

"Haven't seen a white man in ages."
"Where you been?"
"Florida."

The three explorers wandered over tundra after tundra until they finally came to an Eskimo village, where, nearly frozen to death, they were taken to the igloo of the leader. They huddled in a corner when the chief entered and handed them a small, thin blanket.
"What good's this little blanket gonna do us?" asked one of the men.
"You may need it," said the chief. "It gets a little cool at night."

He took a shot at the lord's country seat. Missed it.

Scotland year: two feet eleven inches . . .

"That Scotsman has twenty kids."
"Great Scot!"

Business is holding up in Chicago.

I took off thirty pounds abroad. Took it off an Englishman.

Cubic: Language spoken in Cuba.

Paul Revere was the first American to try and sneak in without his shoes on.

The visitor to London was quite disgusted. "Rain, rain, rain, fog, fog, fog," he shouted at his guide. "When do you have summers in England?"

"I say," replied the guide. "That *is* a difficult question. Last year it came on a Wednesday."

It was so cold where I come from the natives welcome a hot foot.

Hotel clerk: "Er-uh, before going to your room, sir, would you mind wiping the mud off your shoes?"

Hillbilly. "What shoes?"

"Wasn't it Porter who said 'Take no quarter from the enemy?'"

"No. No porter ever said that."

There can't be any life on Mars. They haven't asked the United States for any money.

In California the dew gets so high they have oar locks on all the car windows.

Weather, like morality, is a question of geography.

The critic, a naval reserve officer, was called to the colors and given command of his own ship, which he ruled with an iron hand. At night, when all was black and quiet, he used to stand on the bridge and think about all the wonderful shows he was missing. On one such evening the quartermaster came bursting onto the bridge.

"Sir," he said breathlessly, "the crew is acting badly."

The captain stared at him and thought about all the magnificent productions about the sea wherein this identical situation had arisen.

"You, my good man," he said, "are no Barrymore either."

I went on a vacation for change and rest. The waiter got the change and the hotel got the rest.

English cows give tea instead of milk.

Hawaii, where at night you watch the natives rotate their crops.

Sheepshead Bey is in Turkey.

"When we were in London we saw them changing the guards."
"Were they dirty?"

I'm a half-breed. My father was a man and my mother was a woman.

Things are so tough in Miami even the holdup men are taking IOU's.

What does a St. Bernard do to save people? Well, he has a keg of whiskey. The man smells the whiskey—and follows the dog.

"They said Edison was crazy, they said Fulton was crazy, they said Ginsberg was crazy."

"Who's Ginsberg?"

"My uncle. He was really crazy."

It's so cold in Alaska the Eskimos go to Siberia for the winter.

"Where were you born?"

"Tokyo."

"How did that happen?"

"The usual way."

Mexican book: *Forever Hombre.*

What's the use of being a Texan if you're small?

Baltimore is famous for three things: win, place and show.

I learned French in six easy liasons.

"How many successful jumps does a paratrooper have to make before he is ready for combat?"

"All of them."

The Indian was making his first trip to the city and checked into his first hotel. "Me very tired," he told the clerk. "Me go right to bed."

He got to his room, undressed and was about to retire, when he noticed a blanket on the bed. He picked up the phone.

"This desk?" he asked.

"Yes," replied the clerk.

"Me wish make report," said the Indian. "Last fella live here forget'm take his overcoat."

In Florida this season they used antifreeze for sun-tan oil.

A Scotsman is a guy who goes to a wedding with a broom and brings home the rice for dinner.

When I was in Europe I never felt so lost since the time I looked for the men's room at the YWCA.

I came to see her off and she certainly was.

The captain was one of those immaculate tyrants, and the seas were rough. "Hide quickly," shouted the steward to the generous tipper. "They're throwing overboard the most troublesome of the seasick passengers."

"Here's five bucks," said the sport. "See that I don't miss my turn."

The headwaiters in Florida are making a fortune in tips this season. Everyone wants to sit near the radiator.

We've been at the North Pole five months. Might as well stay all night.

It's so dry in my home town they have fishes three years old that still haven't learned to swim.

They eat dry toast—and wash it down with crackers.

"How is everything in Italy?"
"Italian."

Women mummies are wonderful things. Who would ever think they would dry up and stay that way for so long.

The English prefer tea to coffee, rugby to football, left side of the road to right—same as in California.

Broom: A Salem town car.

The actor passed away and found himself, after much travel through darkness, at the gates of hell. He showed his ticket to the devil. "You're in the wrong place," said Mephisto. "This is hell and the ticket you have here is for heaven."

"I know, but the ticket allows a stopover here," corrected the actor. "You see. I'm from Hollywood. And I have to make the change gradually."

The Mann Act: A law passed to discourage travel.

It rained so much the statue of Henry Clay turned to mud.

"How did you make yourself understood in Paris?"
"Oh, I just pointed at the labels."

Visibility was so bad even the birds were walking.

Eiffel Tower: An erector set that made good.

Lots of rain in the Midwest. I asked a native for directions and he said it was ten miles as the crow floats.

Small hours after midnight are now called the *oui* hours.

During the newsreel a picture of two French generals was flashed on the screen. The crowds could be seen holding their umbrellas, with water dripping from their hats. "My God," a voice from the audience called. "It's still raining over there."

My town is so small the city limit signs are back to back.

"You ain't no gal from these here parts," the mountain girl said to the city girl. "Your teeth are on the inside."

Hawaii has the same weather all year 'round. Wonder how their conversations start?

That sailor on watch was the biggest liar. He kept yelling "Four bells and all's well" and I never felt worse in my life.

Kansas has a lot of cyclones. That's one state that raises everything, including its citizens.

The movie company was on location in darkest Africa with the famous actor-producer-director-writer. The famous A.P.D.W. was instructing his leading lady. "I slink through the jungle and I slink through the jungle," he said. "Then you slink and I slink."
"No. It's no good," shouted the temperamental actress.
"Why?" asked the famous A.P.D.W.
"Because," she said. "You slink more than me."

My uncle is a very successful businessman. He exports French post cards—to France.

The refugee, unable to speak any English, and afraid of getting lost, copied the words off the signpost, figuring he could show it to anybody and they would tell him how to get home. He's still lost. The sign he copied read "Curb Your Dog."

Foreign countries are all out of town.

The distinguished American senator was met at the airport by the distinguished ambassador to Spain. "Look, Mr. Senator," said the diplomat, "I'm going to introduce you to the high Spanish dignitary. Do you know what to say to him?"

"I'll say '*Adios, muchacho*.'"

"That means good-bye in Spanish."

"All right," said the distinguished traveler, "don't introduce me then until he's leaving."

It was damned hot in that place. After shaving I'd put baking powder on my face and when I perspired I broke out in biscuits.

"My uncle was killed in a shipwreck."

"Did he drown?"

"No. He was cast up on a desert island with two chorus girls."

"Did he starve to death?"

"No. He worked himself to death tearing down distress signals."

Captain yelled, "Put on your life belts." And there I was with nothing but a pair of suspenders.

They serve a balanced diet in the Navy. Every bean weighs the same.

Rome had senators, that's why it declined.

My folks came over on the *Mayflower* but I don't feel bad about it. We can't all be born here.

"I bought you a dream book. To interpret your dreams."

"Why? I dream in English."

Washington, the father of our country, never had any children of his own. Makes me wonder what kind of people we really are.

The married couple was traveling to the West Coast in their own plane to meet a movie deadline. Suddenly the wife, a brilliant actress, shrieked, "Darling, we're out of gas."

"Don't worry," her husband replied. "Just keep talking."

I came from nowhere and I will return to nowhere. I live in Jersey.

California: A tough state to get away from and a tougher state to go back to.

My cousin, the Scotsman, came to this country but couldn't make a go of it. I feared the worst so I went looking for him. I found him in a saloon, trying to drown his sorrow in free lunch.

Uncle was a hard-drinking sea captain. Traveled all the exotic oriental ports of the East and got drunk with sultans and harem queens. Now he's got the d.t.'s. But he doesn't see pink elephants and snakes, he sees eunuchs with women.

George Washington never told a lie but he was always late. If he wasn't he would have gotten a seat in the boat.

My new girl speaks French like a pastry.

When I was in Kentucky a cyclone tore down ten thousand stills. The atmosphere in the hills was 90 proof. If you took a breath you hadda have a chaser.

Father was one of the three wise men from the East— the East Side.

Women were made before mirrors and they've been before them ever since.

Travel: Something that broadens people and also flattens them.

"Is he cockney?"
"No. He never drinks a drop."

The fastest dogs in the world are in Alaska . . . the trees are so far apart.

New York: A Mix Master with people.

In South Africa there's a race of wild women who have no mouths and can't talk. That's why they're wild.

I stayed at a foreign hotel that had no bathroom. It was uncanny.

The salesman was traveling through the mountains of Kentucky when he was stopped by a moonshiner. "You're a city fella ain'tcha," the mountaineer declared.
"How do you know?" asked the salesman.
"By yo shirt."
"Shirt?"
"Yeah," said the hillbilly. "You're wearin' one."

Cannville is 430 miles from New York on the New York Central. No other city can make that statement.

Uncle is from Scotland. He has a zipper purse that still has to make its first zip.

Broadway is the place where you buy a sandwich named after someone you'd rather bite in person.

The comic had been employed to entertain at a British smoker, but he was having rough going. They just didn't laugh. So he decided to tell his best story.

"There were two people on an ocean trip," he began, "and they both got very seasick. The steward came to the man and said, 'Sorry to tell you your wife is dead.' The man said, 'That's good. I wish I were.'"

There was silence, and then one of the Englishmen said, "Too bad. What was the name of the people?"

"My uncle just got back from his vacation. He stayed at one of those hotels where there were mostly women."

"How did he look?"

"I don't know. The burial was private."

Amour is not important in this country, even though it's almost as big a company as Swift's.

Years ago someone in California hollered "Gold," and people drove from all directions. That's the way they still drive in California.

There will always be an England and we hope we can afford it.

This story was told at one of the famous "cruelty at sea" trials in which the crew brought charges against the shipping company.

The ship was rolling in the turbulent sea. The decks were awash and the mizzenmast was battered. The waves were forty feet high and the rains pelleted the decks like bullets. "The ship is too heavy," roared the captain. "Throw the food overboard."

"We did," shouted the quartermaster. "But the fish keep tossing it back."

This happened in Scotland. "Pop," the little boy called. "There's boiling water coming from the radiator."

"Don't waste it," shouted the old man. "Throw in a tea bag."

Two old maids were thinking of their younger days abroad.

"I'd like to see Big Ben once more before I die," said one.

"Ah, yes," said the other. "Good, wasn't he?"

MARRIAGE... courtship ...dates and the pursuit

(Matrimony is the process whereby love ripens into vengeance.)

The blonde and brunette met downtown for lunch the week the blonde returned from her honeymoon. "Weren't you taking an awful chance in telling your husband all about your past mistakes on the day you married him?" asked the friend.

"I'll say I was," admitted the blonde. "Some of them almost sobered him up."

Bride: "My little peach."
Groom: "My little plum."
Preacher: "I now pronounce you fruit salad."

Since our wedding I haven't looked at another woman. She was enough to discourage anyone.

"I want some arsenic for my mother-in-law."
"Have you a prescription?"
"No, but here's her picture."

"Your honor," said the husband, "the officer had no right to arrest us and bring us into court for disturbing the peace. All we were doing was standing in the street having a little, insignificant difference of opinion. Such as oft times happens with man and wife."

"Why didn't you have your minor quarrel at home instead of in the street?"

"WHAT!" The wife was most indignant too. "And break up all the furniture!"

The bride wore a corsage of orchids, a flowered dress and two cauliflower ears from a previous marriage.

She lay in bed, blissfully happy on this, the first morning of her long-dreamed-of honeymoon. "Darling," she called as she heard him puttering around in the bathroom. "Did you brush your teeth yet?"

"Yes," he cooed. "And while I was at it I brushed yours too."

I brought my wife to the convention. It was a question of bringing her along or kissing her good-bye.

The missus was angry when he came home.

"I saw you wink at that girl this morning."

"Something got in my eye."

"Something got in your car too."

We were off to be married—and to marry her I had to be off.

Baby wanted to stay up for a change, so I changed him.

"I got an awful fright the day of my wedding."

"I know. I saw her."

The bride didn't look happy . . . she looked triumphant.

"How could you endure talking to that homely woman without laughing in her face?"

"That's easy. She's my wife."

"Oh. My mistake."

"No. Mine."

The beauty of marrying an ugly girl is that in twenty years she'll be as pretty as ever.

The drunk was brought into night court, having been picked up on suspicion of being the notorious night prowler. "What were you doing out at 3 A.M.?" the judge sternly queried.

"I was going to a lecture."

"A lecture at 3 A.M.?" The judge was scornful.

"Oh, sure," said the drunk. "Shomestimesh my wife shtays up longer then that."

I never kept any secrets from my wife, even when I tried.

She's a May bride. She may or may not be married.

She's such a lousy cook. Her husband is so thin, when he holds his hands over his head he looks like a fork.

I saved her and she married me. That's gratitude.

Husbands are like photographers. All they ask you is to keep still and look pleasant.

We've a new addition to the family, my mother-in-law.

Baby carriage: Last year's fun on wheels.

"Don't we always exchange presents?"

"I always exchange yours."

"I told her she's got to get a new maid," said hubby.

"What happened to the old one?"

"I quit."

"Young man," said the matron to the hotel employee, "would you find my husband?"

"I'm a bellboy," he replied. "Not a bloodhound."

Marriage: A broken engagement.

An old maid is a yes girl who never had a chance to talk.

I always believed that opposites should marry. She's rich and I'm poor.

I've been married thirty-five years. Now I've got enough points to get out.

Argument: "You said I cured you of the blues. That I was as good as medicine."

"Well, now I claim you're a drug on the market."

They like to do the same things. When she waxes the floors he takes a bottle and polishes it off.

He who marries a chicken gets henpecked.

"She walked down the aisle on his right arm."

"What was her father doing with his left arm?"

"Dragging the groom."

"Just think, John," she whispered. "We don't have to pull the shades down. We're married."

There's a new gadget that does all the housework for the little woman. It's called a husband.

She wanted a formal wedding—so father painted the gun white.

Just tell her who's the boss. Say, "You're the boss."

"You brute," she shouted. "I cook all day and get abuse."
"I'll trade you," he offered. "I get heartburn."

"Honey, when I drop you off at the club dance I'm going to have to leave," said the busy husband.
"How am I going to get home?"
"I'm broadminded. You just get home any way you can. I won't ask any questions."

Only the brave desert the fair.

I have a reservation in the doghouse. She gave me a room with an adjoining bone.

She never said good-bye. That's a nice how-do-you-do.

"Does the mountain air disagree with your wife?"
"It wouldn't dare."

Before marriage a woman expects a man. After marriage she suspects him. After he dies she respects him.

We're married fifty years—seems just like yesterday. And you know what a lousy day yesterday was.

How to tell ladies from men now that they both wear pants. The one listening is the man.

"We've been married for fifty years."

"How does it feel?"

"Who feels after fifty years?"

Her cooking's improving. All the lumps in the mashed potatoes are the same size now.

She: "Don't you think we should get married?"

He: "I'd love to, darling, but I won't be able to afford a home for years and years."

She: "Couldn't we go and live with your parents?"

He: "That's impossible. My parents are still living with their parents."

I never knew what real happiness was until I got married and then it was too late.

Her husband is a writer. She edits his pockets.

The first American joke: the Declaration of Independence.

A husband is a no-good drunken bum who a woman wouldn't give a nickel for. But when he gets hit by a car his price immediately goes up to $50,000.

It was one of those famous society divorce cases. The niece of the embattled couple was on the stand.

"Tell us what happened last May 24," said the attorney.

"Our maid caught my uncle kissing my aunt. She said one of us would have to leave so the maid left and uncle went with her."

"What did your aunt do?"

"She went to a picture with the butler."

"Where was the chauffeur at the time?"

"He was getting a divorce from the maid to marry my cousin."

He married that plump little girl that always giggled. He always believed in a short wife and a merry one.

"We are going to have mother for dinner."
"Make sure she's well done."

On the sea of matrimony he got a leaky boat.

The chilly weather made her think of her poor dead husband. He was always so cold. Poor man, he used to wonder if he ever would get warmed through. He was so miserable when he was cold. But it gives her great comfort to know that he is happy now.

I hated to lose her there. They had a very efficient lost and found department.

After the court awarded the woman a large marital settlement they met once more in the corridor. "I suppose you always had my best interests at heart," the man said with resignation.

"I certainly had," she said wistfully.

"Well!" he roared. "Then why the hell did you marry me?"

How can two be happy when one is talking?

It was a B29-C37 wedding. The groom looked like he could be 29 . . . the bride looked like she'd never see 37.

"How much does it cost to get married, Pop?"

"I don't know. I'm still paying on it."

She's lonesome for me, especially when I'm not home.

I've been in love four times and married three times. It's like a football game. Three down and one to go.

"Listen, wise guy, my wife's old man used to be a prizefighter."

"What does that make you?"

"Nervous."

As the gal said when the marriage license was issued, "It won't be wrong now."

After the divorce I married her sister so I wouldn't have to break in a new mother-in-law.

"I've been cooking for ten years."

"You ought to be done now."

Her fingers showed signs of toil. The one with the wedding ring showed she was through working.

Joined in holy deadlock.

"I wonder if John will love me when I'm old."

"Don't you know?"

The woman was explaining the tragic details of her husband's demise. The coroner listened sympathetically. "In his youth he was a famous football player and he could never get over those glorious days," she explained, dabbing away a tear. "He used to walk in his sleep.

That night he tried to kick me between the bedposts. He died of a broken heart when he woke up and found he'd failed to convert."

Sister is so angry at her husband she wishes she had never turned around the first time he whistled.

Marriage may be the real road to happiness, but there are a lot of good side trails.

She doesn't go out at night with her husband any more. The only thing he takes out at night now is his teeth.

It was one of those marriages in name only and he decided to try to make it up to her. "Let's have some fun tonight, dear," he suggested.

"Okay," she said. "And please leave the light on in the hallway if you get home before I do."

"How can you live without her?"
"Cheaper."

Mrs. K., mother of the bride, was attired in a soft-blue lace dress which fell to the floor.

"How soon do you expect the nuptials?"
"Right after the wedding."

It's our iron wedding . . . I gotta be made of iron to be married to her for twelve years.

If she was half as smart as she thought she was . . . I would have been married to a damned smart woman.

"My good man," said the preacher at the memorial service, "you won't find another woman like her."

"Who's gonna look?"

Marriage is all right for people with children.

After five months of marriage she presented her husband with a seven-pound baby boy. "Me thinks this is a bit early," he remarked.

"No," she said. "We only married a bit late."

"Whaddaya yappin' about?" screamed the drunk at his nagging wife. "I got in a quarter of twelve."

"You did not, you drunken louse," said lovey. "I heard the clock strike three."

"Well, shtupid," he cooed. "Ain't three a quarter of twelve?"

The first time she washed her hands the wedding ring went off the gold standard.

What a happy couple. They see lie to lie.

The poor woman lay crying on her psychiatrist's couch. "We were married twenty-five years before he died," she said, dabbing away a mournful tear. "Never had an argument in all those years."

"Amazing," said the doctor. "How did you do it?"

"I outweighed him forty pounds and he was yellow."

"Now, madam, I will take your case," said the lawyer. "But do you think it advisable for you, a mother of twenty children, to accuse your husband of neglect?"

Women try their luck, men risk theirs.

I phone my wife several times a day. I know several men who do the same thing.

When I married her she looked like a slender birch. Now she looks like a knotty pine.

The lawyer liked what he'd just heard. "You say your wife has the worst memory on earth," he repeated. "Does she forget everything?"

"No," said the man. "She remembers everything."

"Do you believe in war, dearest?"
"I do, sweetheart."
"DO YOU REALLY BELIEVE IN WAR?"
"Oh, I thought you said more."

"There's a machine out now that can tell when a man's lying."
"I know. I married one."

"Darling, I have loved you as a child."
"Yeah," she agreed. "Maybe you'll love me as a man yet."

There's one habit I'd like to break her of—breathing.

It was nice of me to send my wife away on a vacation. Heaven knows, I needed it.

The couples were playing bridge for several hours when the man excused himself to go to the gents' room. "For the first time tonight," remarked his partner, "I know what he's doing."

Reno: A civilian separation center.

My right arm is twenty-five and a half inches and my left arm is thirty-five inches. We have twin beds and my wife likes to fall asleep holding hands.

The hotel had been happy to receive the young honeymooners. They looked like such a fine, handsome, respectable couple. But suddenly the most violent argument broke out between them. The language was terrible. "Here, here," interjected the manager. "What's the idea?"

"It's her fault," yelled the groom. "She wants to eat first."

She cooked me these ladyfingers—the lumps in the middle are knuckles.

If at first you don't succeed, try, try a gun.

And so they were married and were a mutual detriment to each other.

"If you make the toast and coffee, dear," said the newly married girl, "breakfast will be ready."

"What're we gonna have for breakfast?"

"Toast and coffee."

"Honey, you look like an old cameo."

"You don't look so good yourself."

"What would you call a man who just lost his wife?"

"Lucky."

She keeps our house spotless. You'd think it was a hospital.

Oh, my darling, we are now a part of each other. You are a part of me, and I, a part of you. Of course there'll be confusion when we get dressed in the morning.

Lost my teeth. The wife gave me a rabbit punch for Easter.

She was all excited about her pending nuptials. "We're going to spend our honeymoon at 822 Wall Street," she confided to a friend.

"Don't you work at 824?" she asked.

"Yeah," said the betrothed. "He doesn't want me to be late for work."

My wife isn't such a good cook. We had people for dinner two weeks ago and they're still sitting there.

"Ever struck by lightning?"

"After ten years of married life I don't remember trifles like that."

"Your wife told me she has an electric blanket that's so warm she can cook on it."

"No wonder she serves me goulash with fuzz."

Mothers-in-law aren't justified. However, jokes about them are.

Two former sweethearts, who never married, met unexpectedly one day. "You're not so gallant as when you were a boy," she remarked.

"And you're not so buoyant as when you were a girl," he answered.

"He is the kindest and lovingest and dearest husband," said the Hollywood actress. "He's letting me have a divorce and stating mental cruelty."

"Darling," she said into the phone. "I sprained my ankle and can't lead the chapter on its annual hike. Would you come right home and do it for me?"

"What!" he protested happily. "Alone with all those girls?" As though he did not relish the assignment. "What will I do?"

"Very little," she replied. "Two of them are friends of mine."

If she married for love she'd be her own groom.

"Every night my wife takes my shoes off," he boasted.
"When you come home?"
"No. When I wanna go out."

The woman sought the hallowed advice of the marriage counselor.

"I just don't know what to do." She was obviously distressed. "The first year my husband spoke to me twice and we had twins. The second year he spoke to me three times and we had triplets. The third year, four times and we had quadruplets. What shall I do?"

"Tell him to just point, you'll know what he means."

There was too much of her and not enough of the dress. She didn't have it on two minutes before she caught a cold.

Husband: A sweetheart with the nerve removed.

"Papa, what's a fiancée?"

"A woman who is engaged to be married."

"And what's a fiasco?"

"The fellow who's going to marry her."

The bride and groom were so ugly—everyone thought they were taking a comedy picture.

She was the light of my life. I put her out ten years ago.

Marriage is a union. A union of heart, a union of soul, a union of minds, but wait till you have to pay those union dues.

"He's the most bashful man I ever met," said the newlywed. "He even took along mistletoe on our honeymoon."

First year is the paper anniversary. After one year you're beaten to a pulp.

Hubby got a little high and started to make a play for the luscious babe playing the piano at the party. But in the course of his exploits he tripped and the piano cover closed on his hands.

"Remind me to put a piece of steak on your black eye when we get home," said the wife.

"But I haven't got a black eye," he corrected.

"You're not home yet," she reminded.

Unlike most brides, my wife can boil water, but I get tired of it seven times a week.

Marriage is like eating just the soup in a bowl of borscht. You're left with a cold potato.

Have a baby my wife just had a cigar.

"Darling, I hear someone on the stairs."
"Go back to sleep. For once it ain't me."

She was crying. "He made me send the hat back," she tearfully told her mother. "WHAT!" shrieked mamma. "Is he trying to act like a man again?"

I never knew what real happiness was until I got married . . . then it was too late.

"My wife is baking a cake. Gotta go home and do some beating."
"The eggs, eh?"
"No. The wife. She knows I hate cake."

Slowly he raised the cup to his mouth, never looking up from his breakfast paper. He took a deep swallow then sent the contents of the cup squirting across the room in a gigantic mist and spray. "WHAT THE HELL IS THIS?" he roared.
"You always say my coffee tastes like two-day-old dishwater," said his wife, surprised at his surprise. "So this morning I gave you some two-day-old dishwater."

Her husband still has the first two loaves of bread she ever baked. He uses them for book ends.

"Won't it be strange when women rule the country?"
"Only to the bachelors."

She said I was slowly digging her grave. So I bought a steam shovel.

He married a checkroom girl. Every time he goes out of the house he has to give her a quarter for his hat.

Marrying for money is better than marrying for no reason at all.

The soldier was given so much saltpeter he began a letter to his wife, "Dear Friend—"

She ranted and raved. She complained and pleaded. She cried and threatened. "You'd think I treated you like a dog," her husband remarked.
"NO!" she screamed. "A dog has a fur coat."

The work done in a preacher's office cannot be depended upon. A great deal of it does not last.

"You're so cockeyed drunk," screamed the little dear, "you don't even know what day it is."
"Itsh Shunday."
"How do you know?"
"You sherved me fishh two days old."

I hit my wife. Terrible thing happened then. The chair broke.

"I don't know what to do. My wife has threatened to leave."
"Won't she promise?"

"I've been trying to remove a ring for five years and finally got it off with soap and water."
"Didn't you wet your collar?"

"Bakery Closed"—read the sign on the door—"Home Baking."

She has all the virtues except virtue.

A wife can be sweet when she wants.

"Do you think young men should undergo special training for marriage?"
"Why not? Every other class of fighter trains before the battle."

Peggy Joyce made ring history. To go to sleep she doesn't count sheep, she counts husbands.

"You're always wishing for something you haven't got."
"What else is there to wish for?"

Our deep love ripened into friendship.

I can say anything I want in my home. But nobody pays any attention to me.

Song title: "If I Had Met You Sooner I'd Have Been Rid of You Long Before Now."

My wife is so afraid of scandal she won't send our laundry out in one bundle.

For the tenth consecutive day she served him biscuits for breakfast. The scene was a natural one. "Goddamnit, Shirlee," he yelled. "Is this the only darned thing you know how to make?"
"I-I-I gotta save the biscuit box tops to get a prize."
"Send the biscuits," he said disgustedly. "I'll eat the box tops."

Alimony is the system whereby two people make a mistake and one continues to pay for it.

Women are fools to marry men. On the other hand, what else is there to marry?

"Come, come, my good man," consoled the funeral director. "Tears cannot restore your mother-in-law."
"I know," said the grief-stricken man. "That's why I cry."

She calls him a model husband. She caught him out with a model.

"Before we were married you used to bring me flowers."
"I thought you were dead."

My wife walks in her sleep and I go around all night opening windows.

"Shweetheart," said the drunk to his wife. "Thish ish delishious stuffing. How did you ever get the turkey to eat it!"

Alimony is like paying for a meal after you've lost your appetite.

The car in which the elderly couple was riding went over the cliff. It was an awful wreck. "Where am I?" moaned the woman when she opened her eyes. "In heaven?"
"No," said her dazed husband. "I'm still with you."

"Is your wife living?"
"Yeah. But not with me."

She waited at the church so long that she forgot who she was waiting for.

She burns everything, even her cookbook.

My brother, who is twenty-eight, is married to a lovely woman who is eighty-nine. She's very rich. It's what you call a football romance. He's waiting for her to kick off.

He's married eighteen years and is in a lot of trouble. It took him a long time to find out.

We used to sit in the parlor and turn off the light. Now the man comes and turns 'em off.

"Gee whizsh," said the drunk, "4 A.M.—I'd better get home before the shtorm."
"But there is no storm," said his lady of the evening.
"There will be," he said. "Before or after I get home."

Marriage takes the fun out of being a bachelor.

"I spent all her money," he told his lawyer. "Do you think there's any hope for me?"
"Plenty," said the lawyer. "If you play your cards right she'll leave you."

The groom looked high and low for his bride and finally found her in their room passionately kissing the best man. "Darling," she cooed. "I bet you must think I'm an awful flirt."

My wife is a vegetarian. Every time I get home she says, "Where's the cabbage?"

Marriage: Where the groom brings home the bacon . . . and the bride burns it.

"Our fifteenth anniversary. I haven't forgotten, honey darling. You look the same as you did when I married you fifteen years ago."

"I should. I'm wearing the same dress."

He's a father. They must have lowered the requirements.

Tom was really tight-fisted and his pinch-penny antics applied even to the dinner table. "What shall we have for dinner?" his wife asked.

"One of your lovely smiles," said the tightwad. "I can dine on that every day."

"Well, I can't."

"Well, then," said Tom good-naturedly, and at the same time thinking of the buck, "take this kiss." And he kissed her.

That night there was steak for dinner. "Say," he beamed, "this steak is fine. What'd you pay for it?"

"Not much," she said. "What you gave me this morning."

I found a way to settle my wife's hash. I take a spoonful of bicarbonate.

The man who will make a fortune from husbands alone is the man who will build a better mouth trap.

"Before sending you to the chair, is there a last request you would like to make?"

"Yes, Judge. I would like my wife to cook my last meal, then I'll feel more like dying."

The poor fellow had a bad memory so he kept notes about everything, but he often didn't remember what his notes were about. While going through his papers one day he came across a name, and try as he would he couldn't figure out who the man was. So he wrote to him and in the letter asked, "Do you know me? Was there something I was supposed to do for you?"

The reply read, "You already did. I am your wife's first husband."

The reason the average man and wife are not happy is because they treat each other like man and wife.

All men are born free and equal, but some of them get married.

I have the best wife in the country. Sometimes I wish she'd stay there.

"I was down to the station to see my wife off on a one month's vacation."

"But how black your hands are."

"Yes. I patted the engine."

Izzy felt foolish as he told the boss why he needed the day off. "I want to see my eighty-five-year-old grandfather get married," he told Mr. Siegel.

"Why the hell does he want to get married at his age?" Siegel demanded.

"He doesn't want to," Izzy replied. "He has to."

Then there was the sleepy bride. She was so tired she couldn't wake up for a second.

She: "I was a fool when I married you."

He: "Guess you was, but I was too infatuated to notice it."

"My wife beat me up."

"Why?"

"For speaking."

"For only speaking, she beat you up?"

"No. For not raising my hand."

There have been a lot of great war songs. Songs like "Over There" and "Keep the Home Fires Burning." Then during World War II there was "Praise the Lord and Pass the Ammunition" and "Hot Time in the Town of Berlin." But the greatest battle tune ever written is still "The Wedding March."

This little red book is my scrapbook. Every time my wife finds it we have a scrap.

Love is a three-ring circus. Engagement ring, wedding ring and suffer-ring.

Not all women are talkers, some of 'em are hollerers.

Axelrod was having trouble remembering the city where he spent his honeymoon. "It's a place on the seashore what starts with a 'T'," he said.

They racked their brains for an hour trying to remember such a place but with no results. Finally, one of them brought out a map.

"There it is," Axelrod shouted triumphantly. "Tlentic City."

Most husbands get very tender after the silver wedding anniversary. But then any hunk of meat gets tender if you keep it in hot water long enough.

Rice: A product associated with the worst mistake of some men's lives.

It was a dark, dreary night. The wind was howling, the sky was overcast and Becky couldn't sleep. Suddenly, as a bolt of lightning lit up the sky she thought she saw a burglar staring at her through the blackened window.

"Sol, Sol," she shrieked hysterically, "there's a burglar coming in through the window."

Sol rolled over, stared weary-eyed through his sleep and spied the thief working with burglar tools. "Shh," he cautioned. "Don't scare him. Maybe he can get the window up. It's the one we couldn't open since the painters left."

The henpecked husband and his wordy wife were walking down the country road having one of their arguments in the usual way. She was winning. Suddenly she turned and saw a bull charging down the road. There was no time to warn her husband so she jumped into a hedge. The bull caught the man on its horns and sent him spinning fifty feet into the air. He came down in a ditch. When he finally managed to crawl out he saw his wife standing on the road.

"Maria," he said, "if you hit me like that again you'll really make me lose my temper."

When my wife wants anything she uses sign language. She signs for this and she signs for that.

When I married her she was so naïve. But when she packed, boy she packed like she was married before.

We had a bureau-type marriage. She went through my drawers and I went through hers.

"Don't you ever look at a man and wish you were single again?"
"Yes."
"Who?"
"My husband."

He has an impediment in his speech—his wife.

Remember, the little woman still enjoys candy and flowers. Let her know you still remember. Speak of them once in a while.

"I want to express my sympathy over the loss of your husband."
"Nonsense. He's at home this very minute very much alive."
"So is your maid."

"I landed in this dirty, filthy, rotten jail 'cause I had five wives."
"How does it feel to be free again?"

"Who's there?" she called into the darkened room.
"It's only me, darling," a voice replied.
"My husband never calls me darling," she shrieked. "POLICE!"

Many a man loses his voice on his wedding day.

I married my wife because I was lonely. Then one morning I looked at her and said to myself, "How could you ever have been that lonely?"

"My wife took everything and left me."

"You're lucky. Mine didn't leave."

A grocer was delivering some groceries in his wagon one morning when he ran down and badly injured an old lady. The old lady sued him and collected big damages. A few weeks later he ran down an old gentleman. The old gentleman also sued and collected big damages, which almost ruined him.

One Sunday the grocer was sitting at home when his son came running through the door. "Father, father," the little boy cried, "mother's been run over by a hundred and eighty horsepower touring car."

The grocer's eyes filled with tears and, in a voice trembling with genuine emotion, he cried, "Thank the Lord the luck's changed at last."

Or, as the matchmaker says, "What they wish me the first year I should have. What they wish me the second year you should have."

A wedding ring is like a tourniquet. It stops your circulation.

"My alarm clock woke me this morning for the first time."

"How come?"

"My wife hit me in the head with it."

She was his childhood sweetheart. When they married he was in his second childhood.

Imagination: Something that sits up with a wife when her husband's out late.

Last week I had some terrible luck. The chauffeur ran off without my wife.

"What did her father do when you told him you wanted to marry his daughter?"

"He behaved like a little lamb. He said, 'Bah—'"

"Haw-haw, saw you sewing a button on your own coat, henpecked."

"No you didn't."

"Yes, I did. I saw you with my own eyes."

"You did not. It was my wife's coat."

"You better lock me up. I just hit my wife over the head with a club."

"Kill her?"

"I don't think so. That's why I want you to lock me up."

Aubrey Meek was brought before the court on the charge of refusing to obey a police officer. "Why did you refuse to move on when asked to do so by the officer?" the judge inquired, obviously wondering what unexplained force could have given such a man strength to buck a strong minion of the law.

"It's like this, your honor," explained Meek. "My wife said I was to meet her at exactly twelve noon at that spot —and I was forced to choose between man's law and wife's law."

Kalish was coming home from a dance when he suddenly collided with someone who was running wildly in the opposite direction. When the two got to their feet he saw that it was his old friend Goldberg.

"Why, Ralphie," Kalish exclaimed, "what's the hurry?"

"Let me go, Leo. I'm going for the police," Goldberg panted.

"For the police? What's the matter?"

"There's a rough-looking burglar in our house."

"But surely you haven't left your wife alone?"

"Oh, no! She's holding the burglar."

"How's the old bus, Ed?"

"Fine. And how's *your* missus?"

It is true that opposites should marry. That's why there's usually a male and female involved.

What is it all men eat sometime or other, yet it's the worst thing for them? Wedding cake.

"I'm going to my best friend's silver wedding anniversary."

"Oh, married twenty-five years."

"No. Twenty-five times."

A woman's mouth is like a rosebud until a man marries her. Then the bud opens.

Midwife: The second wife of a man who marries three times.

The victim of the robber put up a terrific fight before the robber finally downed him. "Say," the robber exclaimed. "How come you put up such a fight? You have only sixty-five cents in your pocket."

"I'll kill that Becky," the victim exclaimed. "Going through my pants again."

It was his one hundred and fifth birthday and he was sitting there crying. "My wife would have loved to be here today," he said, dabbing away a tear. "She died when she was eighty-five, you know. What that poor woman went through. But thank God, at least the baby lived."

There are only three kinds of women. Those one cannot live without, those one cannot live with and those one lives with.

They're making wedding rings lighter and thinner these days. In the old days they were meant to last a lifetime.

My girl said she wanted something to go with her appearance. So I bought her a set of horseshoes.

"I can't see anything good-looking about her."
"Oh she doesn't carry her money where it can be seen."

Wedding: The stage of the romance when a man gets billed for the times he cooed.

In her lifetime Gussie was sure her husband had bought her only the best. Now that he was gone there didn't seem to be any reason to keep the diamonds so she took them to the jeweler for appraisal.
"My husband examined many diamonds before he selected those," she said. "They're the flower of them all."
"You mean f-l-o-u-r."
"Why?" asked Gussie.
"Because they're made of paste."

The man was telling how he met his wife. "I whistled for a cab, but she got there first."

The best way to preserve your wedding ring is to dip it in dishwater three times a day.

Yetta was amazed at the affluence of her girl friend Zelda.

"How do you get so much money out of your husband?" she asked.

"Oh," replied Zelda, patting the back of her head, "I just tell him I'm going home to mother and he immediately hands me the fare."

Happiness is the only thing that multiplies by division.

Merscen used to play cards with the boys every Thursday, but then he got married. Three years later he showed up again. The boys were naturally curious about his wedded bliss. "Does she feed you well?" they asked.

"She gave me chicken three times last week and three times this week," Merscen said proudly.

"Then you have no cause to complain."

Merscen's face dropped. "Yes, I do. It was the same chicken."

"Somehow I don't think my wife knows her way around the kitchen."

"Why do you say that?"

"This morning I saw her trying to open an egg with a can opener."

A friend of mine married a woman who, right after the ceremony, shot up to three hundred pounds. Now he leads a double wife.

"Will your father permit you to take the piano with you when you get married?"

"He says he will insist on it."

My wife threw every bit of pottery in the house at me. I'm sure gonna miss those familiar vases.

Please, don't leave me," he implored.

"I didn't think I mattered to you," she said, hesitating in the doorway.

"You don't," he replied. "But twelve wives have gone already and thirteen is my unlucky number."

"What was he doing during the quarrel with his wife?"

"Listening."

My girl has a figure like a deck of cards. She's been shuffled around quite a bit, but she's well stacked.

Her old man wanted me to help him clean up the house. He said, "Come into the kitchen, you little squirt, and I'll mop up the floor with you." I stuck my tongue out at him. I always do that when I'm being choked.

She has a musical face. Sharp in some places, flat in others. She looked like a doll. Her hair was pasted on.

Her teeth were like pearls. They needed restringing.

She may be an heiress but she looks more like an heirloom.

She used so much makeup that she became my powdered sugar.

Her previous boy friend looked like George Washington. He wore a wig too.

She missed being Miss America by two feet. Twelve inches on each hip.

The waiter approached the college boy, who was sitting with a friend and two girls.
"Pardon me, but did you order the zombie?"
"Naw," said the college man. "This is a blind date."

His friends were trying to discourage him from calling on the girl. "They're nothing really," they said. "They have no piano, no summer home, no fur coats, no phonograph, no washing machine, no automobile, no TV set, no radio."
"Gee," gasped the boy. "They must have money."

Blind date: When a boy or girl generally hits the jerk pot.

PSYCHO... *psychiatry, psychiatrists, neurotics...* and just plain nuts

(She tried to kill him with a look. But she was cross-eyed.
So she killed another man.)

"Hey, stop applauding at a wedding."

"No applauding?"

"No."

"Can I hiss?"

"I just ate a worm in this apple," said the inmate.

"Well," said the keeper. "Drink some water and wash it down."

"The hell with him," answered the nut. "Let him walk."

Guppladel was awakened by the striking of the clock. It kept striking until it hit thirteen. He looked at his wife, horrified.

"Lulu," he yelled. "Wake up. It's later than I ever knew it to be."

"I want $600 for the operation," said the doc.

"Can't you do it for $300?"

"Sure. But I'll use dull knives."

Hospitals are so crowded they won't admit you with double pneumonia, only single.

The cow called upon the psychiatrist with her calf. "Doctor," she said. "I don't know what to do with him. He keeps asking for malteds."

We were playing with three dice. I rolled three sixes and my point was eighteen. Made it the hard way—two nines.

"Do you know Nance O'Neil?"
"Maybe. What's his first name?"

"I feel like a new man," said the patient.
"Yeah?" The psychiatrist was surprised. "Anyone I know?"

I have a racing form at the office. I don't read it. I keep it in case a horse drops in.

When I was a kid I used to love to sit at home in front of a roaring fire. Father used to get mad. We had no fireplace.

Uncle is the author of a book of reminders—for elephants who forget.

It was another one of those famous society divorce cases. The gentleman farmer was hauled into court by the missus, who was seeking a nice chunk of the family property. "I don't know what to do with him, your honor," the matron sobbed. "He always talks about his cows."
"Make him jealous," advised the judge. "Go dancing with a bull once in a while."

"I was left on a doorstep with a note on my dress."
"What did the note say?"
"I don't know. I was too young to read."

Bon voyage baskets: You keep bon voyages in 'em.

During the war he gave all his patients local anesthetic. Couldn't get the imported stuff.

I sent my mother daffodils. She's crazy about daffodils, likes the rest of the family too.

The gas leaked. But I fixed it myself. I didn't pay the bill.

The daredevil stunt man had lost his balance. The psychiatrist was attempting to establish a friendly relationship for treatment.

"Tell me about your work," he said. "What do you do?"

"Well," said the stunt man, "I jump off cliffs, I wrestle with man-eating lions, I swim under water for fifteen minutes at a time and jump off six-story flaming buildings."

"My gosh. How do you manage to live?"

"I take in laundry."

"What's that howling?" she fearfully asked.

"A timber wolf," he replied.

"But there aren't any timber wolves here."

"That's what he's howling about."

"I'm a magician," the man advised the doctor.

"That's interesting. What is your best trick?"

"I saw a woman in half."

"Is it difficult?"

"It's child's play. I learned it as a child."

"Are there any more children at home?"

"I have several half-sisters."

The doctor appeared for his nightly visit at the home of the sick man. "Have you been following my instructions closely?" he asked the wife.

"Yes. I gave him juices, just like you said. Battery juices."

"BATTERY JUICES!" He was somewhat surprised. "GOOD LORD! HE'LL DIE."

"No he won't," she calmly replied. "He has a cold. He can't taste a thing."

It was so cold my teeth chattered all night. I finally had to get up . . . and take 'em out of the glass.

My sister is a lifeguard in a fountain-pen factory. Anyone writes under water, she dives in and saves the pen.

"Why don't you wipe that vicious scowl off your face?"
"What for? I'm no hypocrite."

They strolled into the park. It was a beautiful day. Perfect for youth and romance that youth is entitled to enjoy.

"See those humming birds flapping their wings a thousand times a minute?" she said.

"Yes," he answered softly. "And they have their bills together."

"Let's do that," she implored.

"Gee," he said breathlessly, "I'm afraid I can't flap my arms that fast."

"Tell me about your trip abroad," said the analyst.
"I went over on the *Normandy*."
"But that sank years ago."
"No wonder the bread was soggy."

"Now remember, relaxation is very important," the analyst was saying. "What do you do as a means of relaxation?"

"I kill flies with a bow and arrow," Jocko said.

"Isn't that sort of messy?"

"Nawww," said Jocko. "I aim only at their legs."

There was a time when I could speak Spanish as well as I spoke English. When I was a year old.

"See you Friday."

"Supposin' it rains Friday?"

"Then I'll see you Thursday."

"How could *you* join the Campfire Girls?"

"I was cold."

When I was young I went days without sleep. It was a good thing I slept nights.

Uncle suffered from privyphobia. He couldn't resist writing on walls.

The psychiatrist thought it was very presumptuous of the patient to lie down on the couch while waiting for him. "You tired?" he asked, unable to hide his feelings.

"No."

"Then why are you lying down?"

"In case I get tired."

I danced with the Siamese twins and they made me get off the floor. I wasn't wearing a tie.

Sinbad was bucking hard for a Section 8. He shaked, rattled and rolled all over the dance floor at the sailors' dance—long before the band arrived. They rushed him to the hospital. "I was on a torpedoed boat," he explained. "All went down on board. Not a soul was saved."

The doctor was skeptical. "How does it happen that you were not drowned?" he asked.

"Well—er—ah," fidgeted Sinbad. "Er—as a matter of fact I was."

"Sit down in the Morris chair."
"I don't want to. I might wake up Morris."

"For years I've been weighing myself on one of those scales that hands out little cards. When I started I weighed a hundred and forty pounds. Now I weigh a hundred and eighty pounds."
"How come you weigh so much?"
"My pockets are full of little cards."

I was reading the paper over the man's shoulder but he made me lick his thumb every time he wanted to turn the page. That's how I found out he worked in a fish market.

Someone sent me a cuckoo clock. I heard it ticking, thought it was a bomb and stuck it in a pail of water. I now have the only clock where the cuckoo comes out every hour and gargles.

"Doc, I must speak to you about my brother. He thinks he's an olive."
"What do you say that?"
"He keeps sticking his head in other people's martinis."

The man hurried into the building, entered the elevator and asked to be taken to the sixth floor. "We have no sixth floor," said the operator. "Only five."
"Okay," said the man. "Take me up to the third floor twice."

When my wife was pregnant she kept asking for strawberries and they were hard to get. There was a big shortage of straw.

"Can't you use a quartet with three people?"
"Quartets have four people."
"That's okay. I never studied music."

"What's your name?"
"12325."
"Is that your real name?"
"No. It's my pen name."

Ever since the lot next door had been sold Mrs. Foofnik developed a psychosis about the whole thing. "It's that lot next door," she told the psychologist. "It's been sold, you know. When are they going to take it away?"

"Take it away?" He was making progress. "They're not going to take it away."

"Oh goody," she exclaimed. "That would leave an awful hole."

"Doc, I bought a six-acre farm," Mr. Foofnik told his analyst. "It's beautiful. Absolutely the last word. I have an acre of peach trees, then an empty acre. An acre of cherry trees, then an empty acre. And an acre of plum trees then an empty acre."

"What's the idea?"
"I gotta have some place to throw the pits."

I ate so much chow mein last night . . . I woke up this morning and washed my own shirts.

"Wonder what time it is. I'm invited to dinner at eight-thirty and my watch isn't going."

"Why? Wasn't your watch invited?"

Although the jewelry house was the most reputable in the city the woman insisted upon asking what the manager considered highly insulting questions. After examining a forty-carat ring she finally broke the dam by asking, "How do I know these diamonds are real?"

"Madam," replied the manager. "Just buy one, lose it, offer a reward for it. If it isn't returned . . . it's real."

With this daylight savings time, the cuckoo just comes out, shrugs its shoulders and goes back in again.

"What do you do for relaxation?"
"I like to go fishing during the rain, under a bridge."
"Fishing, during the rain, under a bridge?"
"It's the best place. The fishes keep crowdin' in to get out of the wet."

"Gee, Doc, I don't know what to do. Whenever I lift my arm it pains terrible."
"Then don't lift it."

My girl has a rattlesnake tattooed on her arm. Very feminine though, the snake has a rose in its mouth.

She lay there trembling, her soft, limpid eyes reflecting the horror of her experience. If only someone would come. If only there was someone she could tell.

The sound of shuffling feet outside in the hallway caused her to rise. Was the fiend coming back for more? The thought repelled her. If only someone would come, if only, HE would come.

Slowly the doorknob turned. She recoiled in horror as she pulled the blanket above her shoulders, but then as the light from the hall crashed through the crack in the door, she saw, she saw it was HIM.

"Oh my DARLING," she cried. Then, sobbing on HIS shoulder she told him the story of what had happened. "I'm so glad YOU'RE here. I've been trying to get the police all day." She broke into heavy sobbing. "But there doesn't seem to be any answer."

"Hmmm," HE said, his shoulders rising in anger. "Maybe they're not open on Sunday."

Grand larceny is when you get away with it.

"I saw Henry the Sixteenth."
"You mean Henry the Eighth."
"I saw it twice."

I work twenty-five hours a day. I get up an hour earlier.

It was one of those unusual cases. The man had shown up at the ward with a fountain pen stuck in his head. Psychiatric examination had determined that it was best to permit the man to keep it there as he was of the opinion it was serving a definite purpose.

"Now tell me," the psychiatrist said during examination, "you say you got a bullet in your head. When this happened did you see a doctor?"

"No," said the man. "I took it out myself. Here it is."

He produced a fired slug which obviously had been extracted from a tree. The psychiatrist decided to humor him.

"Gee," he muttered, feigning astonishment. "That was a great idea of yours, keeping the fountain pen in there."

"Yeah," agreed the man. "But last week it leaked and my eyes turned blue."

"I've diagnosed your troubles," said the doctor. "You've got long eyeballs and short eyelids . . . that's why you can't sleep."

"Did you go to a private school to become an imbecile?"

"Whaddayathink I am, snobbish?"

Psychopath: A path where a psycho walks up and down.

The man appeared at his analyst's office in a frenzied state.

"It's a dream I had," he said nervously. "I dreamed I was among three hundred dancing girls. All luscious, beautiful, buxom, leggy blondes, brunettes and redheads. It was terrible."

"Why terrible?"

"I was a girl too."

The man rang the doorbell and when the psychiatrist opened it he saw that he wore a purple shirt, a seventeenth-century cape and a Napoleon hat. On his feet were spurs that jingle jangle jingle and tied around his waist was a braided silk rope which pulled a toy fire engine when he walked. In one hand he had a lollipop and in the other a jelly apple. "Doc," he said. "I come to talk to you about my brother."

"What are you doing wearing a wastepaper basket for a hat?"

"Listen, if I wanna throw my head away it's my business."

"He was no painless dentist."

"Why do you say that?"

"He yelled when I bit his finger."

"Now tell me, do you always stutter?"

"N-n-n-no d-d-d-doc. J-j-just when I t-t-t-talk."

The businessman didn't want to keep a luncheon appointment with the salesman so he decided to call him and tell him that illness had caused a postponement. "I'm very sick," he said on the phone. "I have laryngitis."

"Then why ain't you whispering?" asked the salesman.

"Why should I?" The businessman was surprised. "It ain't no secret."

My uncle founded the family fortune. He made a powder that you give to insects and it stuns 'em. Then you mail 'em to the factory and we kill 'em.

"It was visiting day at the asylum. "Is there anything I can get you?" asked his brother.

"Yes," the nut replied. "I'd like a watch that tells time."

"Doesn't your watch tell time?"

"No," he said dejectedly. "I have to look at it."

"Swell town you got. Lotta big men born here?"

"No. Only babies."

Resort: A snappy comeback.

"Why are you afraid of girls?"

"I'm not afraid of girls. I can lick any girl I ever met."

Things had reached the point where the doctor thought it best to use hypnosis. Now the patient was lying on the couch, completely relaxed and ready. It had taken months to successfully reach this stage.

The doctor turned the lights out, pinpointing the beam of a small flashlight on the patient's face. His other hand swung back and forth across the patient's face, in a circular motion, the reflected light from the watch he held there hitting the patient's eyes in a pre-set pattern.

"Abadaba sleep," said the psychiatrist. "Abadaba sleep. Abadaba sleep."

The patient sprang to his feet. "Doc," he yelled excitedly "It works. It works I say. My abadaba is asleep."

The ocean was so cold that when I came out someone complimented me on my blue serge suit.

The doctor had come to the conclusion that the man's main problem was self-delusion. "How do you make your living?" he asked.

"I built three million fabricated homes."

"THAT'S A LIE!"

"I told you it was fabricated."

I hit my wife with a chair. But I was thoughtful, it was an easy chair.

"He made violent love to me after he won my heart completely," she told the police officer. "I thought at last I'd found the one thing every woman dreams of. I gave him my all. My life, my love, my money, my soul. He took everything. And then drove off, leaving me along with bitter memories."

"The cad!"

"No. He took the Chevy."

The psychiatrist had recommended a visit to a farm as a means of therapy. "Throw yourself into it completely," he told the man. "Transfer your entire being into the life of a farmer. It will do you worlds of good. Can you milk a cow?"

"No," replied the patient. "I don't know which is hot and which is cold."

"Congratulations, my good man," said the doctor. "You're the proud father of twins."

"Twins!" he shouted excitedly. "Boys or girls?"

"Well—er—one's a boy and the other's a-a girl," the doctor hesitated. "Or maybe it's the other way around."

My wife died. Killed by a typographical error in the health hints.

The proper way to hunt elephants is simply to hide in the underbrush and make a noise like a peanut.

The psychiatrist leaned heavily on the bar and began to drink long, hard doubles. His face was wreathed in sorrow and he was, at the same time, ominously sad. Another psychiatrist happened by.

"John!" he exclaimed. "John! My good fellow. You don't seem to be yourself tonight. Care to tell me about it?"

"There isn't much to tell," John replied. "Remember that rich nut I was treating for years? The one who practically kept me in business from the start?"

"I certainly do. You mean the one who kept dreaming for thirty years that he was still in high school?"

John nodded.

"What happened?"

"Last week he graduated."

I was an incubator baby. Every Mother's Day I send flowers to an oil stove.

The speaker, making his first after-dinner speech, had barely started when he fainted from the excitement. "Quickly," a friend called to the host. "Bring me some ice and spirits of ammonia."

304

"Hey, that ain't nice," said the host. "He fainted and you want to mix yourself a drink."

"What does one get from a goose?"
"Pimples."

The oral IQ was proceeding quite well. The man seemed to have undergone a complete transformation from an idiot into his old self. The doctor was now trying to determine which was best.

"Can you tell me what the hump on the camel's back is for?" he asked.

"The old camel wouldn't be much use without it," came the reply.

"Why not?"

"You don't suppose people would pay twenty-five cents to see him if he didn't have a hump on do you?"

"Your name and place of birth," the nurse said to the patient.

"They call me Jersey City. I was born in Newark."

"Why didn't they call you Newark?"

"What kind of a name is that for a boy?"

Thirty days has September, April, June and November. All the rest have thirty-one except February, which has twenty-eight. Is that fair?

I practice smiling in front of a mirror and can't keep from laughing.

"My boy friend is in the hospital and I wrote him a note telling him I was coming up to see him tonight to surprise him."

"If you told him you were coming, where does the surprise come in?"

"He doesn't know I can write."

"Doc, there's something wrong with me."

"What is it?"

"I get dizzy reading a circular."

The bebop artist was invited to a private recital but arrived a little late. "What was that you just played?" he asked, to be polite.

"The end of Tchaikovsky's fifth opus," explained the musician, to be equally polite. "Shall I play the beginning?"

"No use now," said the bopster. "I know how it comes out."

I once won a newsboys' contest. I sold more newsboys than anybody else.

"I couldn't get up until twelve," the man told the couch doctor, in explaining his tardiness.

"What was the matter?"

"I was asleep."

I had a case of insomnia, but I wouldn't open it in front of daddy.

What is the Order of the Bath? First the water's too hot, then too cold. Then you're short of a towel. Then you slip on the soap, and finally, the telephone rings.

The mob was meeting the big guy, and what the big guy said, went. The buzzer rang and the Shiv went over to answer the door. He peeked through the slot in the frame, and, recognizing the visitor, allowed the panel to swing back. "Leave your umbrella at the door," Shiv told the visitor.

"I ain't got one," he answered.

"Then get one," the Shiv sneered. "The boss told me everyone must leave their umbrella at the door."

"Has a deer got a horn?"

"No. A deer has two horns."

"Then it must have been a car that ran over Uncle."

"Is my wife home?"

"No. Who shall I say called?"

It happened at a marijuana party. "I just flew in from the Coast," said a movie producer.

"Yeah?" queried his host. "By plane?"

Asylum inmate: "I've been abroad."

Second Asylum inmate: "I'm not interested in your private life."

The nut skipped merrily into the psychiatrist's office and gaily announced, "I took the elevator to the fortieth floor."

"The fortieth floor?" The receptionist was amazed. "But our office is only on the fourth floor."

"I know," said the happy one. "But I like to slide down the banisters."

There was a loud rap on the door and the psychiatrist hurried to answer it. "Doc," said a frightened voice. "I must speak to you about my brother. He breaks thermometers, drinks the mercury and throws the glass away."

"WHAT!" shrieked the horrified doctor. "That's the best part."

"What you got there?"
"A pawn ticket."
"Wish you had two. Then we could both go."

If I had my life to live over again I'd drop dead.

They asked me my views about the scriptures and St. Paul. I told them before I express my opinion about St. Paul I think we should hear from Minneapolis.

If I was insured I'd kill myself.

"You've been convicted of the same offense fourteen times. Aren't you ashamed of yourself?"
"No, sir. I don't think one ought to be ashamed of his convictions."

The man was a congenital coward. He therefore sought analysis to tell him why. "The other night is a typical example of what I mean," he informed the couch man.
"What happened then?"
"I heard a noise so I put a pillow over my head."
"Didn't it suffocate you?"
"No," said the coward. "But I'm way behind on my breathing."

I won a prize for saving fifty thousand box tops. They sent me a big box to put the box tops in.

"Can't find any soap or towels to wash with."
"Haven't you got a tongue?"
"Sure. But I ain't no cat."

I didn't know a trombone from a hole in the wall. Then I studied for fifteen years. Now I'm the only guy that can play a hole in the wall.

"What do you think is the motivating factor in your psychosis?"
"I once lived on nothing but water for a week."
"When was that?"
"On my way over to England."

"Hello, Bill."
"Hello."
"Gee, you got an answer for everything."

"I want a man like putty," said the gorgeous, lusty, beautiful blonde. "One that I can mold."
"I'm not putty," I said. "But I'm plenty mouldy."

The man rushed into the elevator. "Tenth floor," he shouted.
"There're only six floors in this building," advised the operator.
"Okay then," he said. "Take me up to the sixth floor. I'll walk the rest of the way."

Them seasick pills are no good. I took a box and I haven't been seasick yet.

The lap dog they sold me was a fake. The first time I sat in his lap he bit me.

Failing business had driven the textile man out of the industry and into an asylum, where his relatives came to visit him. They stood around for a while, and then—as the end of visiting hours approached—one of them asked, "What time is it?"

"Fifteen to," said the textile man.

"Fifteen to what?"

"I don't know," he replied. "Times got so bad I had to lay off one of the hands."

"Refuse me and I'll throw myself in the reservoir."

"That's for drinking."

"I'm not only heartsick. I'm thirsty too."

Life is wonderful. Without it you're dead.

I ate breakfast raw, lunch raw and supper raw, but they made me dress for dinner.

"You say you heard unusual sounds when you went into the grocery store. Describe them to me."

"I heard sardines talking in a can."

"What did they say?"

"Who ya shovin'—"

We played post office. All night long they kept saying there was a letter for me in the next room. I went in. It was only a girl.

The boys were sitting around doing a little bragging. It had been a good year in the garment center. "I just put up a fourteen-room mansion with a toilet in every room—and three swimming pools," said Seidman, the cloak and suit tycoon.

"Why three swimming pools?" Dubin, the accountant, was curious.

"One for people who like hot water, one for people who like cold water."

"What's the third one for?"

"That's for people who don't like to swim."

I tied her hair in knots but it didn't make her mad. She never even heard me take it out of the drawer.

She's very near-sighted. Lost her glasses. Now she's trying to knit a sweater out of spaghetti.

"What's the difference between orchids and geraniums?"

"They taste different."

I dropped my watch out of a second-story window onto a concrete pavement, and it ran for three days. Musta been scared.

I'm not bald. I'm just too tall for my hair.

Buddenbender was invited to the country estate of the influential Smillman for the weekend. After dinner the host outlined the plan of events for the following day. "We are going fox hunting," he declared. "We get up at four, breakfast at five, mount at six and commence the hunt at seven."

"I don't like it," said Bud.

"But why?" asked his puzzled host.

"Because," said Bud, "we get up at four and the fox don't get up till seven."

"Aren't you ashamed to stand here on the street, my good man, and beg?"

"Whaddaya want me to do? Open an office?"

I was invited to a dinner but my watch isn't going. It's on a diet.

"My kid is losing weight," said the worried father. "He gets plenty of sunshine, air and sleep."

"What do you feed him?"

"Hey, I knew I forgot something."

"What kind of weather did you have yesterday?"

"It was so foggy I couldn't see."

Title of a proposed article for *Time* magazine: "Why Play Handball by Hand When Everything Else Is Done by Machine."

I opened my mail by mistake. I thought I could read.

You can tell the age of a horse by the teeth. But who wants to bite a horse?

Two happy mothers were exchanging hints on how they care for their individual infants. "I bought five gallons of olive oil," said one. "Filled the baby's tub and set him in it."

"Did the olive oil help the baby's skin?"

"I don't know," said the mother. "We haven't been able to catch him yet."

I invented a nonhabit-forming sleeping pill. You don't wake up, that's why it isn't habit forming.

If soap is made of waste why don't we wash with garbage?

"How can you be so dumb and live?"

"I ain't tellin' ya."

312

I got a room at the Z. That's a little place back of the Y.

"Doctor," said the patient. "I'd like to take a picture with you. That'll teach my girl back home to go with girls."

It was indeed a rare case. The man kept insisting that he was, in reality, a female lamb chop. The psychiatrist questioned it.

"Do you mean to say," he said skeptically, "that lamb chops have sex?"

"Certainly."

"Then how can you tell a male lamb chop from a female lamb chop?"

"That, sir," said the patient, "would be of interest only to another lamb chop."

"What are you doing?"

"Drawing my bath."

"I paint a little myself."

I had a terrible accident as a child. I was hit on the hand by a falling napkin.

She didn't have a washing machine. She just sat in the bathtub with the laundry and kicked her feet around.

I wanted to get her a corsage, but I didn't know what size she wore.

Hollywood Story Conference:

"In the story you've just written, why does the hero go to the South Seas?"

"A million reasons."

"Give me one."

"He wants to camp out."

"This paper says it's going to rain today."

"Why don't you buy some other paper?"

The analysis was concluded. The man seemed perfectly content, normal and happy. The psychiatrist was happy with the job he'd done. He was about to bid the man adieu for the last time when the patient turned and said, "There's something—something I haven't told you. Doctor, I'm part Indian."

"Really?" The doctor was startled. "What part?"

"The part that sits around the fire."

"Are you a contributor to the *Atlantic Monthly?*"

"No. This is my first ocean voyage."

I enjoyed the hike in the country, but I had to walk most of the way.

Insurance: Something that costs you thousands of dollars so that when you're dead you'll have nothing to worry about.

My uncle is very superstitious. He won't work any week that has a Friday in it.

The psychiatrist was late for the appointment. He came barging in and was very apologetic. "Think nothing of it," said the patient. "I kept busy."

"How?" asked the doctor suspiciously.

"I was in the corner talking to myself."

"Was it an interesting conversation?"

"Not very. You know me."

"Darling, there's a man with the new telephone directory at the door."

"Tell him to go away. I haven't read the old one yet."

"I'm getting gray-haired from worrying."

"Why do you worry?"

"Cause I'm getting gray-haired."

It was a disastrous year for the farmers. The snow fell and fell and fell until finally the government relief agency had to step in and lend a hand. "It must have been terrible," said the government man to a farmer. "All that snow."

"Could have been worse," calmly answered the farmer. "My neighbor had more snow then me."

"How's that?" asked the government man.

"More land."

"Your mouth's open."

"Yeah, I know. I opened it myself."

I tried mustard plaster. Somehow I just can't get plastered on mustard.

It is recommended that you put sleeping pills in coffee so that the coffee doesn't keep you awake.

Benny arrived home to find the kitchen a mess of broken crockery.

"What happened?" he asked his wife.

"There's something wrong with this cookbook," she explained. "It says that an old cup without a handle will do for the measuring—and it's taken me eleven tries to get a handle off without breaking the cup."

I sent my brother a birthday cake, air mail. I wanted him to get it while the candles were still burning.

The boy was running around with too many women so the old man decided to send him to the leading psychiatrists. It was a long-drawn-out analysis and the bill was very high but he felt it was worth it if a cure was reached. Finally, when the son returned, he demanded to know what had been covered in the treatment.

"Did you tell the doctors how we caught you with the maid when you was ten?"

The son nodded.

"Did you tell them we couldn't keep a cook for the last ten years because of you? Twenty-three cooks we ran through?"

The son nodded.

"Did you tell them about the five models from the place, the thirty-three girls in college and what happened with the superintendent's wife?"

Again the son nodded.

"So tell me, what did they say?"

"They said I have homosexual tendencies."

The young bachelor appeared at the psychiatrist's office with his problem. "I've got pictures of Lana Turner, Marilyn Monroe, Betty Grable and Hedy Lamarr pasted all over my room."

"Then what's your trouble?" asked the doctor.

"All night long I keep dreaming about Gene Autry's horse."

Terrible tragedy on Highway 13. A tree surgeon ran into a tree and nearly fainted when he learned it was one of his patients.

My brother has a tapeworm. Comes from eating tape.

I just invented a convertible hearse. Before they lower you down you get a little tan.

An asylum inmate had been complaining about a cat in his stomach tearing around and clawing him something fierce. One day he got an attack of appendicitis and the surgeon decided this was a good time to effect a cure. He sent for a black cat, and when the inmate came out of the ether the doctor held up the animal and said, "You're okay now. Look what we got."

The inmate stared, grabbed his stomach and yelled, "You got the wrong cat. The one I swallowed was gray."

The great novelist had gone insane but now there seemed to be some hope for his recovery. For three months he'd been sitting at a typewriter in his room and pounding out a novel. At last he announced it was completed and brought it to the leading psychiatrist at the institution who grasped it eagerly and began to read:

"General Jones leaped upon his faithful horse and yelled, 'Giddap, giddap, giddap, giddap, giddap.'" Then the doctor thumbed through the rest of the book. "Why there's nothing here but five hundred pages of 'giddaps,'" he exclaimed.

"Yeah," said the writer. "Stubborn horse."

I've been reading a swell tome. It's called the phone book. Doesn't pull any punches. It names names.

The limousine pulled up in front of the nuthouse and the aristocratic-looking gentleman got out. "Is this an asylum for the insane?" he asked the gate attendant.

"Yes, sir," said the gateman.

"Do they take inmates upon their own recommendation?"

"How should I know? Why?"

"Well, you see, I've just gotten hold of a package of my old love letters and—"

Goldberg was suing Levy for money Levy owed him. When they put Levy on the stand he flattered Goldberg. "He's a gentleman, a scholar, a wonderful husband, a terrific father, a real friend in need, clean-cut indeed and I'm very proud to know him."

Goldberg told his lawyer to tell Levy that flattery would get him nowhere. Then Levy jumped up and said, "Judge, yer honor, I want you should throw out this case. I'm asking you as a special favor to throw it out. I didn't know vhat I vuz doink ven I borrow from Goldberg. I vuz crazy, I musta been."

"You seem sane to me," the justice replied.

"Judge," said Levy, bewildered. "I said vhat I said about Goldberg and you tink I am sane?"

"My brother is a great inventor. He just invented a cake of soap eight feet long and five feet wide."

"How do you lift it to lather yourself?"

"You don't. You just sit on it and slide up and down."

The man walked into the restaurant, ordered a cup of coffee and then proceeded to put twenty heaping spoonsful into the cup. Then he sipped daintily at the contents.

"Why don't you stir it?" the boss asked angrily.

"Why should I?" he said. "I don't like it sweet."

They laughed at Lincoln. But he went right ahead and built the highway.

318

I nearly got killed yesterday. I went to an antique show and said, "What's new?"

It was one of the greatest manhunts of all time and Detective O'Sherlock was hot on the trail of the killer. He trailed him into a department store, then he trailed him into a restaurant, then he trailed him into a trailer. But he lost him eventually.

"How in God's name did you lose him?" the chief roared angrily.

"I followed him into every hole in town," explained the great O'Sherlock, ace of the force. "Into everything from men's toiletries to men's toilets but I didn't follow him when he went into the movies. That's where I lost him."

"AND WHY DIDN'T YOU FOLLOW HIM INTO THE MOVIES?" the chief calmly queried, bursting a blood vessel.

"Because I already saw the picture."

Everybody should pay their taxes with a smile. I tried it but they wanted cash.

The man lay on the couch telling his psychiatrist a woesome tale.

"I see my brother, Doctor," he said. "He is walking down a long corridor, walking up thirteen steps into a green door. There are lots of people standing around. They're bandaging his eyes—ooh—Doctor, Doctor, what does it mean?"

"Well," said the psychiatrist, "if they ain't playing blind man's bluff he's in real trouble."

"I heard a knock on the door and thought it was my landlord so I jumped out the window onto the fire escape, but I was fooled."

"No landlord."

"No fire escape."

"What was the idea of kicking this man while he was tying his shoelaces? The officer tells me that you've been walking the streets kicking strangers while they were bending over tying their shoelaces. Why do you do it?"

"After all, Judge, a man must have a hobby of some kind."

Here is an excellent system for remembering telephone numbers. First think of cheese. That reminds you of Swiss. Swiss reminds you of Alps. Alps reminds you of mountains. Mountains remind you of ocean. Ocean reminds you of Columbus. Columbus discovered America in 1492. And my number is HIllside 7593.

"I must charge you for murder."

"All right. What do I owe you?"

I know a family of air pioneers. The father was the first to jump one thousand feet from an airplane. The mother was the first to jump two thousand feet from an airplane. The daughter was the first to jump three thousand feet from an airplane. Now the son is going to be the first to jump ten thousand feet from an airplane. You see he figures he has nothing to live for anyway. He has no family.

"Your honor, on the Fourth of July he threw fire-crackers at me, on Thanksgiving he smacked me with a turkey and on Christmas he conked me with a Christmas tree."

"What have you got to say for yourself?"

"After all, Judge, what's the sense of holidays if a guy can't do a little celebrating?"

The judge was pronouncing sentence.

". . . remand you to Glocca-morra State Penitentiary, where you will be put to death in the electric chair the week of August 3. And may God have mercy on your soul. Now, just for your own information, visiting hours are from two to four."

"You mean you'll let me go visiting?"

The nuthouse was organizing a swing band and invited the inmate to join. "But I don't know a bassoon from an oboe," he protested.

"That's all right," said the leader. "We don't use them stringed instruments."

"The best cure for absent-mindedness," said the professor, "is to associate names with things. For example, if you were to meet a gentleman by the name of Baker, associate his name with cooking. If you should meet a gentleman by the name of Gold, associate it with jewelry. And so on."

"What happens if I meet a fellow by the name of Mabenclabber?"

"Go back and speak to Baker."

"I have a most unusual watch to offer you. It never needs any repairs or winding. It has no hands, no sweep second dial and no face."

"But how can you tell the time?"

"That's easy. Ask anybody."

The woman had been undergoing psychiatric treatment for some time when she asked the doctor if it was all right for her to go to Florida. He gave his approval. A short time later the psychiatrist received the following telegram: HAVING A WONDERFUL TIME. WHY?

The lawyer was trying to explain the seriousness of the charge against his client. "Perjury," he said. "What does a cat do when it licks up its milk? PURR."

"That's right," said the client. "They purr."

"Now what do they call twelve men who decide the fate of a criminal?"

"A jury."

"Correct. Now put them together and what have you got?"

"Twelve men who lap up cats' milk."

"I object to everything he said," shouted the lawyer.

"Why?" asked the judge.

"It makes it sound as if I was listening."

The police chief hurriedly phoned his wife to say he'd be late for dinner. "I'm having police headquarters searched. It's that Bureau of Missing Persons," he explained. "We can't find it."

An icicle is a kind of permanent wave.

"Doc, remember the girl I told you about when we first started the treatments eight months ago," the patient said as he relaxed on the couch. "You know, the girl whose hair I used to stick in the inkwell."

"Oh, yes. Ever see her?"

"Only when I want to fill my fountain pen."

Song Title: "I'm Dancing with Tears in My Eyes 'cause the Girl in My Arms Is a Boy."

"I wish you'd fix this cuckoo clock."

"But this isn't a cuckoo clock."

"Yes, it is. It just struck thirteen."

"Who goes there?"

"You won't know me. I'm new here."

"I was getting ten dollars a week and the boss just doubled my salary."

"Yeah? What are you getting now?"

"Ten dollars every two weeks."

Finklestein was frantic. For five weeks now he hadn't been able to do anything in the way of business because he'd forgotten the combination to the safe. His partner, Kanubowitz, had gone away on an extended motor trip and there was no word from him. Then one day the phone rang. "Izzy," Finklestein shouted into the phone, "thank God you called. I can't do any business. I had to lay off the whole shop, fire the salesmen, refuse orders from our biggest accounts and just stay here in the office and wait for your call."

"What happened?" Kanubowitz asked.

"It's the safe. I forgot the combination."

"That's simple. Turn once left and twice right."

"But how about the numbers?"

"It doesn't matter," Kanubowitz said. "The lock's broke."

After the treatment was over John spoke very calmly to the doctor. "When I was a kid," he said, "they told me if I didn't stop biting my nails I'd grow up to be an idiot."

"Well," said the doc, "then why didn't you stop?"

My brother is a great inventor. He just invented glass-bottom boats for fish. So they can see how big the fellow is they got away from.

An autocrat is a crat that drives a car.

The phone rang at 4 A.M.
"What do you want?" he shouted into the instrument.
"Nothing," was the reply.
"Then why did you call me in the middle of the night?"
"Because the night rate is cheaper."

Two Irishmen were standing in a bar. "Ye say ye fell from a window. How far was it?" one asked.
"Tin stories," replied the other.
"What did ye think of on yer way down?"
"Whoi, I didn't think of nothin' until I passed the fifth story. Thin I remember I left me pipe on the window sill."

Cinderella: "Godmother, must I leave the ball at twelve?"
Fairy: "You'll not go at all if you don't stop swearing."

I know a cannibal medicine man who can grow hair. Well, he can't exactly grow hair but he can shrink your head and make the little you have look like more.

The psychiatrist was advising the unhappy man.
"Get a girl who likes to do the things you do," he said.
"Aw, Doc," protested the patient. "What would I want with a girl who likes to whistle at other girls?"

Margie went to the psychiatrist with her psychosis. "Doctor, when I'm in the next room I develop a dreadful fear. I'm so afraid I won't hear if the baby falls out of the crib. What can I do about this?"

"Easy," said the head doctor. "Just take the carpet off the floor."

The woman rushed out of the house and ran smack into her next-door neighbor. "Going somewhere?" asked the neighbor.

"Yes. I'm baking a cake from a recipe I heard on the radio. It said to put all the ingredients in a bowl and then beat it for five minutes. Sounds silly, but I'm on my way."

The tail gunner was being tried for dereliction of duty and the court-martial proceedings were very stern. "Tell us what you heard in the headset," the court demanded.

"I heard a squadron leader hollering, 'Japanese planes coming in at five o'clock—Japanese planes coming in at five o'clock—'"

"Then why didn't you do something?"

"Why should I? It was only four-thirty."

The judge was being interviewed by *Time* magazine.

"How do you manage to render more decisions than any other judge today?" the reporter asked.

"I hear the plaintiff and render my decision."

"Don't you listen to the defendant?"

"I used to, but I found it confused me."

"In the moonlight your teeth are like pearls."

"And when were you in the moonlight with Pearl?"

The tall, beautiful, blond, blue-eyed secretary was explaining to her roommate exactly why she'd consented to accompany her boss to Florida. "He's giving me 500,000 palarados," she said.

"But we have no such money," protested her girl friend.

"I know," said Blondie, "but if we ever do I'll be rich."

The police chief was angry. "Now you've been on the force for two years and never made an arrest," he shouted at Patrolman Pat. "I'm gonna give you one more chance. Someone is stealing Squire Davis's apples. Go up there and catch the thief."

So Pat goes up there and around midnight he pounces on a masked man in the orchard trying to sneak away with a pack on his back. He opens the bag and finds it contains valuable silver so he returns it to the masked man. "Sorry, my mistake," Pat says. "But you can thank your stars it wasn't apples."

"Didn't I tell you to notice when the soup boiled over?"

"I did. It was ten-thirty."

"Call me a taxi," said the fat man.

"Okay," said the doorman. "You're a taxi, but you look more like a truck to me."

I went to the country on my vacation and the little birds sang so merrily under my window every morning that when I left I went out and thanked them for the beautiful melodies. The landlord came out and said, "I hope you don't think those birds were singing for you?"

"Why, of course I do," I told him.

"Those birds are singing for me," he said, angry-like.

I knew I was right and we got into a big fight over it. When we were brought before the judge he fined us both $10. "Those birds," he said, "were singing for me."

A man walked into a boat store and announced that he wanted to buy the front of a boat and wanted to know how much it would cost.

"Well now, a whole boat is $100,000. A half would therefore be $50,000," the clerk said, thinking it was a joke. "Then there is a charge of $15,000 for sawing it in half. Making a grand total of $65,000."

"What will you do with the rear end of a yacht?" the man asked the clerk.

"Sell it to a man with a short dock. And what will you do with the front half?"

"It's like this," the man said, whipping out his checkbook. "I'm a perfectionist of sorts. My daughter is christening a battleship next week and I'd like her to have a little practice."

"This is a waffle iron. Now we can eat waffles."
"I don't think I've ever eaten any ironed waffles."

"Your new girl looks like a hundred."
"But she just had her face lifted."
"Maybe she dropped it again."
"Yeah. This time she broke it."

She sat there with her fur neckpiece. When I went to remove it she screamed. How should I know it grew out of her neck?

"Well," yawned the moth as it slid off the overcoat, "I enjoyed that nap."

Chinese checkers are census takers in Chinatown.

A grimitzer is the lowest form of human being. Runs errands for a kibitzer.

"This morning one of my guests put on his bathing suit, dived out the window and landed on his head. Badly bruised."
"No water?"
"No pool."

"Do you claim this man hit you with malice aforethought?" asked the lawyer.
"Look, smartypants, you can't mix me up that easy," the witness replied. "I said he hit me with a Ford and I stick to it."

It was during World War I, when Pat was in France, that his wife wrote to him. "There isn't an able-bodied man left in Ireland," she said, "and I'm gonna have to dig up the garden meself."
Pat wrote back. "Don't dig up the garden. That's where the guns are."
The letter was censored and soldiers came to the house and dug up every square foot of the garden. "I don't know what to do," Pat's wife wrote him. "Soldiers came and dug up the whole garden."
Patrick wrote back, "Plant spuds."

"This picture doesn't do you justice."
"It's not justice I want. It's mercy."

MECHANICS...science... automobiles...inventions

(My car is so old they gave me license plates with Roman numerals.)

"I just invented a machine that does the work of fifty men."

"What is it?"

"Fifty women."

I've never been pinched for going too fast, but I've been slapped.

There's a remarkable new domestic appliance on the market. You push a button and it lights the gas by rubbing two sticks together.

"I had a flat tire last night."

"I saw her. She was a mess."

Change my auto license from 1975 to 1976 . . . I just hit another man.

Daddy is missing for three years now. When last seen he was standing in a safety zone on Hollywood Boulevard.

"Can you imagine that guy, offering us $9.00 for the car!"

"He must be crazy. Let's take advantage of him."

This is the Machine Age. The only thing people are doing by hand is scratching themselves.

Uncle has a terrific business. He makes dice out of Ivory Soap—for floating crap games.

She gave me one of the new kind of pens. Fill it with water—it writes under ink.

I like to take my girl's husband along with us when we go riding. He's a mechanic, in case something goes wrong with the car.

The patient had his phobia concerning automobiles and the psychiatrist was old-fashioned. "If you had a horse you wouldn't have to drive a car," he told the patient.
"Aw, go on, Doc," he scoffed. "Horses can't drive cars."

Grandfather patented a rip cord for pajamas—so you could bail out of bed.

Fluid drive: When there's a drip at the wheel.

I had a terrible accident. My mother-in-law fell asleep in the back seat.

There's a new device on the market to keep the inside of a car quiet. It fits right over her mouth.

"Uncle tried to make a new kind of car. He took wheels from a Cadillac, radiator from a Ford, tires from a Plymouth—"
"What'd he get?"
"Two years."

I received a lovely gift. A pen that lasts longer than a lifetime. If you die it writes six feet underground (it's also known as a pallpoint).

Years ago you lived till you died, not till you got run over.

Navy surplus vacuum cleaner: It whistles and picks up everything in sight.

"I bought a second-hand hearse."
"Why?"
"When I drive I like to stretch out."

I'm selling my car and becoming a pedestrian. I got guts.

They just invented a new dandruff to stop falling Vaseline.

"Here's a ticket for parking."
"Thanks. Where's it playing?"

There's something new out now that's terrific for people who can't sleep. A mattress soaked in ether.

The car traveled along at a five-mile-per-hour clip. "At least we won't be arrested for speeding," the driver told her husband.
"No," he agreed. "But we might for loitering."

She came home rather late. "Oh, sweetheart," she called, "your car's on Main Street."
"Why didn't you bring it home?"
"Couldn't," she called. "It's too dark out there to find all the parts."

"My wife was arrested for parking."
"For parking?"
"Yeah. For parking one car on top of the other."

My car was manufactured second-hand.

No wonder luck is tough. Too many autos. Can't find any horseshoes any more.

I rode twenty thousand miles in a jeep and got decorated with the Order of the Purple Seat.

I put a penny in one of them weighing machines. A card came out. It said, "You are intelligent and trustworthy"—got my weight wrong too.

"Why do traffic lights turn red?"
"You'd turn red too if you had to stop and go in the middle of the street."

Uncle invented a sun dial that keeps daylight savings time.

I got a pen with a meatball point—writes under gravy.

Remember a while back when the cars were all coming through with wooden bumpers. In those days when a guy was about to hit you he didn't blow his horn. He yelled, "Timber."

Jesse James was the first person to be killed by a Ford.

The lady's car couldn't get started and traffic was tied up for blocks. The light turned green, then yellow, then red. "Whatsa madda, lady," shouted the officer. "Don't you like any of our colors?"

"Your engine's smoking."
"Well, it's old enough."

"YOU'RE TRYING TO BRIBE AN OFFICER OF THE LAW! KNOW WHAT I'M GOING TO GIVE YOU FOR IT?"

"A receipt?"

There's a pen that writes for fifteen years without running dry, but your hands fall off.

The woman protested her innocence to the judge. "I was not going fifty miles an hour," she said indignantly. "Not twenty, not fifteen, not ten. In fact when the officer came up I was almost at a standstill."

"I must stop you," warned the judge, "before you back into something—$10 fine."

He invented a machine that did the work of one hundred men, but nobody would buy it. Took a thousand men to work it.

"Caught my fingers in the milking machine."

"Hurt?"

"No. But my pinky's fourteen inches long."

Jeep: A cocktail shaker with three speeds.

The newest cars travel faster than sound. You'll be in the hospital before you even start the motor.

I hook a trailer on my car when I come to town so I have a place to eat and sleep while I'm looking for a parking space.

I'm working on something revolutionary, animated book ends. It consists of two elephants with an electric attachment. When you remove a book the elephants charge at each other—and close the gap at once.

There's a machine that makes a suit out of lint, but it's no good. It picks up blue serge.

The cab skidded around the corner on two wheels and then shot up the block. "Not so fast, driver," warned the fare. "Not so fast, I say. Do you hear? This is the first time I've driven in an automobile."

"Ya got nuttin' on me," said the driver. "Dis is my foist time too."

"I have no windshield on my car."
"How do you keep the wind from hitting your face?"
"I ride on a bus."

I'm letting my little son drive the car . . . he's still too young to be trusted as a pedestrian.

Father has the first dollar he ever made and the police have the machine he made it with.

The latest automobile will have glass floors so when you run over somebody you can see if it's anyone you know.

An aviator coming down in a parachute met an old lady floating on a cloud. "Hey," shouted the pilot. "Have you seen a Spitfire going down?"

"No," said the old lady. "Have you seen a gas stove going up?"

My wife is learning how to drive the car. Next week she learns how to aim it.

Everybody's crazy to ride with me . . . to tell you the truth I'm a little nuts myself.

It's amazing how they know where to dig for oil—just where the gas station is.

"When the hand of the woman driving in front of you is out, what does it mean?"
"She wants to see if it is raining."

"You were going one hundred miles an hour," reprimanded the judge. "Weren't you afraid of hitting another car?"
"What? On the sidewalk?"

My car works on buttons. I sent it to the auto laundry and it came back with all the buttons missing.

Up where I come from we got no hankerin' for those new-fangled city devices like can openers, for instance. Oh, we got a lotta canned foods up our way—no good cook would be without them—but we just don't go fer those metal openers. They spoil the food. My wife, fer instance, has one buck tooth. She sticks it on the edge of the can and I chase her around till it's opened.

A pedestrian is a man who walks on the suicide of the street.

Auto suggestion: Let's park here.

My business was a dismal failure. I was making red mouse traps, but the mice wouldn't go in. They were afraid of the cover charge.

I told the cop I was speeding to get to Chicago so he arrested me for drunken driving.

My car is so fast the payments are three months behind.

There's a new kind of pen. It just doesn't write.

Thanks to the Democratic depression cars are thicker than red spots on a measles patient.

I bought a car with a glass bottom in the rear. So my mother-in-law can see the white line.

His wife had just learned to drive the car and now they were out in the suburbs racking along at eighty. "Doesn't speeding over the beautiful country make you glad you're alive?" she asked.

"Glad?" He raised an eyebrow. "Glad isn't the word for it. I'm amazed."

"This ticket to the West Coast costs $132 and allows you a three-day hangover in Chicago."

"How much will it cost if I don't get drunk in Chicago?"

I stand behind every car I sell. I help push it.

Father had three cars in five days. You see he uses the phone next door in an auto showroom and he doesn't like to walk out without buying something.

Father has a great business. He makes liquid garters, to hold up liquid stockings.

We were the first people to make shoes with built-in birdseed, for pigeon-toed people.

I hadn't been able to get the top down for years but my wife finally did. She drove fast under a low bridge.

"This is an AC–DC radio. Know what AC–DC means?"
"Sure. AC means around the city and DC means distant countries!"

Among the family inventions is included a thing to keep ice from melting another piece of ice. And a medical typewriter to type blood.

To some husbands taking a wife is like buying a used car. They don't know they're stuck till the paint comes off.

The car knocked down the man on the country road. "Don't just stand there," shouted the driver to a gaping farmer. "Go into town and get the village doctor."
"Can't," said the farmer.
"Why not?"
"That is the village doctor under the car."

The poor old inventor—never really successful—was a bit mixed up those days. So the family sent him to a prominent psychiatrist. He told the doctor about his more glorious days.
"Doctor, I once invented a great device. Would have made me a fortune. It was a new kind of revolving door."
"What happened?"
"It went around so fast that it inhaled me."

There's a new special under-the-car mirror for fastidious people who want to make sure their ties are straight after they get knocked down.

"You've got quite a load on. You're not going to walk home in that condition?"

"Course not. I'm gonna drive."

Uncle invented a machine that could take a car apart in thirty seconds. It's called a locomotive.

"How did you smash up the car?"

"I hit a pedestrian."

"That wrecked the car like this?"

"The pedestrian was on a bus."

The state is abandoning the electric chair. Henceforth criminals will have to cross Times Square against the light.

The sailor was out with his new girl. Suddenly the car stopped. The girl reached into her handbag and took out a flask.

"WOW!" said the sailor boy. "What's that?"

"Gasoline," she replied.

I believe it's true that Methuselah lived nine hundred years. They had no autos then.

His mother-in-law was at the wheel. She turned the corner and suddenly screeched to a halt.

"What you stopping for?" he asked from the floor.

"The road map says to turn north and follow the trolley," she said. "We'll have to wait till one comes along."

"How fast are we going?"

"Can't tell. The needle's pointing to my beneficiary."

Auntie was pinched for stopping on a dime . . . it was in a cop's pocket.

He nicknamed his mother, who was just learning to drive, "O-ma the Dent Maker."

"If a farmer raises a thousand bushels and sells it for $10.00 a bushel, what will he get?"
"An automobile."

"I would like a driver's license for my horse."
"What makes you think we'd give a driver's license to a horse?"
"Well, you give them to jackasses."

The best way to do away with back-seat driving is to install a dual exhaust system—with one exhaust leading into the back seat.

It was a desperate chase but the police car was catching up to the bank robbers when suddenly it swerved into a gas station, from which point the cop driving phoned his chief. "Did you catch them?" the chief asked excitedly.
"They were lucky," replied the cop. "We were closing the gap, only half a mile away, when I noticed our five hundred miles was up and we had to stop and change our oil."

"How's your wife getting along with her driving?"
"She took a turn for the worse last week."

"This car cost me three thousand bananas," the man said, leaning over the mechanic's shoulder.
"You're lucky," the mechanic replied. "You might have paid money."

My wife has driven the car fifty thousand miles and never once had her hand on the wheel.

My uncle's car was so old they issued it upper and lower plates.

"A man took my car."
"Did you notify the sheriff?"
"He's the one who took it."

"I passed my eye test and got my driver's license."
"Was it tough?"
"Not very. They told me to put my hand over my eye and count my fingers."

Tree: Something that stands in the same place for hundreds of years and suddenly jumps in front of a car.

SPORTS AND GAMBLING

(I caught a fish so big I got up in the middle of the night and called myself a liar.)

I got a sure thing in the fifth. The only way it could lose, I was sure, was if someone turned the track around. Someone turned the track around.

The gambler was invited to the fancy houseparty. The butler was announcing the guests. "Swinburne III, Vanderbilt II—"

"Let's get outta here," he said to his pal. "There ain't a winner in the joint."

"Who won the bet, you or him?"
"After he leaves here he has a date in Macy's window."

We hunted grizzlies in the Rockies and bagged nothing but my pants.

The golfer was brought into the hospital suffering from sunstroke. The nurse began to read his temperature. "102—103—104—"

"Hey, Doc," whispered the suffering sport. "What's par for this hospital?"

The art of wrestling is a most improved sport. Today wrestlers grunt and groan much louder than they used to.

Samson, with all his strength, couldn't break away from the links.

The following announcement interrupted the calm day of swimming at the swanky pool:

"Will the gentleman with the blue and pink trunks report to the locker room. You forgot them—"

Percy was walking through the paddock with his terrier when one of the entries tapped him on the shoulder. "Put all you can raise on me today," said the mare. "I'm a shoo-in."

"That's the first time I ever heard a horse talk," said Percy.

"Me too," said the dog.

In ancient times boxing wasn't as modern as it is today.

The horse was named "Fleabag"—he was scratched.

"So this is your trophy room. But where are the fish?"

"They all got away."

Bridge: A game of mind over chatter.

I've been skating for hours on end. Maybe I ought to take lessons.

"When I was your age I thought nothing of a ten-mile walk."

"Well, I don't think much of it either."

Magellan went around the world in 1521—which isn't so many strokes when you consider the distance.

It was the match race of the year, between two of the greatest horses of the era, Ruptured Snail and Lazy

Bones. Bones took it by ten lengths. When Snail got back to the paddock the other horses gave him a big razzing. "Listen, wise guys," Snail said. "If I had as many rests as he had I could have won by plenty too."

To some people the largest diamond is the ace.

My favorite outdoor sport is helping a dame into a cab.

We went fishing. Had no bites, but plenty of nips.

"Why do you play golf?"
"To aggravate myself."

If fish were as big as the stories told about 'em—grocers would have to sell sardines in garbage cans.

What a football team! What an attack! Even their breath is offensive.

The man sent the following wire to his friends to let them know about the poker game: THERE WILL BE AN EXHIBITION OF FINE DRAWINGS AT THE NEWTON HOTEL TONIGHT.

All I ever got from hot tips was some nasty money burns.

They made him judge of the flower show—because he smells so good.

"We need a fifth for bridge."
"You mean a fourth?"
"No. A fifth. We're thirsty."

The bookie was testifying before the crime-investigating committee to determine the honesty of horse racing. "The boss gimmie $250 to try the fix," he said. "D'ere wuz four horses in dis race so I gives da jockeys fifty bucks apiece."

"That's only $200," interjected a brilliant senator.

"I know," said the book. "I need da udder fifty in case it's a photo finish. Tuh fix da photographer."

My horse was winning all the way. Suddenly he saw a lady horse—and stopped to tip his jockey.

The crowd was on its feet to watch Battler put the finishing touches to Killer Kohen and become the new champion of the world. When the fight was over the sports announcer rushed through the ropes, grabbed Battler and shoved a mike in his face.

"I ain't got nuttin' tuh say," said the Battler. "I'm an orphan."

They invited me to play water polo and I can't even ride a horse.

I got the hardest luck. Even when I'm cheating I can't win.

It was a very affectionate race. The horse hugged the rail, the jockey had his hands around the horse's neck— and I kissed my money good-bye.

Marilyn Monroe yelled "fore" on the course—and eight or ten showed up.

"You're a fine horse, coming in twelfth," bawled the trainer.

347

"I can't help it," protested the horse. "Thirteen is my unlucky number."

The two hunters sat in their boat, hidden from the view of any ducks that might happen by. They waited and waited. Suddenly they heard a noise in the growth alongside them and upon parting the reeds found another hunter—cockeyed drunk and working on the death of another fifth. "Hey," they warned. "This is our spot. Get the hell downstream."

The drunk said nothing. He just killed the bottle and then paddled two miles away.

A single duck came skimmering by a short time later. The two hunters each fired two shots and missed. Then they watched downstream as the drunk took one shot and bagged it.

They paddled down to offer congratulations. "Say," they told him, "that was pretty fast. How'd you do it?"

"Aww—" said the drunk. "With all them ducks up there, how could I miss."

The man walked over to his bag and pulled out the club he wanted after hurriedly scanning the distance. "You're gonna use a putter three hundred and fifty yards away?" asked the caddie.

"Listen," said the man. "When I want a surveyor I'll ask you."

The horse I bet on ran such a lousy race that his parents are turning over in their glue bottles.

Cardroom: Where men are men and spades are double.

The Scotsman wore a black band on his sleeve . . . he was in mourning for a lost golf ball.

. . . and so it came to pass, as the gambler would say.

I own a model horse. He poses for glue bottles.

"This horse is over a hundred years old, dear."
"You're looking in *my* mouth."

Fights ain't like a wedding. In a fight you don't know who will lose.

"My girl has an archery set."
"Has she a quiver?"
"Yeah. But black coffee fixes her up."

I always thought horse racing was the national pastime . . . then one day I saw *Playboy*.

"Some champ," complained Bruiser's wife. "Can't even put his baby to sleep."

My wife took up gardening. All she grew was tired.

The runner rounded base and headed for third as the outfielder uncorked a tremendous peg from deep center. Ball and runner arrived at the hot corner in a cloud of dust. "You're out!" shouted the umpire.
"I'm not out!" roared the angry runner.
"You're not?" The ump was surprised. "Well, just take a look in tomorrow's paper."

Father was a boatman. I always heard him say, "I'm going out for a schooner."

Golf helped the actor in one way. It gave him something to lie about besides his salary.

First prize: $2,000.
Second prize: $1,000.
Third prize: $500.
In case of ties: ties will be given.

The boozer took careful aim at the bird, but hit a frog. He picked it up, studied it, scratched his head and said, "Well, anyhow I knocked its feathers off."

A golf ball is a golf ball no matter how you putt it.

I came from a family of great gamblers. My name is PL9-0097—named after my father's bookmaker. Mother's name is Nick the Greek.

"Did you see the Straight of Magellan?"
"Yeah. But he beat me. I had only two pair."

"You know, Henrietta," said the impassioned courtier, "every time I see you my heart beats faster. I feel the urge to do bigger and better things. I feel so strong and virile. Do you know what that means?"
"Sure," said Hennie. "It means in about five minutes you and me is going to have a wrestling match."

Book title: *Learn to Skate in Eight Easy Sittings.*

I'd have gone around the course in par, but I couldn't knock over the flag in the eighteenth hole.

"Loan me $10," said the horse to the trainer. "I wanna bet on myself."
"Have you got $10?"
"Sure," said the horse. "But you don't think I'd bet my own money do you?"

I lost a big wad—that's the last time I'm gonna bet chewing gum.

Safari. Africa. Big-game hunting—and the woman was driving the handsome white hunter crazy with her barrage of questions.

"How will I know if I trap a tiger?" she asked.

"By his yellow coat and stripes, madam."

"And how will I know if I trap a lion?"

"By the brown color and his flowing mane."

"And how will I know if I trap an elephant?"

"That, madam," sighed the white hunter, "is the easiest of all. By the slight odor of peanut on his breath."

"My father was a runner in his younger days."

"I know. I went through the war with him."

He was the cream of fighters. He got whipped.

She went hunting for rhinoceros and shot two of my dogs. Next day she shot two more of my dogs. Today she's going hunting with a rhinoceros to hunt for dogs.

The drunk saw the duck hunter lying in the brush with gun poised toward the direction of the high-flying flock in the distance.

"Shay, mishter," advised the drunk. "Don't waisht a shot. The fall'll kill 'em."

Polo is golf with fertilizer.

"What happened to your uncle's boat?"

"Ever notice that big rock at the entrance to the Golden Gate?"

"Yes, I have."

"Well, he didn't."

Sister is going with a baseball player. He's so short a grounder goes over his head.

It was a clean fight. The manager threw in the towel every round.

Kibitzer: A guy who'll bet your shirt on somebody else's hand.

She follows sports—and vice versa.

I picked up two girls at the track. It was my daily double.

"Shall I put chlorine in the water?"
"Sure, push her in if she needs a bath."

The only ones who think baseball is the greatest American pastime are those who never strolled through the park at night.

Duke was telling the boys in the poolroom about his day at the track. "I put my dough on this long shot, twenty to one. Comin' into the far turn she was bunched up with the leaders. Twenty to one and I got ten bucks down. They come thunderin' down the line—their noses neck in neck." Duke stopped to wipe away a bead of perspiration.
"What happened?" asked an excited friend.
"It was a photo finish."
"How'd it come out?"
"Don't know," said Duke. "The pictures ain't back from the drugstore yet."

I love the rustle of leaves in the spring—racing form leaves.

I have a terrific formula for beating the horses. Bet more money on the winners than on the losers.

He was married six times in two years—he's on a losing streak.

"I box to reduce. Lost four already."
"Pounds?"
"No. Teeth."

"I was at the dog track and won three races."
"Bet you were tired after all that running."

"My daddy fell through the ice."
"Was he drowned?"
"No. But he was badly diluted."

My wife enjoys sports and anything else that calls for an argument.

There was an ancient city buried under our local golf course. The Sunday golfers dug it up.

We played pinochle golf—a dollar a hundred.

He was one of those prizefighters with artistic leanings. Thus, when the world-renowned painter showed up at the gymnasium, he was awed. "Say—uh—er"—he hesitated—"I'd like you to paint a full-length picture of me on canvas."
"Fine," agreed the artist. "When is your next fight?"

I sat there for hours with my chin in my hands, practicing for the checker championship.

Uncle is a great hunter. He killed two flies with one hit.

Dwarf: A jockey with a long beard.

"What was your biggest scare in football?"
"When I played center on the Navy team with an all-Greek backfield."

I always win at cards but never at the track. It's hard to get a horse up your sleeve.

She went on one of them live-bait boats and caught a fish weighing 180 pounds. The wedding is in June.

One horse can carry more money on its nose than the stage coach carried in all its history.

"What do you call the last three hairs on a dog's tail?"
"Dog hair."

"My uncle went hunting with a marriage license. He caught a bear and the game warden asked him to show his license. So my uncle, the clever one, showed him the marriage license."
"What happened?"
"He had to marry the bear."

The man stood before the bar of justice. "Have you ever taken the oath?" asked the judge. Then noting the quizzical look on the fellow's face, added, "Do you know how to swear?"
"Oh yes, sir," he replied. "I'm your caddie."

I always wanted to be a gambler. As a kid I used loaded tiddlywinks.

In two words my favorite sport is po lo.

I got in my daily dozen—twelves games of pool.

The coach says to me, "Tex—grab that ball and run down the field with it."
So I grabbed it and ran ninety yards with nary a one of 'em layin' a hand on me. When I ran back the coach says, "Okay, now take off your spurs and let me see you do it."

Marriage is a gamble. They ought to sell the licenses out of a pari-mutuel machine.

I was in the saddle ten hours. I got the highest bunions in Prospect Park. Big? When I sit down I teeter.

He was punching the bag—and she told him he was no gentleman.

The poor gambler was now under the care of a prominent psychiatrist. Horse racing was his undoing. "I lost all on the gee gees," he told the doctor. "And the lousy part of it is I got all my tips right from the horse's mouth."
"I wouldn't believe anything a talking horse told me," soothed the doctor.
"That's just it, Doc—neither did I," moaned the gambler. "I made them put it in writing."

I made some great runs on the gridiron and never spilled a drop.

Notice on the bulletin board at the wrestling arena: "There Will be a Rehearsal for Tonight's Bout."

"When a lion rushes at you, what is better than presence of mind!"
"Absence of body."

My girl likes sports, she's been engaged to four of 'em.

I bet on a horse that came in so late they had to pay the jockey time and a half.

"Lady Godiva was the first lady jockey."
"Did she win?"
"No. But she certainly showed."

He was the kind of a guy who would bet on anything —provided he was sure of winning. "I'll bet my wife's first words will be 'My dear' when I get home," he said to Lucky.

Lucky took him up on it and they bet $100. When they got to the sport's house he stuck his head in the door and called, "My dear, I'm home."

"MY DEAR BE HANGED," roared his wife. "WAIT TILL I GET YOU INSIDE."

Spring is here. We started spring cleaning. She went to the attic and I went to the track.

"My daddy is eighty-six and has twenty children. Don't you think I should notify the papers?"
"Not yet. Why don't you wait for the final score?"

I won the Davis Cup, donated by the Davis Super Market.

"I guess you don't like me."

"Say, if I could guess as good as that I'd do nothing but play the horses."

They call my favorite fighter "Sweet Chariot"—he always swings low.

Basketball players are the only ones who can dribble and still look neat.

The drunk strayed into the Vegas gaming room and plunked down ten cents at the swanky roulette table. "Hey, mister," said the croupier, "we don't bet that kind of money here."

"Okay," said the drunk. "Take any part of it."

I knew there was something wrong when the jockey got inside the horse.

The horse was so weak I didn't know whether to play him to win, place or live.

He behaved very nicely at the post, even after the others left.

In college I developed a bad case of athlete's lip . . . from blowing up footballs.

"Son," said the father, "if you must indulge in horse-play—take up polo."

"I'm surprised that fellow that married the tall, blond, luscious, rich woman hasn't applied for a divorce."

"Does a man with four aces howl for a new deal?"

I bet on a polite horse. He kept holding out his hoof on the turns.

"What do you call a man who rides a horse?"
"That depends on how close he comes to me."

The girl was about to take her first horseback ride. "That's an adorable creature," she said, pointing to a chestnut stallion.
"That horse has never been ridden," said the groom.
"Oh, goodie," she cried gleefully. "We'll learn together."

I stopped playing with the hockey team. They finally got a real puck.

I always pay my gambling debts with a smile and hope they spend the money on doctors.

When I rode the horse they said I was a tenderfoot, but I made the grade a little higher up.

The lady saw the little boy peeking through a knothole. "Come with me, little boy," said the lady, who was really the wife of the club owner. "I'll get you inside."
"Aww—" said the kid, "How're you gonna get me in?"
"Really, we'll get in. I got lots of drag."
The kid studied her closely. "I know," he said after awhile, "but how you gonna get it over the fence.

I went out hunting with a bird dog, a pointer, a setter and a big bag. In three hours I came back and the bag was full. In it was a bird dog, a pointer and a setter.

"I shoot in the high three-sixties."
"I shoot in the low four-eighties."
"Okay. We'll play for a nickel a hundred."

My idea of royalty is a pair of jacks or better.

I took my horse to Florida, put green sunglasses on him
. . . and he ate up $30,000 worth of beach.

"I'll bet you've been at my whiskey again, Charles."
"Pardon me, sir, but I never bet."

It looked as if this long shot was gonna come through
at last.
Then suddenly he turned around, saw another horse's
face for the first time and dropped dead.

My girl is like a horse. She says "Nay, nay" all the
time.

Golf is okay. It got some of the best people to take
showers.

Race track: The place where windows clean people.

The tracks were crowded. I never knew there were so
many people in the publishing business.

"She's a great trick rider. Sometimes she's on top of the
horse and sometimes she's underneath."
"So what? I did that the first time I rode."

I fished the Alaskan streams for salmon . . . and never
caught a single can.

She had all the curves and I did all the pitching.

We beat them in doubles. They were handicapped. They had only one racket between them.

When learning to swim use the same principle as skating. Try to keep from touching the bottom.

I'm a lover of horseflesh, but not between two slices of bread.

Queensberry had the right idea when he divided waltzes into three-minute rounds.

"For three nights straight I dreamed about salami, baloney and liverwurst. Is a hunch, no? I go to the track and in one race is running a horse named Salami, a horse named Baloney and a horse named Liverwurst. So I bet all three to win. Coming into the stretch is running in dead heat Salami, Baloney and Liverwurst."
"What horse won?"
"A long shot by the name Cold Cuts."

Two industrialists were seated in their club arguing.
"I tell you there's a hat shop on Forty-ninth Street between Madison and Fifth," said Mr. Lotterdoe.
"I say there isn't," challenged Mr. Giltedge. "Let's make a sociable bet on it. Say one million dollars."
"Okay, and a box of cigars," Lotterdoe agreed. "Let's make it interesting."

McGoo was telling McGee why the people in his town had to go to the city to be united in wedlock.
"Our minister is so strict he won't even perform a wedding ceremony," he said.

"Why?" asked McGee. "What has that got to do with morals?"

"He says his conscience will not let him take part in a game of chance."

"Surely you don't believe your husband's story about fishing," the catty neighbor said. "Notice he didn't bring any fish back."

"That's what makes me believe he was fishing."

I just bet on an aristocratic horse. He was the last of his race.

I'm managing a crossword-puzzle fighter. He enters the ring horizontal and leaves vertical.

"What made you put off your wedding for two days?"

"I figured out that my silver wedding anniversary would come out on a Saturday and I always play golf on Saturday."

The exact extent of the unemployment menace can be carefully measured by the daily attendance at the race track.

An old gambler was talking to his son as he lay dying.

"Son, promise me you'll never touch a card. Above all, never play blackjack. It's a game that will cost you a fortune, waste your time, ruin your health and cause you untold moments of anguish and pain. Do you promise me, here on my dying bed, with the merciful angel of death hovering about and Almighty God as a witness, that you will never play blackjack?"

"Yes, Father," muttered the pious son.

"And remember," shouted the old gambler, "if you must play, always be sure to take the bank."

I played with Snead on the links yesterday, and there was only one point difference in our scores. He had 68 and I had 168.

The minister drove into a sand trap. He picked up his golf club and broke it but didn't say a word. Then he picked up the golf bag and tore it to shreds but didn't say a word. Then he took out all the golf balls and flung them into the woods but did not say one word. Finally he muttered, "I'm gonna have to give it up."

"Golf?" asked the caddie.

"No," he replied. "The ministry."

My brother crossed a chicken with a racing form and got a chicken that laid odds.

The wife had been berating her husband for losing his money gambling and threatened him with dire results if he persisted in this folly. One day she found a slip of paper in his pants pocket.

"What's this?" she demanded.

"Aww, honey," he pleaded, "it ain't anything really. Just an old ticket for the Irish Sweepstakes."

"Yeah?" she said. "I can see the name of the horse on it. One Gold Watch."

It takes years of practice before a ski jumper stops looking like someone being thrown out of a saloon.

Seymour was an inveterate baseball fan but one day his friends prevailed upon him to go to the race track with them. Being a beginner, he picked a long shot, Ruptured Snail, to win and bet two bucks on the nose at fifty to one. Sure enough, coming into the stretch Snail was neck and neck with the favorite. As they neared the wire, with the naked eye unable to tell who was leading, Seymour could restrain himself no longer. Jumping to his feet he yelled, "Slide ya bum, slide!"

"You say Billy Hill killed a man, is that right?"
"Yep. He chased him three days with a shotgun, finally got a bead on him and biffed him in the right lung."
"Killed him?"
"You bet."
"How is it they didn't lynch Bill?"
"Well, the feller he shot didn't have a friend on earth, so the game warden just fined him $2.00 for hunting without a license."

"I'm interested in the sport of kings."
"Horses?"
"No. Queens."

Know what killed six-day bicycle races? They struck for a five-day week.

I used to put the shot. But I could never remember where I put it.

I took a correspondence course in athletics. I used to receive fifty pounds of equipment a day via the mails. It didn't help me a bit, but now we have the world's best-developed mailman.

The football star had to pass "Legal Terms" in order to be eligible to play. "What is a hand-over clause?" asked the prof.
The gridder thought awhile and then said, "When you sign the contract you put your hand over it."

363

"Got into a poker game with your father and uncle last night."

"Did you?"

"You bet they did me."

The abolition of bingo should be done away with.

"I haven't seen my husband for eleven years," the wife said.

"Be patient," advised the lawyer. "Maybe he's taken up golf."

I wanted to eat one day so I looked for a restaurant. One said, "Dinners 12 to 2." Another said, "Luncheons 11 to 1." So I went there. They gave better odds.

Herb Gordon fanned at the golf ball so many times it caught cold.

"You've seen me play better than this," he said to the caddie.

"I did?"

"What do you call a man that holds the bag?"

"A taxpayer."

It was at a famous actors' club that an unemployed comic suggested a game of billiards. "Billiards?" questioned one of the members. "And in the winter?"

"Why on earth not?" the comic persisted. "In every game of billiards there comes a time when those three balls creep into a certain formation and at that time one thinks of one's winter coat."

An angler at the fishermen's club was describing his toughest catch. "After three hours I landed this terrific monster of the sea," he said.

"I saw the pictures and he was only six inches long," said one member.

"Sure," admitted the angler, "but in three hours of fighting a fish can lose a lot of weight."

He asked for a putter, then drove three hundred yards onto the green. Then he asked for a driver and drove the ball to within two feet of the cup. Then he asked for a niblick and got the ball into the cup. "Now I'm in trouble," he told the caddie.

"Why?"

"I don't know what club to use to get it out."

"I want a $2.00 ticket on myself," said the horse, walking up to the pari-mutuel window.

"WHAT?" exclaimed the man in surprise.

"Shocked that I can talk?" asked the horse.

"No," he replied. "I just don't think you can win."

"I love horses," said Mrs. Van Gottit.

"Ah," said the stable boy, "that is why you ride with your arms around their necks."

WOLVES AND WOLFESSES

(When I told her my proposition her face grew crimson and gold—her old school colors.)

"I had a good time last night at Helen's party."

"Who was there?"

"Me and Helen."

Familiarity breeds attempt.

Mañana, meaning tomorrow. Pajama, meaning tonight.

Make for the hay when the sun shines.

A wolf is a guy who goes into a restaurant and, instead of ordering a steak, orders a waitress.

He's some sheik, he's getting into the best circles. Circles? He's crashing the best triangles.

He picked her up in a bar. She wanted someone to talk to.

"My husband calls me a dumb bunny," she whimpered. "I don't look like a rabbit, do I?"

"No you don't," he soothed.

"It ain't my fault I have ten children, is it?"

"Ten children!" He seemed surprised. "I suppose that will be all."

"I don't know," she said. "My husband is a very stubborn man."

A playgirl is a gal who's out to make pin money . . . but doesn't sew.

The curse of denial: "In other words, NO!"

"Is that your heart beating?" she whispered in the dark.
"I hope so," he murmured.
"Why do you hope so?"
"If it isn't my heart," he said, "it's your husband knocking at the door."

In a taxicab it's mileage, in a parlor it's fun.

Busman's holiday: A postal clerk playing post office.

He swallowed one of her earrings. He whispered something and got too confidential.

It's difficult to remember her. She was nonhabit forming.

A girl's weakest moment is after her strongest drink.

"How did you meet that swell looker?"
"I rescued her from a lifeguard."

My sister went out with a few aviators and can't figure out how they rate wings.

She was watching her figure. That made two of us.

"Did you take your girl home last night?"
"No. I left her at her house."

"This is my debut."
"I thought it was your first time."

She won't play ball unless you furnish the diamond.

Their lips met and he held her closer, tighter, firmer. "Oh, darling," she whispered. "I've been saving my love for you."

"All right, honey," he breathed. "Be prepared to lose the savings of a lifetime."

He parked the car. "Move over close to me," he said.

"Didn't I tell you I was a lady?" she asked.

"I don't care what you were," he answered. "Move close."

"I forgot my glasses last night," he told his wife at the breakfast table. "Then what are you smiling at?" she wanted to know. "I remember where I left them," he said.

"I'm so discouraged. Everything I do is wrong."

"What're you doing tonight?"

"Wanna go to our dance?"

"I'd love to."

"You have to."

The lady said yes. "But wait till I'm drunk," she qualified. "So I don't remember."

"Can I see you home?"

"On a clear day it's easy."

The dame-on-the-prowl entered the restaurant and sized up the situation. She saw a prosperous-looking gentleman sitting all alone in a corner. So she tiptoed over, opened her handbag and let her handkerchief flutter to the floor. "Oh dear," she sighed, "I've dropped my handkerchief."

"Madam," said the gentleman, rising, "my weakness is beer."

"Let me go on the trip with you," said the gigolo.

"No," said the dowager. "You'll throw your arms around me and kiss me and hug me all the way."

"No I won't," protested the professional lover. "I want to have some fun on the trip."

The giddy dame decided to put her cards on the table. She sneaked up to the playboy and whispered, "I'm footloose."

He looked her over carefully and said, "The rest of you can stand tightening too."

"Care for a drink?"

"I'm sorry. I'm married."

"I'm married and just as sorry."

Women bring out the Boy Scout in me. I scouted around and oh boy.

A wolf is a guy who barks up the wrong she.

"Do you still see that pretty chorus girl you went with last summer?"

"She's married now."

"Answer my question."

She laughed when I sat down on the park bench, but when I started to play—

"Can I take you home?"

"Sure. Where do you live?"

Most wolves are fresh-air lovers. They get you out in the air and get fresh.

"How much do you love me?"
"How much do you need?"

I'm in bad company—that's why I'm having a good time.

He bent over to kiss her. Her arms shot from beneath the blanket and twined around his neck. "Don't go, Henry. Please don't go," she breathed. "Tell me how long you've loved me."
"Three hours," said Henry. "And it's darn hard on the arms."

"What would you take for spending a weekend on my yacht?"
"A life preserver."

All men have their price and some women their figure.

I have a way with the ladies? If I have my way she's no lady.

He invited her up for a scotch and sofa.

"Why did you break your engagement with Mary?"
"She wanted to get married."

A wolf is a guy with two eyes and two legs. The two eyes are on two other legs.

"Lovely date you had last night. Have a good time?"
"Rotten."

"Whatsa matter?"

"Did you ever enjoy a book with the last chapter left out?"

The tall, handsome, cocksure gentleman walked over to the girl and made a remark about the type of escort she was with. She laughed gaily. "When I don't want a man's attentions," she confided, "and he asks where I live, I just say I'm visiting here."

"Ha-ha," he laughed, relishing her humor. "Where do you really live?"

"I'm just visiting here."

"I know a funny old expression."

"You have a funny old expression."

My girl is very forward in some ways. Last night she turned the lights lower than my intentions.

I thought romance was in the air, but it was only the wind blowing from the zoo.

Sid finally wangled a date with his showroom model and now the evening was over and they were in her apartment.

"Hey," exclaimed Sid as he examined the closet where he was putting away his coat, "twenty fur coats. That's quite a collection. You certainly don't get them overnight."

"Dearie," she said, chucking him under the chin, "that's exactly how you do get them."

She summers in Atlantic City, winters in Florida and springs at sailors.

Two chorus girls were comparing notes on the techniques of their respective boy friends. "He kissed my hand," complained one.

"That's the way a man with experience kisses."

"A man with experience should have better aim."

When I was a boy I played with toys. Didn't know any girls.

I called her "Statue of Liberty"—'cause she's always lit and stands for everything. Her friends call her "Channel 2"—'cause anyone can pick her up, especially at night.

A lawyer is a man who will stay up all night to break a girl's will.

Don't tear your hair out over a woman. It will be harder to meet the next one if you're bald.

"The doctor ordered me not to have anything to do with her."

"Was she sick?"

"No. Her husband was the doctor."

When she was a kid she used to want an all-day sucker. Now she just wants one for the evening.

She asked me if I was Santa Claus and I said, "No." Then she said, "Then leave my stocking alone."

Lulu and Lizzie were talking about Percy. "He's an awful pest," said Lulu. "He doesn't know when to stop."

"That's strange," said Lizzie. "I was out riding with him and he found a dandy place."

When a bachelor walks the floor with a babe, he's dancing.

A wolf is man who likes to go window shopping and prefers to deal with well-established forms.

"You act like a child. I'll get you a doll and games."
"Get me the doll. I'll make up my own games."

Three textile men were seated in Feuerstein's, the Lindy's of the Lower East Side, and discussing the finer things life has to offer.

"The best," said Nat Pineus, "is a nice juicy steak, smothered in onions and mushrooms with crisp french-fried potatoes."

"I don't agree," answered Lou Goldberg. "The best is borscht, a boiled potato and a good piece of herring."

Sharfman shook his head. "I'm sorry, gentlemen, to me the best is a date with Lana Turner, Jane Russell and Marilyn Monroe."

"Aha," replied Pineus and Goldberg, "and who's talking about the very best?"

A reformer is the kind of guy who would have you believe that he gave Eve back her apple.

Two girls were comparing notes about the previous evening.

"Where we were the moon was so romantic and bright you could read a newspaper by it."

"Yeah?" squealed the other excitedly. "What did he do?"

"He read the newspaper."

The girl tried to make the minister. She wore stained-glass spectacles.

A wolf is a guy a gal has to eat, drink and be wary with.

Where do bad little girls go? Most everywhere.

She talked him into a new dress. He talked her out of it.

The doctor was explaining the unique case of the man who baffles medical science. "To all medical knowledge the man was dead," he explained. "Yet we buried him twice."

"When did you know he was really dead?"

"When he canceled his subscription to *Playboy*."

"What kind of oil do you use in your car?"

"I usually begin by telling them I'm lonely."

Two things that are over-rated: home cooking and home loving.

Uncle was arrested today for shopping. He walked through the store, squeezed a doll and it said "Mamma." He squeezed another doll and it yelled "Floorwalker."

"I love you," he said as they lay on the hotel grass.

"But we just got acquainted."

"I know," he replied. "But I'm only down here for the weekend."

376

Some years ago an ancient piece of papyrus was unearthed. For months science worked at deciphering its message. The final translation read, " 'What are we going to do now?' [signed] Anxious."

Johnny showed up at the poolroom with his head swathed in bandages. "How'd you come to get banged up?" asked his buddy.

"You know that brown-eyed babe on the first floor whose husband is in jail?"

"Yeah."

"Well, he ain't."

"How do you like bathing beauties?"

"I don't know. I never bathed one."

I call her "Checkers"—'cause she jumps when I make a move.

Wolf: A guy who likes his liquor straight and women curved.

What a beaut. We were down at the beach last summer and I was teaching her how to swim. Everything was going fine until the lifeguard came along . . . and made us go into the water.

"We're running out of gas."

"No fooling?"

"That's up to you."

Wolfess: A Campfire Girl who still likes to play with fire.

"How dare you? [smack] I'm a home girl."

"I'll see that you get home."

The usher showed him down the aisle, pinpointing an empty seat next to a gorgeous blonde. He started across the row of seats and was excited to see her beckon him to lower his head. "I'm saving this seat for a gentleman," she whispered.

"That's me," he whispered back. "How did you know I was coming?"

"Do you believe in clubs for women?"
"If everything else fails."

Nice girl. She used to be my dancing partner. First we went into the rhumba, then we went into a fox trot, then we waltzed into my hotel room.

"Wilt thou?"
"Only in hot weather."

Dear sir: Your library card will be canceled unless you bring back the librarian you took out two months ago.

She got mad because I stole a kiss. I stole it from her sister.

Old: An extinguished-looking gentleman.

He set his mark, and though she was a married woman he persisted. But she was afraid. "What if we break one of the Commandments?" she asked fearfully.

"So what?" he whispered. "There'd still be nine left."

"How's your new girl?"
"Not so good."
"You always were lucky."

"If you don't leave now," she informed the persistent Casanova, "I'll call the whole fire department to put you out."

"Can I drop you someplace?"
"No. I'm just getting over the last drop I had someplace."

A wolf is a drool person.

"Tony boy," she drooled, running her hand through his hair, "come on up to my room and have a bite before you go home."
"No thanks, Rose," said Tony, who'd been up to her room before. "You can bite me here in the hall."

The landlady called the female roomer. "I thought I saw you taking a gentleman up to your room last night," she said.
"Yeah," said the roomer. "That's what I thought."

"So long have I waited to see you. So long have I waited to meet you."
"I'm her husband."
"So long."

A wolf is a guy that knows all the ankles.

She kept following me for ten blocks. I couldn't get rid of her. She kept right in front of me all of the time.

Even Mason and Dixon had to draw the line someplace.

My uncle was a little embarrassed in Washington. He trailed a woman in a black gown and found out it was a Supreme Court justice.

"Come up to my apartment and I'll show you my etchings."

"How thrilling. You're the only man I've met in quite a while who has an apartment."

The English course didn't do him any good. He still ends every sentence with a proposition.

"Say when."
"After this drink."

He didn't give her a present . . . but he gave her a fine past.

The doctor is watching my diet. He took out the potatoes on Monday and he took out the meat on Tuesday. I'm looking forward to Friday. I'm taking out the nurse.

Song title: "I'll be Seizing You in All Those Old Familiar Places."

Big wedding. I got in line twice to kiss the bride and nobody noticed it.

"I don't mind you looking up my family tree," she said, "but leave my limbs alone."

"You look sweet enough to eat."
"I do eat. Where'll we go?"

Wolfess: The kind of a girl a fellow picks up instead of out.

She's only a rag, a bone and a hank of hair, but every man she meets wants to become a junk dealer.

"Don't you remember me?"
"Your face is familiar . . . but I don't recognize your drinking."

She didn't like the gleam in his voice.

"How'd you like the date I got you?"
"Nothing much."
"He's a lawyer."
"I thought he was an explorer."

They were out on their first date. He drove into the country, pulled off the road and parked the car. The girl was obviously frightened. "You shouldn't be scared," he soothed. I'm a nice guy."
"I know all about you," she said trembling.
"Yeah?"
"Yeah!" she replied. "My mother does your laundry."

"How about a date?"
"Why, I don't know you."
"I don't know you either."

The man burst angrily through the door, threw his wife off the stranger's knee and angrily demanded, "How do I find you kissing my wife?"
"I don't know," said the stranger. "Maybe you're home early."

SHOW BUSINESS...
radio...television...
burlesque...movies...
night clubs

(They couldn't afford a rising orchestra pit, so they made the musicians stand up slowly.)

Bing Crosby met an old East Side café owner on Hollywood Boulevard. They threw their arms around each other and were glad to renew old friendships. "Remember, Bing," said the old-timer, "twenty years ago you worked my club and you said someday you would become a big star on the radio, the stage and the screen?"

"Yes," said Bing wistfully. "I do recall."

"So tell me," said the old man. "What happened?"

He is now an agent. He must know talent. He gave up acting.

I held the audience open-mouthed. They yawned all at once.

The unemployed musician went into the pawnshop. "How much will you give me for this cornet?" he asked.

"One dollar," said the broker, after careful deliberation.

"What?" He was indignant. "Why the neighbors offered me more than that."

"They're calling for the author."

"But I can't make a speech."

"Just go out and say you're sorry."

The audience not only slept through my performance, they brought along their pajamas.

This is a story of the alleged honesty of the music business. Two nice young chaps wrote a song. They took it to a music publisher who changed one or two words and, in order to publish it, made them give him a piece of the song. The artist and repertoire men at the recording company (the brains who pick the songs to be recorded), in order to record it, had to be given a piece of it. The singer, in order to sing it, had to be given a piece of it. And the disk jockey, in order to play it, had to be given a piece. By the time the sheet music came out it didn't look like a song . . . it looked like a petition.

The way he reads clean lines is a dirty shame.

"Do you ever get stage fright?"
"Every time I see an egg or a tomato."

Comic: A guy who knows how to take a joke.

The Hollywood actor was being an ingrate when asked to appear at a benefit for a beleaguered friend. "But he saved your life in vaudeville," pleaded the poor man's agent.
"Nobody saved my life in vaudeville," protested the ham. "I died everywhere."

He never forgot his parents. Each week he sends them a box of apples, which they sell on the corner of Forty-second Street and Broadway.

I don't have an agent any more, I'm laying off direct.

The couple celebrated their twentieth anniversary by going to a movie show. It was a passionate, torrid, flaming picture and excited the animal instincts in the woman. When they got home that night she snuggled close to him but he ignored her. "Why is it that you never make love to me like the hero in the picture?" she cried.

"Don't be stupid," said the man. "Do you know how much they pay those fellows for doing it?"

The fan dancer was shy. She took off her clothes with one eye closed.

Opera house: Jukebox with a chandelier.

"Can you play an instrument?"
"No. I can't even play the violin."

Janice, the half-man half-lady, is ill. She hasn't been feeling himself lately.

"What do you think of my execution?"
"I'm in favor of it."

It was at the local poolroom that he developed his interest in the drama. There he took his first cue.

The actress had her own ideas about production props. "I insist upon real liquor in the drinking scene," she said.

"Okay," agreed the producer, "if you let me use real poison in the murder scene."

He is comedy relief. He relieves the picture of all its comedy.

We sang the cuspidor song: "Oh How I Miss You Tonight."

"Remember how I used to kill 'em on Broadway?"

"Did you ever get your license back?"

The procession wound its way slowly along Broadway.

"Whose funeral?" asked Hammy.

"Jim the actor's," said Shoofly.

"Is he dead?"

"Must be. Unless it's a rehearsal."

"My great-grandfather drove the Indians out of Kansas."

"What program was he on?"

The critic was at the opening night incognito—he was awake.

There was a big woman sitting in front of me, but I saw everything okay. She had a pierced ear.

"Hey," whispered the girl to her escort as they entered the theater. "Look who they've got tonight. My favorite actor. Nosmo King." She pointed to an electric sign.

"Darling," said her boy friend. "That sign says 'No Smoking.'"

Arthur Schnabel used to play impromptu home programs with Albert Einstein. One day Schnable detected a glaring error in Einstein's metre. "No-no-no," he shouted. "Albert. Cahn't you count—one-two-three-four."

When they said they shot the picture, they weren't kidding.

The usher, while showing the patron to his seat, stepped on his foot. "Why aren't you more careful?" berated the theater goer.

"Whaddaya want for sixty cents?" bawled the usher. "Fred Astaire?"

The film actor returned home from the testimonial dinner angry at the world. Finally, after much coaxing, his wife learned the reason. He had not been called upon to speak. "What makes it worse," he cried, "is that I spent all afternoon in the makeup department having a lump put in my throat."

"Experience taught me to be an actor."
"Why blame it on experience?"

It's so damp in Hollywood that the footprints in Grauman's are wearing galoshes.

"I feel sorry for Lady Godiva riding without a saddle," said the burlesque queen.
"Why?"
"Did you ever sit down on a horsehair sofa?"

And for your pleasure we have a small musical aggravation.

A show with a message closed out of town. They should have sent the message by Western Union.

A "yes man" is a guy who kisses his boss on all cheeks.

The actors were out of work when they met in Lindy's one day.
"Say, I got an idea," said one. "Why don't we team up. Do an act together?"
"Sounds good," said the other. "What kind of an act have you got in mind?"
"Well, I come out and sing. The curtain comes down.

Then it goes up and I come out and dance. Then the curtain comes down. Then it goes up again and I come out and juggle. Then—"

"Hey, where do I come in?"

"The curtain don't go up and down by itself."

Broadway: Where they sell cut-rate tickets for bad shows and cut-throat tickets for good ones.

The acrobat was having a rough time. Every time he'd come on everybody'd get up and walk out. "Why don't you get a new act?" advised his agent.

"What's the use?" moaned the acrobat. "Nobody's seen this one yet."

TV slogan: The show must go off.

Hollywood actress: One who would never dream of being seen twice with the same husband.

"Last week he was in a picture where he had to jump out of a fifty-story window."

"Didn't it kill him?"

"No. I saw him in another picture this week."

Song title: "When it's Banana Time in Sicily I'll Come Sliding Home to You."

"I'll give you a sporting proposition," said the conductor to the musician. "I'll break my leg if you'll break your violin."

It is better to have pink bloomers than a pink tooth-brush.

The actor wouldn't leave his car to go into the lunchroom. He explained that he had a bad memory, might forget the car and be left behind. "Your car number is 1492," said the attendant. "Associate it with Columbus."

He got out, entered the lunchroom and was just starting on his dessert when the whistle blew. "Er-uh, pardon me," he said aloud. "Can someone tell me what year Columbus discovered America?"

I don't like to pan, so I'll just say it isn't as good as her bad pictures.

The circus giant was only ten feet tall. He smoked when he was a kid.

The backer of the show demanded a part for his talented nephew. The producer, unable to refuse, called the young man to him. "You realize of course," said the producer, "that you have no experience despite your 'terrific' talent. Therefore you must be taught gradually. The first year or so your part on stage is to say 'George is waiting outside.' Should the show run five or six seasons we'll change the line and you'll say 'George is waiting outside. Shall I show him in?' "

". . . and after that?"

"After that you will play George."

My song was on one side of the record. On the other was an apology from the record company.

The new show was called *The Farmer Meets a Skunk* —formerly *The Farmer Takes a Whiff*.

Even his jokes about old jokes are old.

I knew Tom Thumb when he was a pinky.

The actor died and went to heaven. "What did you do on earth?" asked Saint Peter.

"I was an actor."

"You can't come in here." And he slammed the gate.

So he went down to hell. "What were you on earth?" asked the devil.

"An actor."

"You can't come in here," screamed the devil, and shut the furnace.

"Gosh," moaned the actor. "Must I go back on the Orpheum circuit?"

After they played "The Star-Spangled Banner" there was a helluva letdown.

Two ballet dancers were talking. "Your pants are so tight I can see what you have in your pockets."

"I have no pockets."

"What's that lump there?"

"That's a mosquito bite."

He was one of the greatest actors that ever cleared his throat.

An original wit is a guy who hears the gag before you do.

It was one of the great show business funerals. Everyone who was anyone was there. Right after the services the deceased actor's agent asked his friend, another famous actor who had delivered the eulogy, what he thought.

"A very fine funeral," said the actor. "But the acoustics were very bad."

Television has proved that sight has a definite odor.

A little dying, a little guying, a little spying, a little ryeing, a little buying and a great deal of lying—that's show business (also marriage).

"I like to go to the theater at 8 A.M.," said the Scotsman.

"Ah," said the manager knowingly. "Before prices change?"

"No," Scotty replied. "Before there's any prices."

The audience was so tough they knew the words to the Bronx cheer.

Right after the sumptuous dinner given in his honor he rose and sang a few songs, which is a nasty way of showing appreciation.

As a composer I was always able to write verses easily but had trouble with the chorus. None of them would go out with me.

Comedian's byword: Seek and ye shall file.

Monotonist: A single that only talks.

The two playwrights met at the theater where one of them had his show playing. "Nothing on the boards for you this year?" said the working one. "Too bad. But you're really not the best available, you know. By the way, what made you come to see my play?"

"I have a cold," said the unemployed one, "and the doctor told me to avoid crowds."

She was so dumb they had to rehearse her two weeks for a pause.

Incognito in Hollywood means "I wish someone would recognize me."

If the person or persons who found my gold watch at the theater will get in touch with me they may keep the gold if they'll return the inscription.

He loves those female night-club singers. He listens with both eyeballs.

The eggs missed me. They hit the scenery and improved the looks of it.

The comic was down in the dumps. "Don't worry," said the agent. "They laughed at Fulton."
"Who's he?" asked the comic.
"I don't know."
"Gee," sighed the comic. "I wish I was Fulton."

What's worse than Thursday night on TV? Thursday afternoon.

Crime doesn't pay in the movies.

The two girls went up to see the agent. "We would like to get café jobs," they said demurely.
"What experience have you had?"
"We used to sing for the Army."
"Union or Confederate?"

Uncle Jim was a tightrope walker . . . until one night he was tight and the rope wasn't.

Most of my professional acting career was spent south of the border. It's a lot easier to starve when you're warm.

She had everything a singer should have and a good voice too.

The company was performing *The Beggar Student* in front of an Irish audience. "Be true to steadfast Poland, our Poland for liberty, our country will be free," emoted the actor. Then, waiting for applause that did not come, he added, "And God save Ireland too."

We staged a bullfight for the benefit of the Society for Prevention of Cruelty to Animals.

"I'm the backbone of television," said the comic.
"I wouldn't go that high," said the critic.

He was a modest actor who had plenty to be modest about.

The show was all right but the theater had been constructed badly. The seats faced the stage.

Comedians don't need straight men any more, they're all talking to themselves.

I'm a stooge to no one man. I free-lance.

For a solid week they'd rehearsed until 3 A.M., then another such rehearsal was called. "I object," said a chorus boy.
"Why?" asked the director.
"Because," said the boy. "If this keeps up I'll have no sparkle in my eyes opening night."

394

Two of the best-known works in show business: "Okay, two" and "IOU."

The young actor was awed when the theater owner told him that his was the most traditional theater in America. "Gosh," said the embryo. "Did John Barrymore play here?"

"Yep," boasted the owner. "But he won't again. He fell off the trapeze three times."

She finally got a break after years of struggle, mostly against assistant directors.

"Your act is lousy," said the agent.

"All right," said the modest young man. "I'll write all those comics and tell them their material is lousy."

"Ever hear of a minstrel show?"

"No. Does that make me a jerk?"

"I don't know what did."

Nudist national anthem: "You're an Old Smoothie."

The burlesque show had to close because of a shortage of raw material.

The neighbor burst unexpectedly into Mrs. Hyman's apartment. "Look," she yelled excitedly, waving a circular. "A vaudeville show with five name acts and two name bands, a set of dishes, two double-A pictures, amateur night and bingo. All for thirty-five cents. Let's go."

"Aw, what's the use?" said Mrs. Hyman. "I never win."

In technicolor her hair photographs yellow. When she sticks her tongue out it looks like ham and eggs.

He bowed just to keep his end up.

"Speak louder, mister speaker. I can hardly hear you. LOUDER."
"Why don't you pay more and come nearer?"
"It ain't worth it."

The belly dance was originated by someone trying to take off a union suit in an upper berth.

She wasn't exactly anything to look at, but she had heart and a desire for show business. "I'm going to London's Theatrical Agency about a job," she told a friend.
The friend eyed her carefully. He saw her bulbous figure, her ugly face, her stringy hair. He thought about her scratchy voice and her sloppy dress. "There's no use going there," he said diplomatically, "unless you've got good legs."
"Why?" she was genuinely puzzled. "Haven't they got an elevator?"

"What have you in the balcony?"
"Four hundred seats and three ushers."

"There ain't no palm trees in Alaska," the technical adviser told the stubborn movie director.
"There ain't, hey?" The director was angry. "I'll show 'em. Bring on more palm trees."

And now I would like you to meet a man who has never done a thing in his life and is ready to stage a comeback.

He'd be the most popular man on television if he was as well known as his jokes.

He sings for charity. He needs it.

"Did Philadelphia scream when they saw him in person?"
"It was about 50–50."

The incessant ringing of the phone woke the actor at an awful hour. Three in the afternoon. "Yes?" he said groggily into the mouthpiece.
"Mr. Dumore, please," a voice said.
"Dumore speaking."
"Mr. Dumore, we would like you to appear at a benefit."
"What kind of benefit?"
"It's a benefit for a fella who beat the rap—money's to go to his lawyer."

Hollywood is the place where a fella never worries about making a living till he makes $3,000 a week.

A musician has a pen that will write under scale.

Soap opera: Singing in the bathtub.

"Did you see *The Hairy Ape?*"
"Yes. I sat in the first row and didn't miss a hair."

In show business a gentleman's agreement means nothing. There aren't any gentlemen.

The popular master of ceremonies was down on his show-business luck and was happy to get a job at the leading train terminal as an announcer. A train announcer. "All right, folks," he called over the PA his first day on the job. "Now coming in on track number four, the Century Express, ten minutes ahead of time, from Chicago. Let's give it a great big hand."

Yasha Loeffitz, the famous musician, was once invited to a fancy cocktail party. "And bring your cello," said Lady Bigceet.

"Sorry," said Yasha. "My cello doesn't drink."

"Your sax is flat," raved the bandleader.

"It was in tune when I bought it," said the player.

"That was five years ago."

"If you'd been out of work as long as this sax you'd be flat too."

"I'm a finished dancer."

"I'll say."

I played my trumpet until 3 A.M., and the fella next door kept knocking on the wall for encores.

The waitress kept staring at the leading man every time she brought him a course. "Say," she finally said, "don't I know you from somewhere?"

The actor was coy. "Possibly you've seen me in the movies," he said.

"Maybe," she said thoughtfully. "Where do you usually sit?"

The ardent actor pursued the damsel. "Marry me," he implored, "and make me the happiest man in the world."

"I promise to marry you when you make a fortune."

"That's not an engagement," cried the actor. "That's an option."

"What will you give me for this joke?"

"Ten yards head start."

I used to love to take my girl to the movies and put my arms around her. But that's all over now. I might drop the dishes.

What's the difference between drama and melodrama? In drama the heroine throws the villain over. In melodrama she throws him over a cliff.

I had 'em in the aisles—heading for the exits.

"Will you ever forget my first appearance?"

"Sure. What am I offered?"

The romance is off between the fat lady and the midget. He used to sit on her lap. One day she forgot and sat on his.

He's fast on the ad-lib. All he has to do is hear it once.

The agent liked the guy's appearance. There was something about the way he carried himself, the way he walked, the way he looked at you that showed he was the kind of man who knew what he was doing.

"What kind of an act do you do?" he asked.

"I take a high hat. Put eggs, butter, bread and kerosene in it. Wave my hand and—"

"What comes out?"

"The lining."

The following is offered as evidence in the murder of dame vaudeville:

"There's a cattle boat sailing for Greece tomorrow and

I can book passage for you. I'm a personal friend of the head cow."

"I think you're giving me the wrong steer."

"I just thought I'd horn in."

"Well, we certainly milked that one."

She thinks she's still in *The Student Prince*. She's always looking for soldiers.

She's a burlesque girl. She told her doctor she wanted to be vaccinated where it wouldn't show. He gave it to her in a spoon.

The houselights were up. The theater was empty and everyone was preparing to go home when they noticed a woman still sitting is the orchestra. "Why don't you go home?" the manager advised. "The show is over. The hero is dead."

"He was such a nice man," she said. "I thought I'd wait for the funeral."

The woman met the angry little boy coming out of the baby-incubator exhibit. "It's a fake, lady," the boy said. "They don't do no tricks. Just sleep."

"Sorry, you can't take that dog into the theater."

"What harm can pictures do to a little dog like this?"

"Judge, my husband is the cheapest man in the world. He hypnotized me into thinking I was a canary and then fed me birdseed."

"What have you got to say for yourself?"

"I could have made her think she was a sparrow and she'd have to hunt for her own food."

He wrote his own gags to keep the wolf from the door. He told them to the wolf.

They wanted to have a sneak preview. Couldn't round up enough sneaks.

The two comedians met in Sardi's one day. One was on the way up, television contracts, guest shots, personal appearances, etc. The other was just drifting. "I tell you these guys who supply me with material are awful," said the drifter. "If things keep up like this I'll be glad to get a booking in a flea circus."

"I have an idea that keeps my writers from giving me bum jokes like yours," said the riser.

"What's that?"

"I pay them."

"I talked all through your performance last night."

"That was rude."

"No. I was talking in my sleep."

During a most serious performance one of the actors was annoyed by a woman eating a large club sandwich in the front row. "Go down there," he told an usher, "and embarrass her."

Despite the fact that the lady was a famous first-nighter, the usher obeyed. "Pardon me, madam," he said. "Maybe you need a little salt or pepper?"

"No," said the dowager. "But a little ketchup wouldn't hurt."

Two couples met in Europe and were speaking nostalgically of good old New York. "Do you know if *Arsenic and Old Lace* is still running?" asked one society woman.

"Ask Horace," said the other. "He knows all about horses."

When uncle was on the stage he never had to worry about transportation. At the end of each engagement the audience would ride him out of town.

He did a two-hour act. One hour to see it and one hour to regret it.

He was a number one actor. Remember there's nothing lower than number one.

He was born to the stage. His first grade teacher picked up his option after twenty-six weeks.

He laid so many eggs that he released a hen for active duty.

His wife made her reputation . . . by losing it.

She had pear-shaped tones and a figure to match.

She couldn't be on key if she sat on a Yale lock.

"Shay," said the drunk to his pal, "letsh get outta here and go downtown. Heifitsch ish playing."
"Against who?"

"Last night I had a wonderful experience in the theater."
"Where?"
"In the balcony."

Thousands wouldn't buy his act and I'm one of the thousands.

Song dedicated to a friend in the hospital: "You've Got Everything . . ."

"Did you hear about my singing?"
"Yes. What's your version?"

The dance act had been laid off for six months when one day the male partner rose and announced, "I'm going down to the booking office."

"Whatsa matter with you?" asked his partner. "You getting stage struck again?"

Announcer: A guy who knows his N-B-C's.

One Siamese twin to the other: "You musta had a swell time last night. I look a wreck today!"

"You can't make this into a picture," advised the screen writer. "The captive lead is a lesbian."

"So what?" said the sharp producer. "We'll make her a Hungarian."

"Sh-h-h-h—I'm doing my act."
"Sh-h-h-h—the audience is asleep."

Song title: "When the Roll Is Called Up Yonder, Will the Frankfurter Be There?"

The natives applauded—when I left town.

The critic died. Sometime later a friend decided to visit the plot and was surprised to see that the body was reposing in a vault, contrary to the deceased's wishes.

"Why don't you bury him?" the friend angrily asked an official.

"He used to be a drama critic," explained the custodian. "And we're having a lot of trouble finding a grave on the aisle."

Philly is the Quaker City. They paid me off in oats.

"Where do you get your material?"
"Why, I write my own jokes."
"I see. You're much older than you look."

"Hello? Theater manager? Did you find a little piece of taffy candy last night?"
"Why are you concerned about a small piece of taffy candy?"
"My teeth were in it."

The contortionist tied himself in a knot, so he wouldn't forget.

A screen writer was invited by a producer to see a preview of a show he, the writer, had missed doing the screenplay for. The lights went out and just as the screen flashed the words "Stupendous Pictures Presents" the writer leaned over to the producer and said, "Drags, doesn't it!"

Producer: A guy who sells 75 per cent of a show but won't bring it in until he sells the other 75 per cent.

So-and-So is a rapid-fire comedian—he should be fired rapidly.

He played Schubert's Fourth while the girls killed a fifth.

My cousin has an important job. He runs ahead of Hildegarde and points out what tables she should sing at.

I saw Spitalny and his old-girl orchestra.

The sign on the marquee said "Now Playing *The Farmer's Daughter*." Wonder how they could make that story into a picture?

"Ma," said pa, "Zephrim is growed up now and I think it high onto time we showed him the facts of life. What say we let him git into town to see one of them there moving pictures? All by his self."

Ma agreed, after all a boy of eight might be getting notions, so Zephrim trotted to one of them there moving pictures to learn the facts of life. Ma and pa waited up till they heard the pitter-pat of his naked toes on the manure pathway.

"How'd ya like the picture, son?" ma asked.

"Twas dark. Tweren't no picture show there," Zeph talked. "But a lotta cowboys came a shootin' at me. They'da got me too if I didn't get under the seat."

The tattooed lady had all the states tattooed on her . . . and where she had Georgia was an insult to the South.

We musta had the wrong ticket. The man at the door got mad and tore it in half.

"Mistuh, yore a might disappointin' as an act," said the southern vaudeville manager. "Yo tell me yo does a monologue. The agent tole me yo does a talkin' act."

Uncle Saul was one of those painters. Temperamental too, that's how he lost his job with the circus. He painted a poster showing the bearded lady with a clean shave.

He had a defect, which to a comedian might be fatal. He wasn't funny.

I sang on one knee like Jolson. He was singin'. I was duckin'.

"When I played in Carnegie Hall the audience whistled and hollered."
"What did you do?"
"I kept on playing."

Just before opening night the producer went to church and lit a candle. Then he stayed there to make sure some other producer didn't blow it out.

"I want to sing but I don't know what to do with my hands."
"Hold them over your mouth."

Business was so bad they were selling loose cigarettes in the lobby.

Then I wrote my first hit song. It was called "Murder of the Bearded Lady" or "She Died Like a Man."

The teacher called on the son of the theater couple to answer a question about history.
"The twenty-second day of this month is celebrated by all Americans. Can you tell me what day it is?"
"Sure. Matinée Day."

He was billed as the greatest sword swallower of all time, but when he showed up it was with somewhat smaller items. "I thought you were a sword swallower," said the manager. "These are pins and needles."

"I know," said the wonder. "I'm on a diet."

He's been in show business thirty years and has the jokes to prove it.

Everything about it was bad. They even panned the architecture and the ushers.

"I've got a great act," the performer told the agent. "One dog stands on its hind legs while I juggle. Another dog jumps on the first one, kneels and sings 'Swanee.'"

"That's nothing," said the agent.

"Yeah, but the dog on the bottom is a ventriloquist."

She made her debris in grand opera.

There are so many hotdog stands on Broadway that the shoplifters carry forks.

"In this skit you play the part of an old farmer," the director told the actor. "You get up at four in the morning. Milk the cows, feed the horses, feed the pigs, chop the wood, clean the barn. Then you go into the chicken coop—"

"Wait a minute," interrupted the ham. "If I gotta lay the eggs I quit."

The actor was out of work for three years so they cast him as a banker.

The MC coughed and coughed and coughed. The minute he caught his breath he said, "Be sure and buy Christmas seals this year."

The half-man and half-woman act was ready to kill itself. The male half caught the female half going through his pockets.

"How'd you like the play?"
"I think it stinks."
"I can't say I like it that much."

The telephone jangled in the Hollywood director's office.
"I'm getting married tomorrow." He recognized the voice of his leading lady. "And I've promised to give up motion pictures."
"Maybe I can get them to hold up production," he said. "How long do you think it'll last?"

At a very early age he showed signs of belonging to the theater, he put gum under the seat of his high chair.

"Won't you sing for us?"
"I'm sorry. I sing only in the bathtub."
"I'll put you down for a song and mention that you're out of practice."

Next week he appears in a fashionable lineup in Boston.

It wasn't that he lacked confidence, still at every performance he left his brother outside with the motor running.

"Don't you want someone to meet you with outstretched hands when you get home?"

"I already have an agent."

She has a three C range: low C, high C and louse C.

The man was singing "I Love Life and I Want to Live" when the other man shot him and announced, "Those of you who love life can now live."

She's been in a lot of pictures. Two of them were movies.

"Hand me my fiddle. I wanna put it under my chin."

"Put the piano under your chin."

"Okay. Hand me the piano."

If you saw a big crowd leaving the theater you knew he was on. And so was the audience.

For the wedding of the popular Hollywood actress the studio sent out nine thousand exclusive invitations.

A Hollywood producer is a man who knows what he wants, but can't spell it.

He was so bad he couldn't stop the show if he fell from the gallery.

The agent in the booking office sent the actor an offer by mail and closed with a request for an immediate reply. "Do I know you?" wrote back the actor.

"Yes," the agent wired. "Once I was a manager in Boston."

"You've got a nerve to expect me to start a correspondence with you upon such short acquaintance," the actor replied, "when I haven't written a letter to my mother in six months."

Her fan mail is getting big, there're a few from total strangers.

The TV actress was being sued. "I request at this time," said the lawyer, "my client be allowed to change her gown. She hasn't displayed half her costumes yet."

"Your Yo-Yo May Be Broken, Mother, but You're Still the Tops to Me."

Television: The thing that gives a comic thirteen weeks' work and thirteen weeks' worry.

The poor girl was so embarrassed. Her bubble developed a leak and she thought everyone was hissing her.

"May I ask," said the woman at the theatrical function to the handsome man, "are you anyone in particular?"

In burlesque all girls look alike and all men like a look.

The midget was so small they rode him out of town on a nail.

"I had a movie star at my house last night."
"No foolin'?"
"Just a little."

The notoriously cheap agent was dickering with the actor when another performer entered the office. So he wrote down an amount on a sheet of paper and handed it to the actor. "That's the figure I'll pay you," he whispered.

"Oh," whispered back the actor. "I thought that was the commission."

He made that joke up in a second. It's a whole day's work for a chicken.

There's a certain night club in town where so many acts died that instead of a contract the management gives you a will.

"Have you seen my latest show?"
"No. But I've seen other shows as bad."

He was responsible for selling thousands of television sets when he started on the air. I sold mine, my brother sold his . . .

"If you're listening to this in your car," said the disk jockey "and have no license to drive, turn it off. I'm in enough trouble."

I'm not sure you would call the actress ugly. All I know is she caught the 1:30 broom out of town.

"How do you account for the fact that you're not doing as much business this week as you did last?"
"Didn't sell as many tickets."

They padded his part—with commas.

For once I heard of a "no man" getting a job in Hollywood. The producer turned to him at a preview and said, "Did you ever see a greater picture in your life?" And he said, "No."

The fat actress went to the agent every day for work—but he kept telling her she was too fat. Some months later he met her again and she was very trim. "Lulu," he shrieked. "You look wonderful. What have you been doing with yourself?"

"Starving to death," she said.

What an actor! Even when he died his funeral ran a year.

The movie improved the story of *The Last Supper* by adding a cover charge.

"When I hear you sing a lump forms."
"In your heart? In throat?"
"No. You're going in the wrong direction."

I won't say the new comedian's style will be popular. It is popular.

"Boys," said the singer. "I said hit it. Not beat it to death."

The manager asked the great seal act to take a cut while playing Oakland. At the time they were in San Francisco. "I can't," said the master, "And pay transportation."

"It's only across the bay," pleaded the booker. "Can't your act swim across?"

She was a side-show performer and now her new husband wanted to know how many times she'd been kissed. "You mean," she asked, "just counting people?"

In my act I swallow a sword seven feet long. I'm only five feet. I get stuck to more floors that way.

He does magic. He disappears with the host's wife.

Never send a critic to cover a war. He might not like it.

The girl was engaged to a man who called himself a producer but she'd heard so much about phony producers she asked a famous actor friend to audition for him to see what he would think. After the audition the actor started to discuss terms.

"I want five hundred a week and a set percentage," he said.

"No," said the so-called producer. "You'll get three hundred fifty and no percentage."

"Four hundred."

"Three fifty."

"I'll let you know."

The actor left and met the girl at an appointed spot. "What do you think?" she asked.

"The guy must be on the level," said the ham. "He's trying to chisel salaries. When they have no dough they pay anything."

An actor knows more small towns than Rand McNally.

The crowd was on edge. The seats were narrow.

There are two seasons in Hollywood, the rainy season followed by the divorce season.

The man read for the part most eloquently. When he finished there was a stunned silence in the theater. Then the producer huddled rapidly with his director.

"Okay?" asked the actor.

"No," said the director. "Come back tomorrow and read it again in a gray suit."

"Shakespeare would have loved me."
"He did."

Drama editors don't get more money than city editors, they get more sleep.

The farmer, seeing his first marionette show, was so impressed he went backstage to meet the guiding genius. "What really gets me," said the visitor, "is how you make yourself so small."

"If you see my wife tell her to wait for me."
"I don't know your wife."
"Then tell her not to wait."

When I played in my home town they loved me. They gave me a parade. They threw confetti. They got so enthusiastic they didn't even bother to tear up the phone books.

"That's Bomba the wild man. He's been married seven times."
"No wonder he's wild."

The theater was so big that when they threw green tomatoes by the time they reached the stage they were ripe.

At the rehearsal the leader said all oboes out, so we went out.

After weeks of dodging the female half of an act which broke up due to the death of the husband, the agent finally found it impossible to avoid the widow any longer.

"I just can't book you since your husband died," he informed her. "He was the greatest. They still talk about him all around the circuit. Nobody can come near him. Why his memory is revered from city to city."

"Listen," she replied. "Since he died I put a monkey in the act. You oughta see it now."

The trombone looks better in my derby than I do.

"How long you been in Hollywood?"

"Three years."

"I haven't seen you in any pictures. Whatcha been doing?"

"Dickering."

The director said, "The lion will charge you for one hundred yards. No farther. Understand?"

"I understand," said the hero. "But does the lion?"

"How does it feel to have your name up in electric lights?"

"Fierce. Everyone I owe money knows where to find me."

She does a peek-a-boo act. The audience peeks then boos.

If you don't think there is such a thing as reincarnation go see some of these night-club comics.

Two comics met in Lindy's. One of them was furious.

"I saw you at the Palace," he roared. "You told every joke I told on my broadcast. They were my jokes."

"Look, wise guy," answered the accused. "Anything that comes out of my radio is mine."

"I have the theater in my blood."
"If you go on there'll be blood in the theater."

The tickets were sky high and so were our seats.

She did the dance of the seven veils. After she threw off six the prices changed.

Just learned she's been broadcasting from Chicago for five years and I've been blaming it on the stockyards.

Lana Turner was on the screen doing a love scene. The usher came down and told me to stop smoking. There was no cigarette in my mouth.

"That song comes from my heart."
"I knew it couldn't come from your throat."

A notion is a nervous breakdown on paper.

"I like my new picture fine. I got a kick out of it."
"The managers have a few kicks too."

The chorus girl was so dumb she thought lettuce was a proposition.

Actress: A clamor girl.

They laughed when he said he could crack a joke. But they stopped when he cracked it.

With him acting was a gift, but even as a gift the audience didn't want it.

She stayed for all four shows and didn't leave until the houselights were on. The actor sent for her. "Madam," he gushed, "you stayed for all four shows. Did you really like me so much?"

"No," she said. "I couldn't find my shoes."

The show was closed after three performances on account of bad language by the critics.

Song title: "I'd Rather be a Coward for Five Minutes than a Corpse for the Rest of My Life."

I'm not an after-dinner speaker. I'm not invited to dinner often enough to practice.

I laid so many eggs that the chicken picketed every theater I played.

There's no shape you ever dreamed impossible that a burlesque show won't produce.

Saw a sneak preview. I had to sneak in.

I wrote a most unusual play. Nothing happens for the first fifteen minutes. It's for people who come late.

Two ex-musicians, now residing in an institution for the unbalanced, were discussing their careers. "Took me eight years to master the guitar," said one.

"That's a long time to do that."

"No," he replied. "I thought I had to blow in it the first four years."

The actor was exhausted from laying an egg that big.

He was hailed as the second Booth—from the right.

He brought a new error to show business.

"Do you know what George Washington said when he chopped down the cherry tree?"
"No. I never listen to his program."

A "yes man" is a person who stoops to concur.

Actor: A man who often staggers home full of boos.

"Who was that lady I saw you with last night?"
"That wasn't a lady. That was my brother."

The movie actor was making personal appearances, his last picture was that bad.

He played in Key West. It was the first time he knew what key he was playing in.

Last year at my concert in London it was so foggy I had to play the last six bars of "Glow Worm" to see the piano.

"I'm a great artist."
"Okay, here's a pencil. Draw me."

"You play the part of a horse."
"That's the end."
"You said it."

His notes come out easy. They should. He flattens them on the way up.

The show was so bad that four empty seats got up and walked out.

"Where's that singing coming from?"
"The bathroom."
"Gimme a plunger. I'll fix it."

We had dinner in one of those romantic Russian places. The conductor led the band with a salami.

Uncle was great at reciting "Face on the Barroom Floor," when in that position.

"What did Juliet say when she met Romeo in the balcony?"
"Couldn't you get seats in the orchestra!"

She does the most complete striptease in the business. She even removes her makeup.

In Hollywood an understatement is news.

"I'm a sword swallower. One time I really swallowed a sword," he told the agent.
The agent was startled, "Really?" he gasped. "Give you any trouble?"
"Only when I sit down," said the performer. "I have a little trouble getting up."

Marquee sign: *Rebecca of S. B. Farm*

Critic: A panhandler.

"Mother used to look in the lion's mouth."

"What for?"

"For father."

The propman was new at the studio. He approached the important man's receptionist and asked to see him. "The director is playing polo today," she said.

"Oh," said the propman. "Then he won't be in?"

"He's in," corrected the girl. "It's a large office.

He went into the movie and, quite by accident, found his wife in the arms of an usher. "How long has this been going on?" he demanded.

"About fifteen minutes," said the usher. "Plenty of seats down front, sir."

"These dishes are for you, madam. This is dish night."

"Nothing doing. Wash your own dishes."

He knows the secret of comedy and knows how to keep a secret.

Vaudeville is so bad even the elephant acts can't remember when they worked last.

In television your eyes prove your nose was right when it rendered its opinion about radio.

The big clubs are all going in for names. And the names they call each other is something awful.

I used to go with a girl who worked on the Ziegfeld roof, when it leaked.

"What did folks do in the evenings years ago when there was no radio?"

"The same thing they do today. But without music."

A man seen entering a night club with a Bible under his arm was asked to explain. "They say the show is terrific," he replied. "Gorgeous girls, scanty costumes, low-cut dresses on the singers, etc."

"Then why the Bible?"

"If it's as good as they say it is I'm going to stay over Sunday."

The man appeared at the agent's office and demanded an audition for his talking dog. "Okay," said the agent, "make him spell cat."

"K-A-T," said the dog.

The agent hit the roof. "How the hell do you expect me to book him?" he roared. "He can't even spell cat."

Pfefferman the producer looked up when his secretary came into the room. "A woman to see you," she said.

"Is she pretty?" he asked.

"Beautiful," the secretary said.

"Well, show her right in."

Ten minutes later he called the secretary in. "A fine judge of beauty you are," he remarked.

"I had to be careful, sir," she answered. "For all I knew she might have been your wife."

"Damnit, she was," Pfefferman replied.

"I pay $500 a week to the bubble dancer."

"Why so much?"

"Big girl. Small bubble."

A producer can best be described as a man who wears a worried look on his assistant's face.

The stage mother kept after the producer until he finally consented to listen to her offspring perform. After the audition the mother asked, "Do you think she'll make a singer?"

"Well," said the producer, "she has a mouth."

"I held the audience in the palms of my hands."
"You could."

The director was talking in his sleep. "Darling, I love you," he said. "You are my life, my heart. More than anything else in the world—"

Then he woke up and saw his wife glaring at him. Knowing what the trouble might be, he pretended he was still asleep, rolled over and murmured, "Cut! Now bring on the horses."

The director fell in love with the dumbest chorus girl on earth, and the most beautiful. "Susie," he said, "you could go a long way if you were real nice to somebody who could do you some good. Er—uh—me for example."

"Ooh—I think I understand," she cooed. "You want me to be nice to you."

So the next morning when she came to work she brought him a large box of candy.

A famous musician had a dinner appointment. He knew he was on the right block but couldn't remember the house or the number. So he kept going from house to house brushing his shoe against the foot scraper. At the fourteenth he said, "Ah, this is it. I didn't know the number but the foot scraper is in B flat."

The magician strode forward and addressed a member of the audience. "My dear sir," he said. "Would you lend me your hat for the next trick?"

"NO!" shouted the man. "Not till you return the lawn mower you borrowed last summer."

"Listen, Sol, what a bargain. If you go to Radio City before noon it is only a quarter. Such a gorgeous place. Chandeliers, rugs, plush seats, full-length feature movie, short subjects, newsreels, animated cartoons, fifty beautiful girls, a hundred and ten-piece orchestra—"

"All for the same quarter?"

"All for the same quarter. And what is more, when you leave the movie you can go upstairs and see a real art show."

"All for the same quarter?"

"All for the same quarter. And then they give you a delicious cup of coffee."

"All for the same quarter?"

"All for the same quarter."

"Hmmm—must be awful cheap brand of coffee."

The angel was taunting the devil.

"Hey, devil," it said, "we're putting on a great show up here."

"Yeah?" said the devil. "Where you gonna get actors?"

Times had reached a troublesome pass at the Hot Air Broadcasting Network, and a meeting of the directors had been called.

"We've got to have a reorganization at once," the chairman announced.

"Why?" a mere director asked. "What's the trouble?"

"We just discovered we have three more listeners than we have vice presidents."

My teacher is a former actress and very hammy. She takes bows every time I clap the erasers.

Waiter: "I'd like to remind you that I sang in one of your shows. Are you surprised to find me here, a waiter?"

Producer: "No. I remember hearing you sing."

The theater manager was exultant. "There are three times as many this week as last to see Hope's fan dance," he said.

"Did they reduce the price?"

"No, they reduced the fan."

The actor's tour was a great success. He outran every audience.

One good thing about television, you can close your eyes and swear you're listening to the radio.

A prominent British actor missed his connections to London and had to stay in a strange town. He sought out an eating place and accidentally stumbled into the most sordid den he'd ever seen. When the waiter came he recognized him as an old actor with whom he'd played in London.

"Great Scott," he exclaimed. "You, a waiter? And in this place?"

"Yes," was the proud reply. "But I don't eat here."

The temperamental actress was boasting to the director.

"After my big death scene," she said, "they cried all over the house."

"Uh, huh," said the director. "That was because they knew you weren't really dead."

I saw *Tobacco Road* so many times I got nicotine in my eyes.

Two Hollywood children were holding a conversation. "How do you like your new daddy?" asked one.

"Fine," said the other.

"I thought you would," said the first. "I had him last season."

A man started to snore in his seat at the opera. "Please stop your snoring," the usher pleaded. "You are disturbing the others."

"Look, kiddo," the man said angrily, "I paid for this seat and I'll do as I please."

"Yessir," replied the usher. "But you are keeping everybody awake."

"Is the play you are in a comedy or a tragedy?"

"If there are a lot of tickets sold it will be a comedy, otherwise it will be a tragedy."

The striptease dancer was on her honeymoon. The groom put on his pajamas and asked, "Aren't you getting ready for bed?"

"No," she replied. "Not until I get a little applause."

"I want my money back," the man shouted to the cashier.

"Why?" asked the cashier.

"You advertised a chorus of seventy," said the man, "and not one of them looks over sixty."

You know in Hollywood the movie colony does everything on a grand scale. One night after a big dinner instead of being served finger bowls, we all took showers.

"Some actresses are born and some are made."

"I agree with you. First they're born, then they're made."

"I sing sad and happy songs."

"What do you sing that's sad?"

"My happy songs."

TV commercial: The pause that depresses.

Television will never be satisfactory to the viewer until we can turn off the set with a click that will be heard in the sponsor's office.

It was a super picture. It looked like a super made it.

The only thing some actors gain by going to Hollywood is three hours.

"I was talking to three producers yesterday. We discussed the oversupply of theaters. I told them those people were killing the cow that laid the golden fleece."

"Cow that laid the golden fleece? Didn't they laugh at you?"

"Nah. They were movie producers too."

The burlesque fan dancer stopped in the middle of her dance and pointed to a completely bald man. "Burlesque or no burlesque," she said angrily, "you should know better than to be seated wrong side up."

"The front seats are fifty cents each, the back seats are twenty-five cents each and the programs are ten cents."

"I'll sit on the programs."

Musician: A man who helps many a singer with his playing. He drowns them out.

I remember it got so hot in a burlesque in St. Louis the chorus was paying the audience to see them strip.

When things got bad in vaudeville it was nothing to have a mimic play a theater and be asked by the management to impersonate a customer.

Theatrical people are ruled by temperament, pride and sentiment. That's why they are not understood by businessmen.

This actor found it tough to get work so he went to medical school and graduated a surgeon. One day he was sitting in Sardi's with the boys discussing his latest appendix operation. "Hey, fellows," he began, "a funny thing happened to me on the way to this opening—"

After watching a show that dealt with robbers and thieves the farmer complained to the manager that his watch had been stolen.

"If you felt someone take the watch, why were you quiet?" the manager asked.

"I didn't wanna cause no disturbance," said the farmer. "You see, I thought it was part of the show."

It was at one of the old-fashioned nickelodeons that the manager was having trouble with the female customers. So he flashed the following notice on the screen: THE MANAGEMENT WISHES TO SPARE ELDERLY LADIES ANY INCONVENIENCE. THEY ARE THEREFORE INVITED TO RETAIN THEIR HATS. (Every hat in the place came off.)

The film star was worried and his friend couldn't figure out why. "After all, you have plenty of money and everything else you might want," the friend said.

"Bah," said the actor. "What good's money to me? Here I am with everything I want and my poor old mother has to starve in a garret."

In pictures blood is thicker than talent.

Protégé: A performer who is getting ready to be ungrateful.

Some people love to go to the movies. And some people go to the movies to love.

When I walked out of the stage door everyone waved pens at me. They thought I had the ink.

"Cheapies" have ruined Hollywood. A "cheapie" is a movie that is produced fast and cheap. For example: I sent a singing birthday telegram to a "cheapie" producer and he shot the scene as a production number for his new picture.

Movies are out of their infancy, but a lot of their stories aren't.

There was a slight earthquake in Hollywood and two movie directors, Clancy and Callahan, had both felt it.

"Patrick," said Callahan seriously, "what did ye think when first the ground began to trimble?"

"Think?" exclaimed Clancy. "What man that has the use of his legs to run with and his lungs to roar with would be after thinkin' at a time like that?"

A Hollywood director was bawling out a movie extra.

"Don't bawl her out," warned his aide. "She's a relative."

"Yeah," said the brave man, "and who isn't?"

GENERAL...hotels... housing...nature... politics...weather...etc.

(Everything is so overcrowded today that the cemeteries are only selling standing room.)

The man was telling his doctor about his frenzied attempts at slumber. "Last night I dreamt I was the only man in a nudist colony."

"How did you sleep?"

"Fine. But I didn't get any rest."

It was one of those rooming houses where cold water came out of the hot faucet, hot water came out of the cold faucet . . . and nobody ever came out of the bathroom.

"I got so tired of dancing I couldn't sit down."

"You mean stand up."

"No. We were dancing the rhumba."

Expert: An ordinary guy that's a long way from home.

In New York City there's a baby born every minute. Sixty an hour. It's the only way we can tell time.

"Daddy," said the little boy, "is it true that some of the best things in life are free?"

"No, sonny," corrected daddy. "Some of the best things in life are married."

It was so dry I passed a citrus grove and saw an orange sucking a lemon.

The phone rang at the weather station. "Is this the weather bureau?" a voice asked.

"Yes," said the janitor.

"How about a shower this afternoon?"

"Well," said the janitor. "If you need one take one."

"I've been indoors so much I developed a traffic-light complexion. Red eyes and green skin."

"He's writing a book."

"Why doesn't he buy one. It's cheaper."

The culture society was organizing a group to be comprised strictly of virgins, when a young lady carrying a baby appeared.

"But, madam," protested the president, "that is evidence that you are not eligible for this society. Why do you think you will be able to join?"

"I was only foolin' around when this happened," she explained. "So I thought I could get in as one of those foolish virgins."

What this five cent cigar needs is another country.

He was one of those modernistic sculptors. His statues were so unique, they baffled even the pigeons.

Elections: Things that are held to see if the polls were right.

As the woman turned on the lights she screamed and ran to the phone. "There's a rat in my room," she shrieked.

"Send him down at once," ordered the clerk. "He must register."

It was an illicit romance and, like all such marvelous things, the knock on the door tolled the fact that it was about to end.

"How're we going to get out of this?" she whispered.

"Does your apartment have a fire escape?" he nervously asked.

"Yes."

"Well," he said, "that lets *me* out."

"How long can one live without brains?"
"How old are you?"

Poets are born, that's the trouble.

The room they gave me was so small every time I bent over I rearranged the furniture.

I had insomnia so bad the sheep fell asleep.

His honesty has never been questioned. Mine has never been mentioned.

The best way to break a leg is to throw a cigarette down a manhole and step on it.

The poor kid was brought up in the dumps and could never quite get over it. When he was drafted into the Army the sergeant caught him eating out of the garbage cans one day.

"Listen, you," roared the angry sarge, "you'll eat in the mess hall. You're no better than the rest of us."

"What's this under your big nose?"
"My big mouth."

Last year he got four thousand Christmas cards and had to send back three thousand as unsold.

It was the sweetest little town. No garbage in the streets. The natives eat skins and all.

There is nothing busier than the ant, yet it finds time to go to picnics.

Shades of the night were falling, but I got a peek.

"I want the best room in the hotel."
"How about the White Room?"
"Not good enough."
"How about the Pink Room?"
"Not good enough."
"How about the Blue Room?"
"Where's that?"
"Right under the desk here. My inkwell leaks."

Notion: An idea with a smile.

The President has eight Secret Service men, two for each tire.

The two girls stood on the corner watching the gentleman holding the newborn child. "Look at his cute teeth," said one.
"Yes," said the other. "And small ears and blue eyes."
"Right," agreed the first. "The baby is kinda cute too."

Buy a chemistry set for a kid who wants to go places.

Never pan a moron, he may have friends in Washington.

433

There's an empty room in the Boston library for books that are banned.

The returns aren't all in yet, but some of the candidates are.

Father has been having a terrible time. He had some men over to fix the roof on the henhouse and after they left the roof blew right off again. This made him very angry because some of the hens got out—and went home.

"What do you hear from Washington?"
"Same old thing. The rattle of golf clubs."

The only thing in our house that wasn't carried away by the flood was a picture of Washington crossing the Delaware.

The river got so high it took a deep-sea diver to wind the city hall clock.

The wind whistled "Nothing Could be Finer than to be in Carolina." It was a south wind.

The sailor was marooned on the desert island and was rapturously gleeful when he found six beautiful women had also survived.
"Oh boy," he shouted. "I'm in business."
On the third day business fell off.

I hate mornings. They're so early.

"Were you true to me when I was away?"
"Oh yes, Max darling, yes Max."

434

"My name isn't Max."
"See how I lie to Max."

It's the patriotic duty of everybody to vote, besides I need the money.

Sentimental song title: "She's Only a Chambermaid Looking for Her Pot of Gold."

I was a great hero in the last war. To keep the enemy from getting the message I ate the pigeon.

"I found an eight-pound package on my doorstep."
"A baby?"
"No. A Sunday paper."

I got this medal for bravery . . . I talked back to my mother-in-law.

"I'm looking for the people who live here."
"Well, you came to the right place for it."

She was at the age where she was too old for castor oil and too young for Serutan.

All night long he kept walking the floor with the baby. At 4 A.M. there was a knock on the door. When he opened it there was his downstairs neighbor holding a pair of brand-new shoes.
"Listen," he said. "While you're at it break these in for me, will you?"

I picked up a seventeenth-century secretary and she could still take dictation.

I love to go down to Times Square on New Year's Eve and mangle with the crowd.

"I never knew you were such a brave man and had all those medals."
"I got the big one by mistake and all the others for having the big one."

Very nice club. You only need a taxi to get there, they bring you home in a patrol wagon.

Down at the draft board they test you with two girls. One a beauty and the other a hag. If you go for the beauty the Army accepts you. If you go for the hag the Army rejects you. If you go for both they send you to the Navy.

Vampire: The fella that yells, "Strike three yer out."

"Darling, the Browns are coming over for the week-end again."
"Good. Maybe they'll bring back our towels. It's a nuisance drying off with blotters."

There are two schools of thought on the raccoon coat . . . one of them from the raccoon.

Without scruples there ain't much fun in temptation.

"Got a room?"
"I happen to be well-filled."
"I see that lady, but have you got a room?"

I've often wondered why the stork gets blamed for a lot of things some other bird is responsible for.

Boston owl: To whom . . .

It was so hot there was a coyote chasing a rabbit and they both walked.

Last summer I vacationed in the hill country of a famous southern state and was treated admirably by the family with whom I was boarding. Along about Christmas I got to thinking about them so I sent each a pair of shoes. When I got up there this year they were still walking barefoot.

"Didn't you get the shoes?" I asked.

"Yup," said the elder. "But they weren't good. You didn't send no instructions."

It was so rainy the statues were soaked to the skin.

Los Angeles has the greatest floating population. They shout praises of their weather from the housetops.

Hearing of the approach of the hurricane, we stuck a double mattress in front of the door. When the wind came it blew the mattress right through the keyhole.

He was an elk. They didn't bury him, they mounted him.

To keep the thermometer from dropping use strong cord and nail.

The lady invited the tramp in for a bite. "That lazy susan," she said proudly, "is three hundred years old."

"Ma'am," said the bum, "that susan ain't lazy. She's dead."

Her father invented the can opener. It was a dismal failure. Nobody had invented the can yet.

I milked fifty cows today then had to go to town and have my fingers straightened.

The noncom surprised the private in the barracks with a girl.

"Uh-uh, this is my sister, Serge," the private stuttered.

"That's okay," the sergeant soothed. "She used to be mine."

"Robin Hood used to rob the rich to give to the poor. Where would he be if he were alive today?"

"Well, if he did it in reverse he'd be in Washington."

It was so cold on the farm I milked for twenty minutes before I knew I was shaking hands with myself.

A premature baby is one that's born before its parents are married.

It is not surprising to see editors out three days before their magazines.

The reason everyone who goes to Florida stays out in the sun is because they can't find a room.

It was impossible to accommodate the society lady with a room so the hotel manager told her to stay anywhere in the hotel that was comfortable until they could find a room for her the next morning. The following day the manager met the lady in the breakfast room. "Where did you sleep?" he asked sympathetically.

"My standing prevents me from telling you," she answered. "But I can say I was the first one to brush my teeth in the morning."

It was so hot when I was stationed in Texas the eagles on the colonel's shoulder were southern fried.

"What is the difference between a Vice President and a President?"
"Six G-men and a motorcycle."

I don't like to carry an umbrella, it looks like you can't afford to be rained on.

Father-in-law wears a size twenty-three shoe. It's a wonder he doesn't catch cold with so much of his body on the ground.

I love those card parties where they wind up shuffling husbands.

The man hurried to the ticket window. "The train," he panted. "If I run can I catch it?"
"Mister," said the clerk. "If you run you can beat it."

Politics is a game whereby the people want to know what the candidates stand for and the candidates, how much the people will fall for.

"What, in your opinion, is the height of stupidity?"
"How tall are you?"

Rip Van Winkle slept for twenty years. Those were the days before television sets.

As the Londoner said, "Welcome to our mist."

Our furniture was made of genuine cowhide. We had to milk the bureau twice a day.

"If I saw a man beating a donkey and I stopped him, what virtue would I be showing?"
"Brotherly love."

Fun is what they fine you for.

I have a place in my home for that painting . . . but it won't match the title.

What do I think of mud as a beautifier? Well, it hasn't done much for the turtle.

The farmer met his kin at the railroad station. "Uncle, I'm mighty glad to see you," he greeted. "That crate of chickens you sent me bust open just as I was going to take 'em out and they ran all over the place. I chased 'em through my neighbor's yard and only got back eleven."
"You did okay," said uncle. "I only sent you six."

My wife has a rich family and I get the wealthiest advice in town.

"Sneeze the other way."
"I don't know any other way."

I don't take baths, I just stay away from people.

"I'm very proud of our police department. They won't let you change clothes on the beach any more."

"What did you do?"

"I changed on the bus."

Two actors were in a small town. "Hey, Charlie," one of them called. "Good to see you. Where ya going?"

"To a funeral."

"Whose?"

"Listen, you ain't in New York where you have a choice of three or four funerals."

In any municipal parade always place the street cleaners right behind the politicians.

Along about November there starts a widespread rumor that Christmas is coming.

My clock runs fine. It does an hour in forty-five minutes.

It was the first time in twenty years that the flood waters went down. When we started cleaning we found three windows we never knew we had.

The man charged into the jewelry shop, slammed his fists angrily on the showcase, removed a wristwatch from his pocket and shook it under the nose of the proprietor. "You said this watch would last me a lifetime," he roared.

"Yeah," admitted the owner. "But you looked pretty sick the day you bought it."

The grandfather clock was so old the shadow of the pendulum swinging to and fro wore out the whole back.

It was so cold my overcoat was wearing a sweater.

He had lots of get up and go, then he lay down and died.

The politician's automobile was parked in the restricted zone for days. Finally a cop came along and took the vehicle to the station house. "What!" squawked the politico when informed of the action. "Get that cop on the phone."

"Are you going to have him fired?" his wife asked.

"No," he replied. "I wanna find out how he got it started."

Medical bills are high these days. I lost an arm 'cause I couldn't keep up the payments on my vaccination.

The draftee went from department to department until he had been thoroughly examined and passed for his preinduction physical.

"All right, son," said the last doctor. "Go in the room over there and be classified."

A worried look ringed the draftee's face. "Gee, Doc," he moaned. "Will they give me chloroform?"

President's cabinet. A place for liquor.

The housing shortage is so acute the restaurants stopped serving cottage pudding.

"Aren't you dressed yet?" brother called.

"Oh dear," sister said to herself. "I must have left the key in the keyhole."

Use Lubbo Soap. It doesn't lather, doesn't bubble, doesn't clean. It's just damned good company in the bathtub.

Our library is very strict. I owed two cents fine so they attached my house.

The weather was wonderful for a floating population. You could get seasick walking home. I didn't need an umbrella just a rudder.

He was about to go down for the third time when the swimmer, with sure swift strokes, reached him and pulled him to shore. The rescued man was grateful but poor and unable to tender a reward.

"But," he said to the swimmer, "I can do the same for you. I am a poor man. Only a chef. All I can do is tell you never to eat chopped steak. This will one day save your life."

I was taking a bath . . . everybody should have a hobby.

All's fair in love . . . war . . . and California weather reports.

It was so cold in Florida, when I took out my watch the hands were rubbing against each other.

Things are so crowded at the hospital now, they operate two on a table, if the night nurse isn't sleeping on it due to the housing shortage.

"I'll get some cigars. Guests will be dropping over."
"They will if they smoke your cigars."

The two men showed up at the party together. "I thought you two were married," said the hostess.
"Oh, no," corrected the one. "We're just good friends."

"Storekeeper, this mattress is terribly hilly."

"Lady, that's one of the finest mattresses in the world. It's made of camel hair. That's why the hump."

"What do you do when you feel like exercising?"

"I lie down until I get over it."

They recently found a skeleton of a medieval knight over nine feet tall. Knights were longer in those days.

In my home we got a building with a thousand stories. It's called the library.

"You know," said hubby, "I used to think you were dumb."

His wife smiled. "Really?" she asked.

"Yes," he said. "I wasn't sure of anything in those days."

She's a Third Avenue debutante. Next year they're gonna tear her down.

The snooty author walked into the bookshop. "How many of my books are gone?" he arrogantly asked the owner.

"Two," said the man. "And I think they were taken by shoplifters."

Brassieres were invented by communists to uplift the masses.

An island is a body of land surrounded by water. An MC is a body of air surrounded by stooges.

My old flame is not so hot now. She went out too often.

"He sleeps in his sailor pants, eats in 'em, works in 'em."

"Why? Doesn't he have time to take 'em off?"

"With all them buttons?"

They make clothes out of milk. That's why my suit looks so cheesy.

I thought she was wearing a dress that buttons all the way up the back. Found out it was her spine.

"He's twice as dumb as I."

"You mean he's twice as dumb as me."

"He's twice as dumb as both of us."

"It's Mother's Day," the boss told his secretary. "I'm going to give my mother-in-law a table."

"Card table?"

"No." He smiled. "A timetable."

It was so hot the cow gave five quarts of steam.

Sign of spring: Keep off the grass.

Virtue pays but there's no market for it.

"Now, sir," said the judge. "If you become a citizen do you promise to come to the aid and service of your country whenever you are called, if it be needed?"

"Well, Judge, I couldn't say positively. If you need me before six, maybe . . . but my wife won't let me out of the house after work."

If Congress ever goes on television natural gas companies will foot the bill.

I have an intelligent dog. I saw him pouring over Pegler's column.

Always put off tonight what you've got to put on in the morning.

"How did he feel last night, daughter?"
"As much as ever."

Conference: A meeting at which people talk about what they should be doing.

The powder puff covers a multitude of skins.

Uncle was never very smart. When he went in the Army he couldn't even think up the answer to roll call.

I bought a two-way bulb. It goes on and off.

April showers may bring flowers
and wrinkles in ten dollar suits.

It was so cold the snowman was trying to get into the house.

When I was on the road I slept all day. No good hotel ever burned down during the day.

The elevator was fixed. Now it falls all the way.

Never tell a bald man a hair-raising story.

"What's good for biting nails?"
"Sharp teeth."

Success has spoiled many a pleasant failure.

Whatsoever a man sews will rip.

I was down in the dumps and didn't find a thing.

"Is that clock right up there?"
"Yes. It's right up there."

The sentry heard the noise, fired twice, then shouted,
"Who went there?"

Millennium: Just like a centennial only with more
legs.

The psychiatrist recommended, as a cure for homosexu-
ality, that the patient spend some time in a nudist colony. A few months later the patient returned. "How was
it?" asked the doctor.
"Well," said the man, "after all, girls are not boys."
"Ah," sighed the doc. "So you noticed."

The minister was out fishing with a hired boatman
when suddenly the storm broke, sending waves of tremendous force smashing against the side of the craft.
"I wish I'd been a better man," moaned the seaman.
"And I," said the minister, "wish I'd been a better
swimmer."

The country has progressed. Washington couldn't tell
a lie. Now everyone does.

What can you get a nudist for Christmas?

"I was born on the sidewalks of New York."

"Sister, when you were born New York had no sidewalks."

Two lamas were seated outside a far-off monastery. Month after month passed with neither of them speaking a word. Finally one said, "Life is like a well."

Several months later the other one spoke. "Why is life like a well?" he questioned.

Two months passed. Then the first lama shrugged his shoulders and said, "All right, have it your way. Life isn't like a well."

He felt rather stupid. "You know," he said to a young lady standing beside him, "I told that old fool over there that the lady of the house was a perfect old fright. And he turned out to be her husband."

"How perfectly delightful," she shrieked. "What did daddy say?"

An antique is something so old nobody knows what to do with it. So they raise the price.

I don't know how often they wash the linens in that hotel. All I know is I dropped the towel and it broke.

The postman is afraid to ring twice in California . . . on the second push the house comes down.

"I'm glad you stopped complaining about the plaster falling," said the landlord.

"Yeah," said the tenant. "It's all down now."

I'm writing a new book about how to eat everything you want, stay out as late as you like, drink all you can stand, go out with as many women as you would care to —it's called *How To Be Dead at Thirty-five*.

The workman was hanging a sign outside of Congress. It read, "Solicitors, fakers and grafters will not be permitted in the House."

Just then a senator happened by. "Better strike out grafters," he said, "or we'll never be able to raise a quorum."

He told me all about himself. He had a second to spare.

She reminded me of the romantic ocean. She was all wet.

"You must hate me."
"I'd like to."

Bridge player: A man who loves to take it on the shin.

Nero looked across the arena and anticipated the devouring of the slave. When the ferocious lion was released it rushed at the poor man, who simply bent over, whispered something in the beast's ear and it stalked away. Nero called the slave to him. "I give you your life," he said, "if you tell me what you said to the lion."

"Sure," said the slave. "I just told him that after dinner you would be expected to say a few words."

My landlady was upset and I was put out.

"Hello, Operator. You gave me the wrong number." The young man was quite peeved about it. I'm calling HOpe 5567."

"There is no such exchange as ROpe," said the operator.

"HOpe," replied the man angrily. "H like in Harry, O for Otto. P for Peter and E for Elmer."

"Gee," said the operator, "that phone booth must be awfully crowded. But what number do you want?"

Killjoy was here.

The pessimist explained why he always dines in restaurants where music is provided. Sometimes the music helps him forget the food. And sometimes the food helps him forget the music.

Accidents will happen. That's why there are so many different kinds of salad.

Benny had told all his friends about the delicious steak he'd eaten in the Delancey Street restaurant the day before. So they decided to go down there and see if it was really as large and delicious as he said. But much to their disappointment, the waiter brought them the tiniest steak they'd ever seen.

"See here, my good man," Benny barked. "I was in this restaurant yesterday and you served me a big juicy steak, and now today, when I've organized a party, you serve such a small one."

"Yes, sir," replied the waiter. "But yesterday you were sitting by the window."

A man took his wife and daughter into this very fancy, ultra-chic dining club. They ordered caviar and champagne and a rare foreign dish that was featured on the menu. The father asked for the check before the daughter had finished eating. "Hurry and eat your carrot, dear," mother said, "it will make your hair curly."

"If a carrot will make her hair curly," said papa, "let her look at the check. It will give her a permanent wave."

My wife served turkey for dinner and all the guests were tickled. She forgot to take off the feathers.

Indigestion is the failure to adjust a square meal to a round stomach.

Girls who eat a lot of sweets,
Will soon develop larger seats.

Lady: "You here again? Have you forgotten I gave you a pie yesterday?"
Bum: "Lady, I haven't forgotten, I've forgiven."

The millionaire was arrested for speeding and brought before the judge in a small community. When the judge offered him the alternative of paying a $10 fine or serving ten days in jail the millionaire decided to take the ten days.

"But, my good man, you are wealthy," said the judge, astonishment ringing his face. "Why you should prefer ten days in jail to paying a $10 fine is beyond me."

"It's like this, Judge," the rich man explained. "Our cook left and my wife figures it'll take that long to find a new one."

Restaurant owner: "How's the food?"
Patron: "I could get more nourishment biting my lip."

"This is a good restaurant. If you order a fresh egg you get the freshest egg in the world. If you order hot coffee you get the hottest coffee in the world, and—"
"I believe you. I ordered a small steak."

Sadie went running home to mother, tears streaking her dainty blue eyes. "Oh, Mother," she sobbed. "My husband took one bite of my cake and picked it up and threw it at me."

"There, there," consoled her mother. "I always told you it was dangerous to marry a big strong fellow like Bill."

When the waitress came to work the manager met her at the door.

"Look," he said, "I want you to put on your cutest uniform, fix your hair lovely, see that your makeup is on neat and walk with that extra-sexy walk."

"Something special on?" she asked.

"No," he replied. "The beef's tough."

So there I was eatin' fish and I can't swim a stroke.

A chef is a man with a big enough vocabulary to give the soup a different name every day.

Doughnut: A fried halo.

You can't have your cake and somebody else's cookie too.

Julius called the family doctor and complained of excruciating pains in his stomach. "What did you eat?" the doctor asked.

"I had a piece of sponge cake."

"But sponge cake shouldn't make you sick," doc insisted.

"Look, Doctor," Julius continued. "I went to this swell wedding and drank plenty of whiskey and ate shelled peanuts. The sour pickles and sauerkraut were delicious too. Finally the dinner came and I had three portions of roast duck, a triple helping of calves liver, four dishes of pie and coffee. After that they served the most wonderful French ice cream and I had six portions. Then I had to eat that lousy piece of sponge cake and it made me sick."

Pat went into a restaurant on Friday, but didn't bother to look at the bill of fare. "Have ye any whale?" he asked.

"No," said the waiter, surprised.

"Then do ye have any porpoise or shark?"

"No, sir."

"Well, then," said Pat, "bring me a dish of corned beef and cabbage. 'Tis sure the good Lord knows I asked for fish."

A cannibal is a man who sometimes has his friends for dinner.

Too many cooks spoil the figure.

In the fancier restaurants the chefs slice the tomatoes by throwing them through a harp.

The sign outside Epstein's restaurant read, "Cutlets from Any Animal You Desire."

When the waiter approached the young lady she ordered elephant cutlet. The waiter appealed to Epstein, who walked over to the table and, bowing graciously, asked, "Madam ordered an elephant cutlet?"

"Yes," she said.

"Madam is dining alone?"

"Yes," she said.

"Madam is expecting no one?"

"No."

"Then look, madam," Epstein roared, forgetting himself, "for one lousy cutlet you expect me to cut up a new elephant?"

Percival (politely): "Waiter, chicken croquette, please."
Waiter (loudly): "FOWL BALL!"

I got myself a cup of coffee and set it on the table. Then I went for a piece of pie. But when I came back with the pie the coffee was gone. So I set down the pie and went for another cup of coffee, but when I came back with the coffee the pie was gone. So I wrote a card. It read, "I put my finger in the coffee," then stuck the card alongside the cup. I went for another piece of pie, but when I came back the coffee cup was empty and someone had written on the card, "I found your coffee but I couldn't locate your finger."

"I brought you a box of candy. Your favorite brand."
"You should have brought a full box."
"It is my favorite brand too."

In the near future men will eat baked beans and say, "Ah dear, these are just like those in the can mother used to open."

My favorite restaurant serves half and half coffee. Half in the cup and half in the saucer.

The management was stuck with loads of salmon from the previous week. "Push salmon," ordered the manager to the waiters. "No matter what the customers want, recommend salmon."

A few minutes later a man walked in. "What do you suggest?" he asked.

"Well," said the waiter. "The spoiled salmon is very good."

My girl is a terrific cook. She makes the best ice cubes you ever tasted. Her specialty is fried water, but when she gets fancy it's no good. Last week she loused up cornflakes.

Mamma won papa with her cooking. Sort of girl meats boy.

Bacteria: Rear entrance to a cafeteria.

Picnic: A shoe box filled with indigestion.

"What a bump I've got on my head. My wife and I had our first argument and she socked me on the head with a pie pan."

"How could she do so much damage with a pie pan?"

"She had one of her pies in it."

"What's the best way to raise corned beef and cabbage?"

"With a knife and fork."

A balanced meal is one from which the diner has a 50–50 chance of recovering.

"Yep," he said, telling of a harrowing experience. "We had reached the place where we had eaten the last dog."

"It must have been terrible," she exclaimed.

"It certainly was. We were all out of mustard and it was twenty miles to the nearest stand."

A horse with blinders cannot laugh. He cannot see who's driving.

The poor electric eel was sitting disconsolately in the aquarium. "What's the matter?" asked the custodian.

"I'm unhappy because I have no wife," replied the eel.

So the custodian ordered another eel, but still the first eel continued to brood. "What's the matter now?" asked the custodian.

"Damnit!" the eel replied, pointing toward his intended mate, D.C."

A carrier pigeon stopped to rest on the window sill in the Pentagon building. Close behind him came another pigeon who stopped off to talk.

"Where you going?" asked the second pigeon.

"To section M to deliver an order," answered the first.

"What's the number of the order?"

"235XM-Q78966-421SSTX," replied the first.

"Better get a move on," said the second. "I got an order rescindin' it."

If you build a better mouse trap chances are you'll catch better mice.

"My home town is so small our fire department consists of a hose cart and four dogs."

"What do the dogs do, haul the cart?"

"No. They find the hydrant."

Papa Bear: "Who stole my beer?"
Mama Bear: "Who stole my beer?"
Baby Bear: "Hic!"

Mohair comes from a goat called Moe.

In my aquarium there is a very aristocratic fish. His folks swam over under the *Mayflower*.

"Hey, your brother got very fancy since he was in jail. He never misses a contest at the Kennel Club now."
"He goes there only to hiss at the police dogs."

Mamma and papa turtle were talking about their kids catching cold because their necks stuck out of their shells.
"Stop worrying," advised papa. "We'll buy them one of those people-necked sweaters."

"Dear, I don't want to hurt your feelings, but this steak is so awfully tough I just can't eat it," he said.
"Then give it to the dog," she said angrily.
"I did," he replied. "He won't eat it either."

Teacher: "What is the right time to gather apples?"
Butch: "When the dog is chained up."

The great Baldchinny was telling about when he was working with ferocious animals.
"One night I put my head in the lion's mouth," he said.
"What did he do?"
"Spat it out."

Then there was a dairy farmer who said, "All that I am I owe to udders."

The farmer was taking his first boat trip and they seated him at the same table with the rancher. Pretty soon, being homey folks, they go to talkin'.

"I got a ranch with fifty cows and one bull," said the rancher.

"Gosh," said the farmer, "you must be mighty independent."

"No, sir," replied the rancher. "Not nearly as independent as that bull."

I used to have a mountain-climbing concession in the Alps but I lost it when they found my St. Bernard guilty of dereliction of duty. Although they never really proved it, one day I sent the dog out on a rescue and when they found him the poor guy he went out to save was frozen stiff and the pup was yellin' "Yippee."

The chickens on farmer Brown's farm refused to go all out in their egg laying. One day a football was accidently kicked into the yard. The rooster looked at the football and said to the hens, "I'm not complaining, but look at the work they're turning out next door."

The lady walked haughtily into the restaurant with her dog and sat it down on the chair beside her. Then she started talking baby talk to it. "Mamma itsy bitsy baby mansy won't hurty you."

The waiter asked, "Your first dog, madam?"

I went to see my girl and she was crying. "What's the matter?" I asked.

"My dog ate the pie I made for you," she said, dabbing away a tear.

"Don't worry," I said. "I'll buy you another dog."

The farmer bought a watch with a one-year guarantee and took it back to the store a couple of months later.

"You must have had a terrible accident with it," remarked the clerk, examining the badly damaged watch.

"A slight one," answered the farmer. "When I was feeding the pig it fell in the trough a couple months back."

"Why didn't you bring it back before?"

"Brought it back as soon as I could," the farmer explained. "We killed the pig only yesterday."

"Remember me?" the man shouted at the politician, as his hand grasped the gun and his knuckles turned white. "You beat my father, broke my mother's arm, ran my brothers out of town and burned down my home. Just because I ran against you."

"Go away," replied the unperturbed politician. "I hate sore losers."

The politician was making a speech to the Bowery crowd and, as usual, it was crowded with a lot of campaign hash and promises.

"When I'm elected you won't see that long, dreary, unending bread line," he said, his voice filled with emotion. "No, sir. When I'm elected there'll be two bread lines. One for white and one for rye."

Next time the alderman comes around to me to help him at election time he's gonna find mistletoe hanging from my shirt tail.

The campaign worker was demanding his reward from the elected politician.

"But," protested the politician, "there are no jobs open." Just then the worker drew a pistol. "Tell you what," said the official, "I'll appoint a committee to investigate why there are no jobs open and you can work on that."

Candidate: A modest man who shrinks from the publicity of private life to seek the obscurity of public office.

For years organizations had been besieging this reluctant gentleman to address them. Now he was presenting his argument before the party's finance committee. "I want two million bucks for my campaign," he said.

"But your campaign won't cost that much," protested the chairman.

"I know," said the reluctant gentleman, "but in case I lose I wanna be able to live comfortably."

U.N.: Site for sore allies.

A virgin forest is where the hand of man has never set foot.

The landlord was laying the law down to the drunk.

"I'll give you two days to pay the rent," warned the property owner.

"Shay, thatsh shwell," answered the drunk. "I'll take the Fourth of July and Chrishmas."

"You can't come in here," the worried mother warned. "My son is sick."

"I want to catch your son's measles," the man said. "Because if I kissed the nurse she'd get it. She would kiss the doctor and he'd get it. The doctor would kiss my wife and she'd get it. My wife would kiss the landlord and that's the guy I'm after."

She's a nice lady. She believes in live and let live. You should see the things she lets live in my room. I had a leak in my bathroom pipe, so she hung a shower curtain around it. Then there was a gas leak in my room. Fix it? No. She gave me a gas mask.

A good beginning and a good ending make a good speech if they come close together.

"What must we do before we can expect forgiveness for our sins?"
"Sin."

Our local Peeping Tom is at the awkward age. Too tall for keyholes and too short for transoms.

That rug looks terrible. Sweep it under the dirt.

"It's starvation that's staring me in the face."
"It can't be very pleasant for either of you."

Alcatraz: A pen that works above water.

You can easily distinguish between asthma and passion. Asthma lasts.

They just opened up a new theater with all the latest gadgets. Press a button, your seat comes out. Press another button, your program comes out. Press another button, the matron comes out. Press the matron, your teeth come out.

"I'm worried about my son's health."
"What's he got?"
"A motorcycle."

The salesman was trying hard to peddle his insurance quota. "You ought to take a policy out on your husband," he told the housewife. "Maybe somebody will put arsenic in his soup someday."
"How much?" she asked.

"The policy?"

"No." She smiled. "The arsenic."

All teeth will remain white if they are properly cared for. Of course I never drink hot drinks, always brush my teeth morning and evening and avoid all acids. That is all I do, barring the fact that I put them in a glass of soft water every night.

"Are there many mosquitoes here?" asked the man who was thinking of buying a bungalow by the seashore.

"None whatever," replied the agent. "Those screens you see on some of the houses are there to keep out the flying fish."

The rather broad lady showed up at the theater just before the performance started and handed the usher two tickets. "Where's the other party?" asked the usher.

"Well," said the lady, with a blush, "you can see one seat is rather uncomfortable so I bought two. But they're really both for me."

"Okay with me, lady," the usher replied, scratching his head. "But you're gonna have a tough time. Your seats are numbers fifty-one and sixty-three."

"I think I have a cold or something in my head."

"It must be a cold."

"I was invited to a reception in a nudist colony. The butler met me at the door."

"Are you sure it was the butler?"

"I could see it wasn't the maid."

"My wife's diamonds once belonged to a millionaire."

"Yeah? Who?"

"Mr. Woolworth."

462

The mosquito was discovered by the man who was discovered by the mosquito.

Diamond: Worth its weight in money.

Santa Claus takes a week to distribute the presents . . . and we hold the bag for the other fifty-one.

Two giants of the gay set were walking down Broadway when a taxi driver hurled an insult at them. One of them proceeded to give him the beating of his life. "Oh, George," said the other when it was all over. "I'm so exasperated with you. But I guess once a tom boy always a tom boy."

The apartment was vacant but the landlord was very fussy about who it was rented to. One day a young chap appeared.

"Any children, radios, phonographs, cats, dogs or pets of any kind?" asked the landlord.

"No," the young man answered. "But I think I ought to tell you I have a fountain pen that scratches a little."

My eyes are bloodshot on account of my teeth. I was up all night looking for them.

Diet: Triumph of mind over platter.

"I can see this watch at night."
"Oh, radium dial?"
"No. A flashlight goes with it."

"What have you got good in a room?"
"A blonde in 217."

A firm of shipowners wired one of their captains: MOVE HEAVEN AND EARTH BUT GET HERE FRIDAY.

Just as they were getting a little anxious they received the following reply: RAISED HOLY HELL AND ARRIVING THURSDAY.

An ignorant foreigner is one who can speak only seven or eight languages.

A stitch in time saves embarrassment.

New Year's Eve is when old year and old friends pass out.

Song title: "Her Legs May Belong to the Midnight Frolic but Her Heart Belongs to the Farm."

The ground in Texas is so full of oil, farmers there raise french-fried potatoes.

The preacher observed that his whole congregation was asleep except the village half-wit. "What?" he yelled. "All asleep except that poor idiot?"

"Aye," replied the only one awake. "And if I wasn't an idiot I'd be asleep too."

Finger was telling Shimmel about a harrowing experience he'd had out West. "Lou, it was awful," he said. "There were Indians to the left of me, Indians to the right of me, Indians in front of me and Indians in back of me."

"Gosh, Sam, what did you do?"

"What did I do? I bought a rug."

"I wear three watches. Vest pocket, wrist and lapel. One says two o'clock, the other four and the other six."

"How can you tell the time?"

"I look at the kitchen clock."

Did you ever stop to think what might have happened to American history if the British soldiers at Bunker Hill had had bloodshot eyes?

Don't worry when you stumble. Remember, a worm is about the only thing that can't fall down.

Censor: One who puts his "no-s" in other people's business.

Two local citizens were having a bit of a difference.

"I wouldn't vote for you if you were Saint Peter," roared one.

"Yeah?" yelled the other. "If I was Saint Peter you wouldn't live in my district."

"That man is a crook. He's wanted in Chicago."

"Whadda they want with another crook in Chicago?"

"What's the best floor to sleep on?" asked the socialite.

"Lady," said the clerk, "if you're gonna sleep on floors they're all the same."

Christmas Eve is when you stay in to see how you came out.

You shouldn't have sent that suit parcel post. There were enough moths in it to fly.

The diamond is the hardest mineral in the world . . . to get.

465

"What was the most expensive piece of jewelry you ever bought?"

"My wedding ring. It cost me $200 a week—alimony."

I went to a surprise party. I was surprised they let me in.

A failure is under no obligation to tell the truth.

The stationmaster and his staff lined up neatly on the platform. When the train came through the station it didn't stop but there was one man leaning out the window with a notebook in his hand.

"Was that an official checking to see if you were on duty?" asked a fare.

"No," replied the stationmaster. "That was the company's tailor measuring us for new uniforms.

Marcel waves: The French national anthem.

Wedding ring: The difference between wild oats and adultery.

We call my sister "Amber"—because she was born on the way to the hospital between a green and red light.

When joining a fancy club remember, never knock a brother member until he's gone at least a half hour.

Many a true word is spoken in a dialect.

A rumor goes in one ear and out many mouths.

The new clerk at the license bureau was a little deaf. When a man approached his cage he asked him his name.

"New—Thomas New."

"I don't quite catch it."

"It's New. New to you, New to everybody, New to the world."

"What you want is a birth certificate."

The *Time* reporter was fascinated with his latest subject, a moonshiner. "Tell me," said the reporter, "don't the revenue officers you've killed haunt you?"

"Yep, stranger, somewhat," answered the subject. "But not nearly as much as the ones I ain't killed."

"Do you ever go camping?"

"No. We just take the screens down."

Sustaining program: Alimony.

Thank the stars my mother was a real woman.

We heard a joke that was so funny we laughed until our sides were hoarse.

Bikini: Something that begins nowhere and ends all at once.

"Who invented the hole in the doughnut?"

"Some fresh-air fiend, I suppose."

"To be a mummy you had to be rich or of royal blood."

"I thought you had to be dead."

A lazybones may be aptly described as a person who has nothing to do and all day to do it in.

Beastly weather occurs when it rains cats and dogs.

A subway is a mixing bowl with people.

Baldhead: A person who got rid of dandruff by removing its hiding place.

"My uncle lives over a fish market. But he hadda move."
"Couldn't stand the smell of fish?"
"No. They couldn't stand the smell of him."